THIEFING
A CHANCE

THIEFING A CHANCE

Factory Work, Illicit Labor, and Neoliberal Subjectivities in Trinidad

Rebecca Prentice

UNIVERSITY PRESS OF COLORADO
Boulder

© 2015 by University Press of Colorado

Published by University Press of Colorado
5589 Arapahoe Avenue, Suite 206C
Boulder, Colorado 80303

All rights reserved
Printed in the United States of America

The University Press of Colorado is a proud member of
Association of American University Presses

The University Press of Colorado is a cooperative publishing enterprise supported, in part, by Adams State University, Colorado State University, Fort Lewis College, Metropolitan State University of Denver, Regis University, University of Colorado, University of Northern Colorado, Utah State University, and Western State Colorado University.

∞ This paper meets the requirements of the ANSI/NISO Z39.48-1992 (Permanence of Paper).

ISBN 978-1-60732-372-3 (paper)
ISBN 978-1-60732-375-4 (ebook)

Library of Congress Cataloging-in-Publication Data
Prentice, Rebecca.
  Thiefing a chance : factory work, illicit labor, and neoliberal subjectivities in Trinidad / Rebecca Prentice.
      pages cm
  Includes bibliographical references.
  ISBN 978-1-60732-372-3 (paper) — ISBN 978-1-60732-375-4 (ebook)
  1. Clothing workers—Trinidad. 2. Clothing factories—Trinidad. 3. Work environment—Trinidad. 4. Neoliberalism—Trinidad. I. Title.
  HD8039.C6T7 2015
  331.7'616870972983—dc23
                          2014038119

24 23 22 21 20 19 18 17 16 15   10 9 8 7 6 5 4 3 2 1

Cover image: Stitchers working in a typical Trinidadian factory. Photo by author.

Contents

List of Figures   vii
Map of Trinidad   viii
Acknowledgments   ix

1. Introduction   1
2. Being a Factory the Signature Way   25
3. Raced and Emplaced: Signature Fashions Workers   51
4. "Is We *Own* Factory": Thiefing a Chance on the Shop Floor   87
5. "Keeping Up with Style": The Struggle for Skill   111
6. "Use a Next Hand": Risk, Injury, and the Body at Work   143
7. "Kidnapping Go Build Back We Economy": Criminal Tropes in Neoliberal Capitalism   173
8. Conclusion   195

References   205
Index   225

Figures

0.1. Map of Trinidad *viii*
1.1. Map of Trinidad and the Caribbean region *8*
2.1. Layout of the shop floor at Signature Fashions *33*
2.2. At work in the stitching section *41*
3.1. Houses in Laventille as seen from Picton Road *57*
3.2. Bungalow-style houses in a Chaguanas suburb *60*
3.3. Production sequence at Signature Fashions *61*
5.1. A tailor plots a pattern onto cloth *121*
5.2. A garment worker stitching up trouser flies *123*
6.1. Example of a button-tacking machine at Universal Uniforms *156*

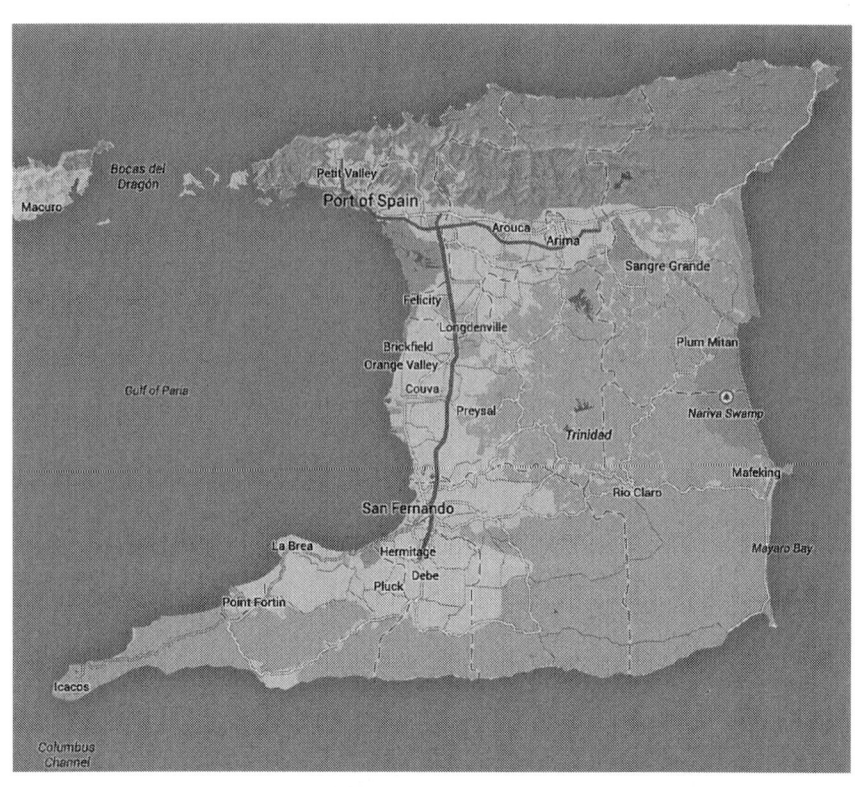

Figure 0.1. Map of Trinidad (map data from Google)

Acknowledgments

Many individuals and institutions have contributed to this work over more than ten years of research and writing. This research has been funded, at various stages, by the Wenner-Gren Foundation for Anthropological Research, Universities UK, the University of Sussex, the Royal Anthropological Institute of Great Britain and Ireland, and the Economic and Social Research Council. I am grateful to each of these funders and could not have completed the book without their support.

In Trinidad, I thank from the bottom of my heart Robert and Helene, the pseudonymous owners of Signature Fashions, who gave me wide-ranging access to their factory as an unpaid employee on the shop floor. They allowed me to disrupt the production process as I made fumbling attempts to learn how to sew and to interview workers during working hours. Mostly, they left me alone to pursue my research project in their midst. Their openness and generosity made access to my field site unexpectedly easy. Because this book contains a great deal of critique, I have felt at times that I have repaid their kindness with disloyalty. I hope it is not taken that way. Signature Fashions is a different place than it was when I conducted fieldwork; the production process and workforce have changed considerably. I hope my commentary is taken as it is offered, with sincere gratitude and a continuing wish for dialogue.

Thanks to the workers at Signature Fashions, who made me feel their workplace was equally my own. As my intended six months of factory ethnography turned into seven, then eight, then nine, I found it very hard to leave their company. I am grateful for their openness and bigheartedness toward me; for inviting me to their churches, temples, and homes; for spending Saturday afternoons shopping together or making a lime. Although I mention them here only by their pseudonyms, Amanda, Donna, and Veena have not only been informants but great and enduring friends. I also want to remember Josephine, whose warmth, generosity, and outsized sense of humor brightened every day in the factory. I am just one of a great many people saddened by her recent death.

Because I have promised to keep my informants in the field anonymous, my thanks to the people of Trinidad are necessarily short. I specifically would like to thank the many garment workers, fabric retailers, trade unionists, independent seamstresses and tailors, African clothing retailers, religious leaders, educators, government officials, health practitioners, *mas* camp workers, and factory owners who shared their time with me and allowed me to record their stories. Thanks also to the workers and owners of Universal Uniforms (a pseudonym), my other factory home in Trinidad. My deepest thanks to my sewing instructor, Donny, my fellow "girls in the sewing," and all those who limed with me late into the evening at Donny's shop in Belmont.

Throughout my fieldwork, Janice Mark, my best friend in *macotiousness*, always kept me laughing. So many of her gentle encouragements and observations are hilarious to me even now: "Becca, you going *whole day* wearing the same clothes?" Without her kind day-to-day advice, I would have made far many more mistakes than I did. I am grateful for her ongoing friendship over the years and for her careful reading of and advice on my book. A big thanks also to Miss Clare Joseph, the Mark family, Joanne Bruno, Nigel, Jamal, Reynold Francis, Rhonda Greaves, Celia Ann Tashie, the Ramkhelawan family, and the Crash Crew.

My debts to the many anthropologists who have shaped this work begin with the professors I had the great fortune to study with as an undergraduate student at Cornell University. Davydd Greenwood, Kathryn March, and Viranjini Munasinghe taught me entirely new ways of understanding class, gender, and race and have thus made an imprint on every page of this book. Viranjini supervised my senior thesis on Hindu youth in London and introduced me to the Caribbean in her class on Asians in the Americas. I could not have known then that my interests in labor, health, and the global assembly line would lead me, like her, to Trinidad, but the education I received from her about the political, cultural, and ethnic complexities of the region has proven indispensable.

The University of Sussex has nurtured this book through many incarnations, first as a doctoral dissertation and years later when I became a member of the faculty and was completing the final draft. My work has benefited from the careful reading and advice of James Fairhead, Geert De Neve, Dinah Rajak, Ann Whitehead, and Jamie Cross. This work has also been nourished by the friendship and ideas of Alice Street, Nick Nisbett, Kathryn Tomlinson, Pauline Von Hellermann, Rubina Jasani, and Nicole Blum. At University College London, Danny Miller served as the external examiner of my doctoral dissertation and has provided valuable advice and continued encouragement, for which I am grateful.

One of the great pleasures of teaching at Sussex is our bright, creative, and outspoken students. Although there are too many to name here, I want to thank them for their critical appraisal of my work during lectures and seminars. Discussions with students have helped me clarify my thinking and refine my writing. Adom Heron, whose undergraduate paper I cite in this book, deserves special mention in this regard.

At the University of the West Indies, I thank Patricia Mohammed, Rhoda Reddock, and Bridget Brereton for advice and encouragement during fieldwork and beyond. Thanks to the Institute for Gender and Development Studies, my academic base during fieldwork in Trinidad, and to the participants in the Lunchtime Seminar Series. My gratitude also goes to the staff in the West Indiana collection of the University of the West Indies Library. Thanks to Kevin Yelvington at the University of South Florida for putting me in touch with these scholars and for his keen advice and support, especially in the beginning stages.

I wrote much of this book during a postdoctoral year at Goldsmiths, University of London, funded by the Economic and Social Research Council (PTA–026–27–2343). I am grateful to my mentor, Sophie Day, who pushed me to publish this manuscript, for her encouragement and timely remarks as it began to take shape. For critical feedback on chapters 6 and 7, I thank the various audiences of students and faculty with whom I shared my work at Goldsmiths, especially in the Anthropology Department Seminar Series.

During my postdoctoral fellowship, I was fortunate to find myself in the company of many young economic anthropologists, particularly through the Work and Labour Seminar Series at the London School of Economics. Thanks especially to Andrew Sanchez, Michael Hoffmann, Max Bolt, and Eeva Keskula for enriching seminars that never failed to push my thinking forward and for their thoughtful discussion of my work.

I have had the opportunity to present parts of this book at various stages of completion to a number of academic audiences. I have particularly benefited from feedback and conversations during invited talks at Brunel University, London School of Economics, London School of Hygiene and Tropical Medicine, University College London, and University of East London, as well as at the meetings of the Society for Economic Anthropology in 2006 and the American Anthropological Association in 2007 and 2010. I thank David Howard and the Society for Caribbean Studies for the invitation to share my work with audiences at the University of Bristol and Southampton University in 2010.

Conversations with Kate Browne and Lynne Milgram were essential in writing chapter 4, which in an earlier version was published in their co-edited book, *Economics and Morality: Anthropological Approaches* (Browne and Milgram 2009). I thank AltaMira Press for permission to use this material. Similarly, conversations with Gavin Whitelaw for our special issue of *Anthropology of Work Review*, "Embodying Labor," helped me think carefully about the multiple relationships between method, analysis, and embodied engagement in the field, which is reflected in chapter 5 (Prentice and Whitelaw 2008). Parts of chapter 5 appear in articles written for *Research in Economic Anthropology* and *Anthropology and Education Quarterly*. I am grateful to Emerald Publishing and the American Anthropological Association for permission to use that material. Chapter 7 is an expanded and revised version of an article written for *Journal of the Royal Anthropological Institute*, and I am grateful to John Wiley and Sons for permission to use that material in this book.

Thanks to Weston Rawlins (Cro Cro) for his generous permission to quote his lyrics at length in chapter 7 and to his manager, Crystal Cowie-Rowley, for facilitating the process. Thanks also to Shawn Baldeosingh for permission to use his photograph of Chaguanas in chapter 3 and to Adam Howse for the line drawings and maps that appear throughout the book.

I thank the whole team at the University Press of Colorado, especially Jessica d'Arbonne, who was an enormously supportive editor. I also thank two anonymous reviewers for their detailed and heartening feedback on my book.

I am lucky to have great friends in Allyson Hobbs, Liz Krieger, Lesley Berry, Manga Fraser, and Ben Peyser. Their conversations have never failed to cheer me, even from very far away.

At long last, I would like to thank my family: my brothers, Steve and Tony, my sister-in-law, Kimberly McCreight, and my parents, Martin and Clare Prentice. Without my parents' loving support, I would not have been able to complete this book or to have accomplished so many other things in my life. I also thank the Blom family for embracing me as one of their own, especially Sandra Blom for her friendship. Finally, thanks to Michael Blom, who has been with me every step of the way, and our daughters, Hazel and Zoe, who came along and disrupted this work in so many wonderful ways. This book is dedicated to the workers of Signature Fashions and to the three of you.

THIEFING A CHANCE

1

Introduction

> A region literally born out of colonialism, export industrialization, and capitalism broadly speaking, for the Caribbean what we now analyze as globalization, modernity, and here, neoliberalism, have arguably been integral to the region's very self-definition. These political-economic systems have insinuated themselves deeply into some of the region's well-established cultural contours, and these, in turn, have given the political-economic systems a vernacular form.
> – Carla Freeman, "Neoliberalism, Respectability, and the Romance of Flexibility in Barbados"

> Rebecca, you wanted to know what is "thiefing a chance?" I'm going to tell you. Some would say it is stealing. *Some* would say. But some would say it's what you could do for yourself.
> – Glenda, Signature Fashions worker

It is early morning at Signature Fashions, but work in the factory is already well under way. Throughout the stitching section, workers are busy sewing the latest line of garments bound for Signature's branded stores in Trinidad, Tobago, and throughout the Caribbean region. Kimberly is quietly at work on the hemming machine, passing T-shirt after T-shirt under its double needles, leaving two neat rows of stitching on the bottom of each garment. As soon as Cissy, the production manager, leaves the shop floor to enter the cutting room, Kimberly stops working and leans forward in her chair. She hisses at Gita, sitting at the straight-stitch sewing machine in front of her.

"Ssssssst," she says. Gita looks over her shoulder at Kimberly. "If I give you a shirt, you could put a pocket on it and keep your stories straight?"

"Sure," Gita says, turning back to her work. I don't see Kimberly pass Gita the shirt and pocket, but I expect that she will do so later in the morning, now that Gita has agreed to "thief a chance" for her. For now, the shirt—an exact copy of the brand-name garments the workers have been laboring over all week—rests in a black plastic garbage bag hanging beneath Kimberly's machine. With the help of fellow workers at nearly every stage of the production process, by the end of the day Kimberly will have completed for herself a precise replica of the shirts that will appear in Signature's stores in time for Easter. She will smuggle it out of the factory either underneath her clothes or stashed in the bottom of her handbag, folded into a tight ball and stitched inside a scrap of cloth to look like a simple, homemade pincushion.

This is a book about life in a garment factory in Trinidad, West Indies. Its ethnographic moment is more than ten years after an International Monetary Fund (IMF)–backed program of liberalization began opening national trade barriers to readymade garments from abroad—an act that crippled the local industry in the face of intense global competition, transformed worker entitlements and expectations, and also presented new economic opportunities for engaging the global market. From the vantage of the shop floor, I examine the lived experience of economic restructuring. Moving beyond approaches that conceptualize factory workers as subjects who are mostly acted upon, I pay special attention to workers' attempts to exploit the interstices of new labor configurations through illicit and informal uses of the factory—practices they collectively dub "thiefing a chance." Despite the intense social coordination involved in "thiefing," workers describe it as a personal, individualistic enterprise rather than a form of collective resistance to workplace hegemony. Thiefing, in other words, is "what you could do for *yourself.*" I suggest therefore that thiefing a chance is not only a material practice; it is also a potent metaphor for how Trinidadian garment workers have confronted the ambivalent returns of the neoliberal era. By making and taking furtive opportunities, workers embrace a vision of themselves as enterprising subjects while actively complying with the competitive demands of a new economic order. An examination of the relationship among these (mis) uses of the factory, the labor process, and the subjectivities of the workforce reveals that thiefing is surprisingly "productive" in all kinds of ways.

Trade liberalization has created a new, global manufacturing landscape in which particular geographic regions now dominate garment production for the world market while other parts of the globe are considered economically untenable as clothing producers, even for domestic consumption. Recent years have seen the ascendance of China, Bangladesh, and India in the export-oriented production of garments and an associated decline of apparel manufacturing in North America, Europe, and the Caribbean (Gereffi and Frederick 2010; Lu 2013; Nordas 2004; Rivoli 2005; Frederick and Staritz 2012). Academic analyses often describe these processes in terms of the "winners" and "losers" of globalization. Yet I present a more complex and nuanced picture of a diverse, variegated, and tenacious local industry in Trinidad that has endured despite global trade liberalization in the form of small and medium-sized factories, illegal sweatshops, seamstresses' and tailors' workshops, and many hundreds of women stitching clothing for friends, family, and clients at home. These heterogeneous sites are connected to each other by the bodies of women who pursue employment, skill acquisition, and illicit enterprises in and through multiple locations. In its ethnographic specificity, this book examines what Neil Brenner and Nik Theodore (2002) call "actually existing neoliberalism," the complex, messy, and contingent ways an economic doctrine of liberalization, privatization, and competition becomes lived as everyday experiences. This neoliberalism is as much constituted through the ways in which people engage and invest in it as by state policies that institute it as a regime of economic governance.

THE PARADOX OF FLEXIBILITY

I spent nine of my fifteen months of fieldwork in Trinidad cutting, stitching, and packaging designer-label clothing alongside workers like Kimberly and Gita. The factory, which I call "Signature Fashions," produces contemporary, high-fashion clothing for the Eastern Caribbean market. Signature Fashions has survived the vagaries of trade liberalization by cultivating a distinctive brand name for its high-fashion garments with a quick turnaround from design and production to retail. As I conducted participant observation in the Signature Fashions factory, two things became quickly apparent to me that later shaped much of my interpretation of garment workers' experiences in Trinidad. First, although Signature Fashions produces a constantly changing, retail-driven product with a short production cycle, the factory's manufacturing process is modeled on the assembly line of classic Fordism—designed for the mass production of standard products by narrowly specialized workers—rather than on a "flexible," dynamic system of continual learning that would seem to suit the production of high-end garments. Workers at Signature Fashions were given little formal training and were not encouraged to innovate, to make decisions, or to problem-solve on the shop floor. Instead, workplace discipline promoted quiet acquiescence to supervisors' demands, invariably evoking the "boss lady" and "boss man" (the company's co-owners) as distant figures of central authority.

Signature Fashions, then, has a fundamental contradiction within its production process: the apparent incompatibility of a rigid, old-guard manufacturing system and a market-adaptive product. How, I wondered, did such flexible goods issue from a seemingly inflexible system? This is a question I call the "paradox of flexibility." The second thing visible to me on the shop floor were the multiple ways workers took advantage of the brief moments when their supervisors' backs were turned to work on illicit projects. Many of the workers maintained their own small-scale businesses in the evening, designing and stitching clothing for friends and neighbors at home. Some workers would copy Signature patterns for their clients by cleverly placing the cut pieces of a garment onto newspaper and tracing the shapes with a pen. ("Have to keep up with style if you sew for people," a worker named Antoinette once whispered to me as I watched her copy the pattern for a designer shirt in this way.) Workers would sometimes bring garments for their clients into the factory to give their homemade items a professional finish. Each of these activities was quietly described as thiefing a chance—a Trinidadian phrase that means taking an illicit opportunity for a small amount of personal gain. In its most sophisticated form, thiefing a chance also meant using company materials and machines to produce exact copies of the designer-label clothing as it came down the line. Workers managed the production of these garments by acquiring fabric from the cutting room and covertly enlisting co-workers to stitch for them during the normal workday.

The clothing produced on this clandestine assembly line would be smuggled home and worn at parties and other social events far away from the factory.

What seemed at first to be two interesting but unrelated features of shop-floor life—the incongruous rigidity of a factory requiring flexible production and workers' practices of thiefing a chance—have proven, with analysis, to be thoroughly entwined. Signature Fashions *did* churn out a constantly changing, market-responsive product. Yet this productive flexibility was not achieved through formal training and learning, workplace democracy, or any of the other managerial techniques that might be valued by a vertically integrated firm in an era of "flexible specialization" (Piore and Sabel 1984). Instead, in a hierarchical, Fordist organizational structure, flexibility became instituted in informal and unacknowledged ways: first, through a periodic intensification of labor and second, through a range of illicit activities workers quietly pursued on their own. When workers thief a chance, they skill themselves up for new sewing tasks—training themselves in a factory that refused to train them—and by managing the production of their own items, workers become invested in the smooth functioning of the entire manufacturing process. Through thiefing (not despite it), workers complied with management's unspoken instructions to become a flexible, self-motivating labor force.

My ethnography therefore contributes to scholarship that troubles conventional readings of "the factory" as a stable institution by emphasizing the intense and covert linkages between formal and informal registers of production. By analyzing how workers' everyday tactics intersect with the strategies of their employers, I show the Signature Fashions factory to be a material and social space in which a wide range of projects, plans, and desires becomes aligned and misaligned, at some moments in deep harmony and at others in rancorous conflict. Industrial ethnographies often highlight the disjuncture between the ideologies and practices of factory production, revealing hidden dependencies between formal and informal labor (Bolles 1996; De Neve 2005; Mollona 2009), the roles of kinship, gender, and racialized processes of subject-making in the manufacturing process (Fernandes 1997; Kim 2013; Lamphere 1987; Salzinger 2003; Yelvington 1995; Westwood 1984), and the importance of sentiments like desire in motivating laborers and capitalists alike (Cross 2009; Freeman 1998; Mills 1999; Shah 2006; Yanagisako 2002). I extend this tradition by examining the productive power of informal, unofficial, and illicit activities by workers on the shop floor, emphasizing the variability of their effects and how they frequently diverge from the intentions of the actors behind them.

Flexible production at Signature Fashions has been achieved less by design in response to the pressures of global free trade than by a paradox of authoritarian discipline and expectations of adaptability that garment workers daily resolve through illicit work practices. My analysis suggests a new reading of "the factory" as a far more accidental, in-deliberate, and serendipitous entity than is usually depicted. The factory here is approached not as a fixed, bounded, or unitary institution but instead as a social and material assemblage constituted through authorized and unauthorized action, acknowledged and unacknowledged interests, planned and unintended consequences. I emphasize that the interests of capitalists and workers are not always known to them and that a successful company can sometimes be sustained as much by the chance alignment of desires as by deliberate planning and activity.

This argument builds upon Sylvia Yanagisako's contention that analyses of economic motivation have been limited by an emphasis on goals and values as mental constructions over the embodied desires that also inspire human action. In her ethnography of the reproduction and maintenance of a capitalist class across several generations in the Italian silk-weaving industry, Yanagisako (2002:7–11) describes an internally differentiated bourgeoisie motivated as much by "sentiments," like the patriarchal desire for filial succession, as by a rational interest in profit maximization. She demonstrates that these sentiments constitute a force of production because they inspire particular forms of capitalist action, shaping the development of the silk industry in ways that are rarely acknowledged. I share with Yanagisako (ibid.:9) a rejection of dichotomizing approaches that separate "instrumental" from "affective" economic motivations. But by focusing on both employers and workers, I show how they bring competing needs to the factory that fall into and out of alignment with one another on the shop floor. My emphasis on the productive nature of these alignments reveals the sometimes incidental nature of capitalist success.

Global Capitalism's Long Embrace

This book is concerned with Trinidad, an island of 1,841 square miles with approximately 1 million inhabitants, located seven miles from the Venezuelan coastline (ILO 2004; see figure 1.1). Although Trinidad is joined with its neighboring island, Tobago, in the parliamentary Republic of Trinidad and Tobago, I follow the anthropological practice of treating the two islands separately. Trinidad has always been shaped by the vicissitudes of global capitalism; it can even be said that "Trinidad has been the creation of the global economy" (Miller 1994a:24). "Discovered" by Christopher Columbus in 1498, Trinidad was colonized by Spain, though neglected by the colonial power until the late eighteenth century. At that time, French slave owners fleeing political turmoil in the French West Indies were invited to settle the island and began cultivating sugar, cocoa, and cotton with enslaved African labor. Britain seized Trinidad in 1797, and the island remained a British colony until its political independence in 1962 (Brereton 1981:1–33, 222). After the emancipation of the slaves in 1838, indentured labor was "invited" from elsewhere in the British Empire, particularly India. The indentured Indian workers introduced to the island between 1845 and 1917 have given the society its diverse, "plural" character, as have the many migrants of European, Chinese, Venezuelan, Syrian, Lebanese, and African origin (England 2008:26).

Trinidad's slave plantations supplied the raw materials to fuel European industrialization; today, the country is principally a producer of oil and natural gas for the world market. Following an oil boom in the 1970s, Trinidad experienced a prolonged recession that culminated in three structural adjustment programs with the IMF and the World Bank in the late 1980s and early 1990s (Hilaire 2000). These agreements marked a shift from a state-controlled to a market-driven economy and entailed cutting public spending in exchange for technical and financial aid to revive the economy; the privatization of state-owned enterprises; a devaluation and floating of the national currency; withdrawal of most subsidies and price controls on food, medicine, and utilities; a reduction of the civil service through early retirement and layoffs; and the dismantling of trade barriers that had shielded local industry from global competition (Bynoe 2000; Henry and Williams 1991; ILO 2004; Riddell 2003; USDS 2001; WTO 1998).

Under the new terms of neoliberal governance, tariff and licensing protections would be mostly shed in favor of free trade (Ramsaran 1992; Sergeant and Forde 1992). The restructuring of Trinidad's garment sector began with a temporary replacement of quantitative import restrictions with "import surcharges," which were then gradually removed (Hilaire 2000:23). As a

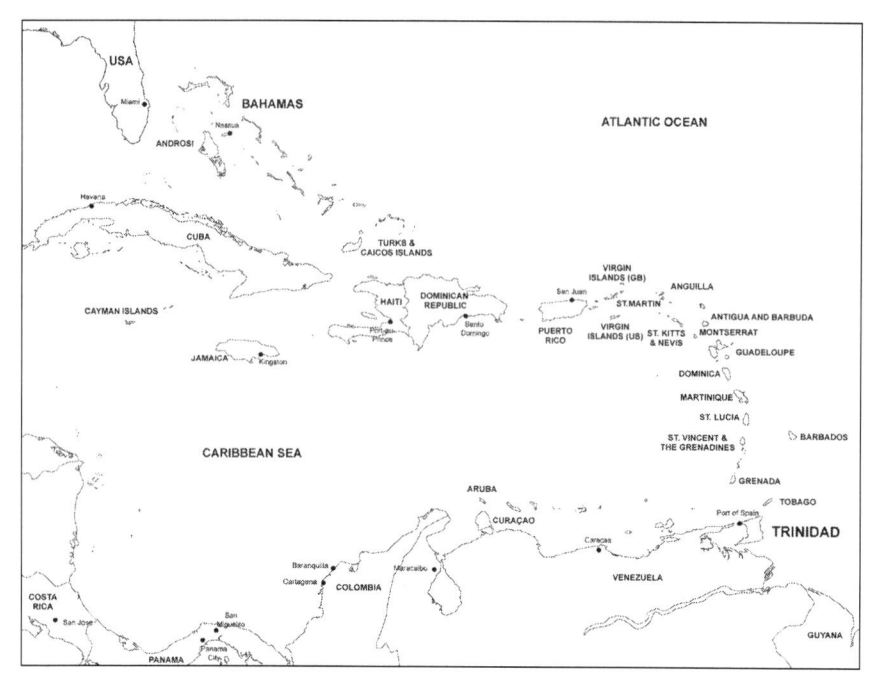

FIGURE 1.1. Map of Trinidad and the Caribbean region (map by Adam Howse)

member of the Caribbean Community (CARICOM), Trinidad adopted policies that would harmonize trade within the region.[1] By 1998, import duties of 45–50 percent on garments produced outside Trinidad had been reduced to 0 percent within the free trade area of CARICOM and to 20 percent on non-CARICOM goods (World Bank 2009; USDS 2001).

As liberalization policies began to take hold, many local companies found themselves unable to compete with the quality and price of clothing newly arriving from overseas. As one former factory owner told me, trade liberalization "was the death of the local garment industry. There is no way [we] could compete with goods coming directly out of China." Manufacturers of commodity garments like T-shirts and trousers have been the most vulnerable; although the lowering of tariffs on non-CARICOM imports to 20 percent appears to offer continuing protection to Trinidadian producers exporting to the regional market, it has been insufficient to offset the comparative advantage of low wages and economies of scale that benefit large Asian suppliers (Rahman et al. 2008; World Bank 2009).

Between 1990 and 2000, Trinidad's garment manufacturing workforce declined 42 percent, although official statistics mask the extent to which garment workers' livelihoods have moved into an informal sector of sporadic employment and domestic needleworking where their labor remained uncounted (CSO 2003:27). The country's dependency on imports to meet basic needs meant that the devaluation of the Trinidad and Tobago dollar raised the cost of living (Hilaire 2000; Riddell 2003). With the doubling of food prices between 1995 and 2005 (Manning 2005), even workers with full-time employment in minimum-wage factories like Signature Fashions frequently supplemented their income by sewing at home.

During the course of my fieldwork and in the months and years since, I have come to see thiefing a chance as a central idiom for how garment workers in Trinidad have coped with the demands of the neoliberal era. Since the 1990s, garment workers have witnessed the withdrawal of both state and trade-union interest in their welfare in the factories and an increasing need to look after themselves in everything ranging from pay disputes to occupational injury. This period has also seen a yearning among Trinidadians for brand-name clothing carrying markers of style and status that are central to modern self-making in this island context (Miller 1994a). Signature Fashions workers maneuver within the material conditions of the local environment, seeking not only economic survival but also the opportunity to undertake culturally oriented projects such as producing, wearing, and gifting high-status clothing.

"Thiefing a chance" is a resolutely Trinidadian phrase. It is part of a wider cultural discourse about how an individual can best "get on" in a constantly changing and competitive economic arena. These kinds of discourses date back to at least the slave era, when trickster tales encoded culturally accepted survival strategies throughout the Black Atlantic (Andrews and Gates 1999; Harris 1995; Roberts 1989). New World slavery demanded modes of coping marked not only by self-reliance and resourcefulness but also craftiness and guile. This cultural complex, both practical and stylistic, is celebrated in local narratives that recast ex-slaves as not just survivors but heroes of their own history. Katherine Browne's (2004) examination of illicit economic practices in Martinique shows how widespread, off-the-books ventures in building, entrepreneurship, and small-scale trading are not only profitable for participants but also serve a cultural purpose in enhancing the esteem of those who participate in them, known locally as *débrouillards*. Martiniquans pursue off-the-books economic activities (which Browne calls "creole economics") to achieve financial autonomy despite the law while at the same time satisfying their desire for a self-reliant economic selfhood. Creole economics contains the pleasures of both risk taking and social recognition, although for men becoming a débrouillard is concerned with being one's own boss whereas women emphasize the need to escape dependency on men.

Browne shows that creole economics valorizes a disregard for the law as long as it is carried out with creativity, cunning, and flair. She locates the roots of this moral code in the slave period, considering it an adaptation to the privations and humiliations of the slavery experience (ibid.:120–22). Débrouillardism therefore embodies a defiant strain of creole culture that has always run counter to the European-derived values of respectability and deference to social hierarchy (Wilson 1973:9). However, by tracing a historical genealogy that emphasizes cultural continuity, Browne overlooks the fact that débrouillardism also represents the entrepreneurial spirit that neoliberalism now enshrines as a foremost value. We live in the age of the daring individual, when success means making and taking opportunities for yourself. In this book I argue that there has been a remarkable convergence between the forms of subjectivity promoted by neoliberalism and the economic selfhood embodied in practices like thiefing a chance. As Carla Freeman (2005, 2007) has observed, this reflects the ways in which a neoliberal economic order confers new respectability on old Caribbean cultural mores by recasting creole values as virtues rather than vices. My aim is to ethnographically document this convergence and consider what it means for workers and workplaces in Trinidad.

A Neoliberal Factory

How can we account for the similitude between the values of neoliberalism and thiefing a chance? Sidney Mintz might argue that they both possess shared Caribbean origins. He observes that the region has been "global" since the fifteenth century, that its colonial position gave rise to the West as we know it, and that the slave plantations—with their technical features, hierarchical structures, and adherence to strict time disciplines—were prototypical industrial factories (Mintz 1996:295, 1998; Williams 1994). The Caribbean is not a non-Western outpost recently penetrated by international capitalism.

Rather, it is where modern capitalism found early and brutal expression and where new techniques of production, surveillance, and the transmutation of persons into mechanistic laborers formed a profitable foundation for New World economy and society.

An interpretation of the Caribbean as capitalism's cradle explains why globalization has been uniquely experienced in the region not as the "radical reversal of relationships of property, culture, and power" but instead as *"the extension of already established relationships . . . a realignment rather than a rupture"* (Robotham 1998:308 [original emphasis]). According to Jeffrey Mantz (2007), the region's centuries-long imbrication in the world market has produced economic subjectivities that render Caribbean people particularly able, confident, and uncomplaining in their encounters with neoliberal capitalism. Writing about the resourcefulness of female agricultural traders ("hucksters") in Dominica, Mantz portrays their entrepreneurial savvy as part of a flexible economic disposition culturally autochthonous to the region. Gina Ulysse makes a similar observation about female informal importers and market traders in Jamaica. She describes how the women have confronted each restriction on their trade, such as increasingly strict customs policies, as a challenge to overcome. As one informant proclaimed: "There isn't a foundation that don't have a crack in it . . . We will find it and we will go right through it" (Ulysse 2007:1).

Trinidadian women like the ones I describe, sitting at rows of sewing machines, toiling beneath fluorescent lights, seem to fulfill the image of generic victims of contemporary capitalism: hardworking, poorly paid, and with little ability to influence the conditions of their employment. Yet such an interpretation represents a limited approach to women's economic agency of the kind criticized by feminist anthropologists in recent years (Lynch 2007; Mills 1999; Ngai 2005; Rofel 1999). Shop-floor ethnographies reveal not only the pervasive and powerful ways workplaces act upon the subjectivities of women workers—subtly disciplining them to become the "docile bodies" of production envisioned by Michel Foucault (1979)—but also how these processes are confronted, resisted, and transformed by those enmeshed in them. Because every economic system presents not just constraints on agency but also opportunities for action, we must resist unidirectional analyses that would portray neoliberal globalization as something that is simply done "to" Caribbean women (Freeman 2001). An ethnographic approach means not succumbing to a view of Caribbean women as perennial victims or as the rational actors of neoclassical economic fantasy; rather, it asks us to consider how women interpret and act upon their world in big and small ways and with what effects.

Kevin Yelvington's study of a Trinidadian factory showed how the proliferation of low-end assembling industries in the global South required their insertion into the cultural, political, and economic matrices that already existed in places like Trinidad (Yelvington 1995). On the shop floor, management mobilized social hierarchies of race, class, and gender derived from the plantation economy to fragment the workforce into separate occupational niches. This move successfully divided workers' interests because they comported with false but commonsensical notions that different races and genders were predisposed to certain types of work. Just as the planter elite once promulgated negative stereotypes of African and East Indian workers to wedge apart their shared class interests, Yelvington shows how these strategies are most successful when groups internalize the unfavorable portrayals of themselves and each other (ibid.:50, 65; Munasinghe 2001:66). The Trinidadian shop floor therefore cannot be understood except in relation to its capitalist history and how that history articulates with local social categories and identities.

For Trinidadian garment workers, the neoliberal turn has meant new challenges but not an upending of life as they knew it before. They have greeted these challenges with a sense of familiarity rather than alarm. The patience, resilience, and readiness to adapt to new labor regimes that have long helped Caribbean women survive also make them exemplary "flexible" economic actors for the neoliberal era.[2] I show in this book that the prevalence of these qualities in the workforce represents an important but neglected reason why Trinidad's garment industry has endured since trade liberalization. In probing how an institutional reliance on the flexibility of labor ultimately disadvantages workers in a context of waged employment, I ask to what extent garment workers have been made accomplices in their own exploitation.

Illicit Acts and Questions of Agency

By placing an analysis of the illicit at the heart of my study, this book explores the role of unsanctioned work practices in a neoliberal labor process. The anthropological literature contains abundant examples of theft, poaching, pilfering, side production, and game playing among industrial workers and other types of employees (Anteby 2008; Burawoy 1985; Haraszti 1978; Mars 1982; Yelvington 1995). Scholars have demonstrated that illicit and informal activities on the shop floor should be considered neither deviant nor ancillary to production but rather must be analyzed in relation to official work processes.

Michael Burawoy (1979) famously described workers in an American machine shop who attempted to gain control over their work through shop-floor games that maximized the financial returns of piece-rate payment without disrupting the ability of others to do the same. Approaching work as a game, employees assessed the likelihood of being able to exceed the piece rate ("making out"). Workers who faced backbreaking piece rates responded by choosing *not* to make the quota, satisfying themselves instead with the guaranteed-minimum base pay; those who were assigned easy-to-achieve piece rates disciplined themselves to keep production below the maximum they could produce, believing that if they overproduced, management would simply recalibrate the rates (ibid.:57). Although making out required cooperation and the enforcement of shared norms, it also had the unintended effect of individualizing workers and enjoining them to work harder. For Burawoy, what is most important is that through these games, workers not only participate in the appropriation of the surplus value of their labor; they also participate in *obscuring* this surplus value extraction. Through making out, workers gain a sense of mastery and autonomy over their work while at the same time consenting to their own exploitation. This element of consent (which obviates coercion) gives such casual "games" a pernicious effect by reconfiguring workers' internal motivations.

In examining thiefing a chance at Signature Fashions, it is important to consider not simply the intentions of workers as active agents in production but also the effects of their illicit practices, both on themselves and on the labor process. Copying garments on the shop floor may act as a strain on the manufacturing process, but, as Burawoy suggests, it may also operate as a lubricant to the smooth functioning of production. We cannot assume prima facie that illicit acts are inimical to the interests of employers but instead must examine them in the context of material and ideological struggles. Over the past three decades, James Scott's concept of "everyday resistance" has rejuvenated a

Gramscian analytic that frames the relationship between unsanctioned activities and the everyday politics of labor in terms of accommodation and resistance (Scott 1985, 2005). Scott described Malaysian peasant laborers' secret and uncoordinated acts of pilfering, gossiping, foot dragging, slander, and evasion not as spontaneous though inconsequential transgressions but instead as evidence of a latent revolutionary consciousness that continually critiqued the prevailing economic and political order. Gossiping and joking about the dominant classes demonstrated the ability of subordinate groups to penetrate hegemonic portrayals of the world; pilfering from landowners without remorse shows the persistence of local moral economies. For Scott, these examples of "everyday resistance" provide evidence that class consciousness can reside behind even the most convincing mask of compliance.

Yet if we are primed to theorize workers' unsanctioned activities as resistance to the exploitative conditions in which they labor, we might be surprised to discover that Signature Fashions workers insist on a depoliticized interpretation of thiefing a chance. Workers do not describe thiefing as a form of redistributive justice and refuse to justify it as compensation for the inequity in earnings between themselves and their employers. Instead, the factory is encountered as a resource containing materials, machines, and know-how that the cunning individual uses for her own purposes. Thiefing a chance is rendered morally acceptable precisely because its participants do not define the practice as *taking* from employers. Workers who thief a chance see themselves as seizing an opportunity that has fleetingly arisen in their midst. Like the débrouillards described by Katherine Browne, they pride themselves on doing so with bravery and style.

To assess worker agency, we must separate intentionality from effects, neither of which can be appreciated without an awareness of subjectivity. It is precisely a neglect of subjectivity, defined as "the ensemble of modes of perception, affect, thought, desire, fear, and so forth that animate acting subjects," to which Sherry Ortner (2005:31) has drawn attention in arguing that anthropology's increasing suspicion of the explanatory value of "culture" has led to an impoverished understanding of human motivation. When garment workers thief a chance, they enact a particular interpretation of the world, structured by their cultural histories and the economic exigencies of the present. An emphasis on subjectivity helps us to move beyond the simplistic notion that choice is constrained by circumstances, to see instead that actors possess an internalized "sense of what is possible and what is not" (Gregory 2007:207). Thiefing a chance is the expression of an individualistic, enterprising subjectivity. I argue that its routine enactment in the workplace has not only direct consequences for the politics of labor but also the insidious effect of validating neoliberal principles of opportunism and self-seeking that make it difficult for workers to find common cause through conventional avenues of solidarity.

Research Strategy and Methods

I spent fifteen months in Trinidad, from August 2003 to November 2004. It was my first experience in the country, other than a short visit in March 2003 to assess the feasibility of my research project and seek the advice of scholars at the University of the West Indies. Inspired by Kevin Yelvington's 1995 ethnography of a Trinidadian factory and hoping to reassess its findings in light of the emerging neoliberal orthodoxies of privatization, deregulation, and liberalization, my first goal upon arrival was to find a factory where I could undertake long-term participant observation. After three weeks of contacting garment factories on my own with little success (I would be given an interview, a polite tour of the factory, and a firm "no" to my request to work as an unpaid employee), I turned for help to a friendly cloth merchant I had met during my first days in the country. He arranged for me to meet Helene Forester, a well-known fashion designer and co-owner (with her husband, Robert) of Signature Fashions, a local company with a small factory in Trinidad and nearly twenty stores in the Eastern Caribbean. With none of the suspicion and wariness I had encountered at other factories, Helene and Robert seemed amused by my proposal to trade my labor for a chance to get to know the workers.

Over the following nine months, I arrived at the factory at 7:30 a.m. each weekday (and occasional Saturdays), leaving at 3:30 or 5:30 in the evening, depending on whether overtime was required. I told the workers I met that I was an American student from a university in England and that I wanted to learn about their experiences so I could write a book about Trinidad's garment industry. Although I was initially reluctant to take notes, by the third month of research I was carrying a small notebook in the front pocket of my apron and openly scribbling in it throughout the day. I was surprised to find my jottings mostly ignored by workers, except when they felt they had been poorly treated and insisted I write it down in my "book." By taking notes throughout the day, I managed to record many conversations taking place in my midst nearly word for word with the speakers' knowledge. These dialogues proved to be rich data, and this book therefore has a strong emphasis on the everyday, vernacular language of the shop floor.

In transcribing forms of Trinidadian spoken English locally referred to as "dialect," I follow the convention of the national newspapers ("ehnt" for "ain't" and "t'ing" for "thing"). Although dialect is socially devalued in official environments such as educational institutions and workplaces, it also serves as a national unifier: a point of pride, affection, and cultural difference for Trinidadians among the community of nations. Dialect is associated with the everyday speech of the working class of all ethnic backgrounds, but Trinidadians of all social classes (and indeed, ethnic groups) selectively play with dialect as a means of marking in-group relations, signaling solidarity, or satirizing themselves and others. In representing the speech of my informants, I try to capture the sound of their words as spoken, explaining meanings when they may not be apparent to readers unfamiliar with the region. In doing so, I attempt to preserve the deliberateness of my informants' linguistic choices without exoticizing the "otherness" of their speech (Mose Brown and Masi de Casanova 2014).

After I had worked in the factory for several months, management gave me permission to conduct one recorded interview with each worker on wooden benches outdoors during slow work days. By the time of these interviews, I knew most of the workers well and already considered some to be friends. After many hours of working, shopping, talking, and "liming" (relaxed socializing) together, these interviews filled in the gaps in my knowledge and provided them with a chance to narrate their own experiences for the record. Every worker but one allowed me to tape these conversations; I also recorded interviews with management and the factory owners, as well as owners and workers at several other Trinidadian factories as part of a wider survey of the industry I conducted in the summer of 2004.

Working in a factory as a major component of fieldwork has both advantages and disadvantages in comparison to other forms of ethnographic research (Hsiung 1996; Salzinger 2003; Yelvington 1995). The primary advantage of participant observation in the factory is that it provides a sustained and intimate look at how the workplace "works," allowing the researcher to distinguish "people in terms of what they actually do" from "merely what they say they do" (Miller 1997:16–17). By internalizing the time disciplines, physical movements, and bodily postures required of workers in the industry, the researcher is able to get a deeper sense of the relationship between the factory as a material and discursive context and the factory as lived space. As an unpaid employee, I could be both witness to and subject of disciplinary power, although always in critically different ways than the other workers. The factory also provides a mundane, everyday context for meeting people and gradually establishing relationships.

Yet the disadvantages of participant observation in a factory are also legion. I found the work physically punishing, especially when I spent ten hours a day carrying, stacking, and cutting cloth during a busy period before Christmas. I pushed myself to do a "good job" on all the tasks assigned to me, not only as a sign of goodwill toward the factory owners but also because my short conversations and joking banter with workers were predicated on a shared acknowledgment that the work had to get done. After a hard day's work, I sometimes could muster only an hour of typing notes while my fellow workers were home preparing meals, cleaning their houses, sewing for private clients, and looking after children. Like many of them, I took a break each evening to watch the 6 o'clock news and *The Bold and the Beautiful*, an American soap opera that has eclipsed *The Young and the Restless* as the Trinidadian media obsession (cf. Miller 1992).

My routine movements during the week shadowed those of the workers I researched. We took early-morning route taxis together to the highway where the Signature Fashions factory was located; we shopped in Port of Spain in the evening for fresh fruit and vegetables on our way home. On Saturday mornings I bought groceries at the open market on the Beetham Highway. I spent Sundays visiting the churches and homes of Signature Fashions workers. The constricted geography of my everyday routine represents a stark contrast to the peripatetic activities of anthropologist Michael Lieber (1981), who followed his male informants across Port of Spain each day as they hustled livelihoods in the informal sector. This difference not only reveals the gendered and occupational patterns of day-to-day motility; it also indicates that although many accounts of Caribbean life emphasize open-endedness, freedom, and movement, some working-class women find it difficult to escape tightly circumscribed avenues because of the high cost of transportation and the arduous demands of daily work. Time for "fetes" (parties), Afro-religious feasts, and liming was carved out of the late-night hours, often at the cost of sleep. The occasional fete at a worker's home was meticulously planned, usually around a child's birthday, with a great deal of cooking and investment in rented sound equipment for music if money was available. Younger garment workers with boyfriends might be taken "out." For many of the older workers, religious worship and family gatherings seemed to be the only time when they were not engaged in income-generating activities, household tasks, or rest.

From the shop floor of Signature Fashions, I followed various threads that led to other research sites. I conducted short-term ethnographic research in two other workplaces: a small garment factory ("Universal Uniforms") that produced vocational and school uniforms for the Caribbean market and a Carnival *mas* (masquerade) camp, where I spent evenings gluing sequins on bikinis leading up to the pre-Lenten Carnival. I also learned about the industry by touring factories and repeatedly visiting the offices, homes, or workplaces of seamstresses, tailors, government officials, businesspeople, educators, and trade unionists. I visited medical clinics where occupational injuries are evaluated and treated, the homes and offices of alternative-care practitioners, and the churches and temples where many workers go to have their bodies rejuvenated and healed. Many of my relationships built during my initial fieldwork have endured over the subsequent ten years, strengthened by visits, phone calls, text messages, and sharing our lives over Facebook.

During my first six months in the field, I lived in a working women's hostel in Port of Spain, sharing a bedroom with a nineteen-year-old student from Tobago. When my partner, Michael, had saved enough money to quit his job in England and join me in Trinidad, we moved into a one-bedroom house in the working-class neighborhood of Belmont. Our house was near the homes of Donna and Jean, two Signature Fashions workers who helped me find the rental. I began taking sewing lessons three nights a week from Donny, a local tailor. I wanted to better understand how to construct a whole garment from scratch (a common skill among Signature's workers) and to gain an embodied understanding of how to select cloth, devise and cut a pattern, and sew a garment together. Learning how to sew became inseparable from fieldwork; in factories, in Donny's shop, and in garment workers' homes, sewing alongside others gave me precious insight into the material construction of garments and their makers' social worlds (Prentice 2008).

Living in a predominantly Afro-Trinidadian area of Port of Spain has undoubtedly shaped my account of garment workers in Trinidad, particularly as compared with the experiences of Indo-Trinidadian garment workers. Like the population of the country, approximately half of the Signature Fashions workers could be described as "Afro-Trinidadian," claiming descent primarily or exclusively from African slaves or settlers, and half could be described as "Indo-Trinidadian," claiming descent primarily or exclusively from South Asian indentured laborers. I got to know both groups well, in part, I believe, because my outsider status (white and foreign) prevented my being too quickly categorized as the "natural" ally of either group; nonetheless, most (though by no means all) of my closest informants were Afro-Trinidadian. Of course, the phrase *Trinidadian garment workers* refers to a diverse and internally differentiated group of people, not simply along demographic lines of race, age, marital status, area of residence, and so on, but also in regard to personal histories, habits, desires, and life projects. I specify in the text where *garment worker* is a useful term that captures commonalities of experience and where important differences may be found within that broad category.[3] Following Viranjini Munasinghe (2001:xi–xii, 97), I use the terms *Indo-Trinidadian* and *Afro-Trinidadian* throughout my ethnography to distinguish etic analysis from everyday, emic speech: "Indian" or "East Indian" to denote Trinidadians of predominantly or entirely South Asian descent and "African," "Negro," "Black," "Creole," or "Afro-Creole" to denote Trinidadians of predominantly or entirely African descent.

Many anthropologists have noted that the intimacies of long-term ethnographic research in complex fields of power generate particular predicaments, both in the field (Brown 1987; Ulysse 2002) and during the writing process afterward (Behar and Gordon 1995; Clifford and Marcus 1986; M. Wolf 1992). A feminist orientation attuned me to multiple, shifting power dynamics in play, not only among individuals and groups in the factories but also in my own relationships with informants and friends. Anthropologists get close to informants and then write about intimate details of their lives—a situation so laden with power disparities that some scholars have questioned the viability of a "feminist ethnography" altogether (Enslin 1994). I am heartened by Judith Stacey's conclusion that although ethnography is more perilous than the supposedly masculinist research strategies of objective social science (wherein both researcher and researched have defined and limited roles), the "uneasy fusion" of feminism and ethnography produces critical knowledge with a subtlety and perceptiveness unachievable through other means (Stacey 1988:26), the loss of which would diminish our understanding of the world.

I have honored my promise to keep my informants anonymous by using pseudonyms for all named persons and factories in the text and, on rare occasions, subtly altering an informant's distinguishing features. In writing about illicit practices in the Signature Fashions factory, I have chosen to focus on workers who are no longer employed there. I have used similar tactics to disguise the identity of Signature Fashions, which is one of several brand-name clothing producers in Trinidad. The long lead time in academic publishing has meant that both the company and workers about whom I write have moved on in many different ways. As the Trinidadian garment industry continues to shrink and transform itself, some workers have taken up employment in other areas, such as food service. Many of the women most devoted to working "in the sewing" now operate entirely in the informal sector of own-account work; several factory owners have cut costs by closing operations and sending workers home with industrial-grade machines and sewing to complete on a piecework basis. But that is a story for another time.

Assembling the Factory

This book pivots around the organizing concept of "thiefing a chance," which here connotes Trinidadian ways of constructing a livelihood by seizing formal, informal, and illicit opportunities. I present thiefing a chance as a metaphor for life under neoliberalism, where workers are expected to be adaptive and enterprising, resilient and uncomplaining. These "flexible" economic qualities are embraced and indeed embodied by Signature Fashions workers—in part because of the exigencies of contemporary life in Trinidad and in part as a result of the historical ways Caribbean subjectivities have been shaped by capitalistic imperatives since the region's founding.

The next chapter serves as an introduction to the factory and brand at the center of this book. Anthropological studies of factory life tend to make two assumptions: that capitalists know their own interests and that they act upon them. These assumptions too often generate ethnographies that pit capital against labor in an interlocking struggle over interests. Here I show the factory to be a much more in-deliberate and serendipitous entity, constituted through the competing and frequently unarticulated desires of factory owners, managers, and workers. By portraying how the factory "works" both materially and socially, I reveal the productivity of the informal and the illicit and how a flexible factory might come to rely on these hidden registers of production.

Chapter 3 serves as an introduction to the Signature Fashions workers. With emphasis on the life stories of three garment workers, I show the role of emotion and pleasure—rather than just economic necessity—that draws Trinidadian women into and out of the garment industry. As highly skilled seamstresses, they often describe themselves not as "garment workers" but instead as women "into the sewing," committed to making a living through the production of clothing in factories, small workshops, or at home sewing for private clients (and often all three). This chapter introduces the workers' home communities and shows how racial identities and communities of origin shape hierarchy and authority through the classification of working bodies on the shop floor.

Chapter 4 describes illicit labor practices secretly (and not-so-secretly) performed by workers each day. These practices, which workers dub "thiefing a chance," include furtively producing extra garments on the assembly line to distribute among themselves, as well as quietly trying out new machines without managerial permission. Workers' categorical rejection of a discourse of resistance to justify "thiefing" suggests that these illicit shop-floor activities would be best interpreted within a creole cultural schema that celebrates cunning self-reliance. Thiefing as a do-it-yourself enterprise represents not a rejection of the values of neoliberalism but rather their elevation.

I describe how Trinidadian garment workers gain expertise in sewing in chapter 5. Workers rely on their technical sewing abilities and knowledge of fashion to forge livelihoods in an unstable and demanding industry. Signature Fashions workers describe skills not as a functional capacity but instead as a cumulative project of self-actualization located in the body. I show how "love" of sewing ties together formal and informal sectors of Trinidad's garment industry yet also how the willingness of women "into the sewing" to embrace opportunity and change is exploited in contexts of waged employment.

Chapter 6 explores how the shop floor is experienced through workers' bodies by examining how they perceive and navigate shop-floor risks of injury and ill health. The factory is an environment in which workers try to protect their bodies and maintain health by asserting control over the pace and progress of their work. These relations of "normal" exploitation are thrown into disarray by episodes of injury that become flashpoints of debate. With the post-liberalization withdrawal of state and trade-union interest in factory workers' welfare, the romantic image of workers as dynamic, flexible, and autonomous agents encapsulated in discourses of thiefing a chance is continually challenged by what Elaine Scarry (1985:14) has called "the sheer material factness of the body."

Chapter 7 looks outward from the shop floor onto an epidemic of kidnappings for ransom that rocked Trinidad during the period of fieldwork. Garment factories were uniquely entangled in the kidnapping crisis because the owner-managers of small family enterprises were often represented in the public imaginary as prime targets for abduction by poor urban criminals, making the shop floor a site of a potentially risky mixture between antagonistic categories of people. The widespread accusation that fabric importers were smuggling drugs and guns into Trinidad interpreted the wealth of industry leaders as ill-gotten and their abduction as morally justifiable. At the Signature Fashions factory, workers and managers grappled with the notion that the neoliberal era is deeply criminal, in which financial gain is a dirty business. I also show how local critiques of the global economy can become mired in internal feuds over race and politics.

Notes

1. CARICOM countries include Antigua and Barbuda, the Bahamas (though not a common-market member), Barbados, Belize, Dominica, Grenada, Guyana, Haiti, Jamaica, Montserrat, St. Kitts and Nevis, St. Lucia, St. Vincent and the Grenadines, Suriname, and Trinidad and Tobago (Griffith 1990:50; ILO 2004).

2. An emphasis on economic and cultural continuities before and during trade liberalization in Trinidad represents an important corrective to an analytical preoccupation with the "exceptional" nature of neoliberal capitalism (Ong 2006; Sanders 2008:111). As Jamie Cross (2010a) has argued in relation to workers in India, the adverse labor conditions formalized in neoliberal enclaves such as

export-processing zones are not very different from those long found in the informal economy outside of them.

3. As I explain in chapter 3, many Signature Fashions workers reject the label "garment worker" and describe themselves instead as women who are simply "into the sewing." For the sake of clarity, I retain the phrase *garment workers* to refer to the diverse group of individuals who make their living from producing garments, including women who prefer to represent themselves as "into the sewing," noting (where relevant) the importance of the distinction between the two categories.

2

Being a Factory the Signature Way

As markets become fragmented and the pace of innovation faster, everyone seems to agree that production methods and labor need to become more flexible; but there agreement ends, because "flexibility" is a dangerous substance . . . From now on workers must be prepared to learn new skills and turn their hand to any kind of work, familiar or unfamiliar, in whatever conditions suit the employer; but workers do not participate actively in decisions about production since that is the manager's prerogative.
– Mark Holmström, "Industrial Districts and Flexible Specialization"

[The boss] tell us what to do, and we will do it that way . . . until she walk away. Then you see we do it our *own* style.
– Glenda, Signature Fashions worker

In the departure lounge at Tobago's tiny airport, a large advertising poster depicts a young Afro-Caribbean man in carefree repose, resting against a sunlit white background. He wears sunglasses and a loose-fitting linen shirt. His face is a picture of calm relaxation. A company logo, *Signature Fashions*, and its tidy tag line, "lovingly made in your T&T," adorn the poster and, along with the serene beauty of the man's face, make up its most prominent features. Just steps away from where travelers will board their aircraft for the twenty-five-minute flight to Trinidad, the poster is located along one of the well-traveled circuits of potential Signature customers: wealthy, cosmopolitan, and country-proud Trinidad-and-Tobagonians. While the poster's imagery may appeal to foreign tourists, it is to the regional passengers' aesthetic sensibilities and native pride that the advertisement is directed.

Signature Fashions is a Trinidadian clothing company with a factory near Port of Spain (the capital city) and a chain of stores throughout the Eastern Caribbean. It was founded in 1990 by a celebrated Trinidadian fashion designer, Helene Forester, and her husband, Robert. With attractive retail outlets in upscale shopping malls, Signature Fashions presents itself as the brand of choice for Trinidadians seeking unique, good-quality garments with an up-to-the-minute fashion sense. Signature Fashions is one of the most expensive local retailers of ready-to-wear clothing, competing with imported brands like Benetton, Levi's, and Tommy Hilfiger. Like those foreign labels, Signature's clothing is prominently emblazoned with the distinctive "Signature" logo, but unlike them, Signature Fashions is tightly tied to local circuits of culture, reflecting and reshaping the aesthetic sensibilities of its core market. By "working" its localness through exclusive fetes, televised fashion shows, and print advertising, Signature has been able to escape the provincial image that frequently plagues Caribbean brands (Yelvington 1995:99; Naipaul 1981:48).

When Signature Fashions began producing designer-label clothing in 1990, garment factories were already disappearing from Trinidad's manufacturing landscape. After a devastating recession in the 1980s and the International Monetary Fund (IMF)–backed reduction of trade barriers to readymade garments from abroad by the end of the decade, many local factories—whose supremacy in the domestic market had been secured by high tariffs and import-licensing restrictions on foreign clothing—slowly began to shut down (TIDCO 2003a). Global free-trade policies, including the dismantling of the quota system that existed from 1974 to 2004 under the international Multi-Fibre Agreement (MFA), have meant that local firms lost preferential access to North American markets (Economist Intelligence Unit 2005:31; Özden and Sharma 2006:243). At the same time, the importation of Asian garments into the Caribbean region has priced Trinidadian producers out of competition (Ramprasad 1997:185–86; Singh 2004; World Bank 2009).

Three types of garment firms have remained profitable under Trinidad's liberalizing regime, each of which possesses the agility and resilience to contend with these rapidly changing market conditions. Low-end sweatshops casualize labor by paying cash wages below the statutory minimum, hiring and firing workers in accordance with contractors' varying demands (Momm 1999). High-tech firms have adopted new technologies to rationalize production and achieve efficiency with small workforces (Jayasinghe 2001). Signature Fashions has pursued a third strategy: cultivating a recognizable brand name and design sensibility for its high-cost clothing, with a quick turnaround from design and production to sale.

With niche marketing and responsiveness to consumer demand, Signature Fashions has achieved a form of industrial flexibility that is supposedly crucial in an age of neoliberal capitalism. Scholars like David Harvey (1990) have described this flexibility as an innovation of post-Fordism, as firms attempt to meet the manufacturing requirements of a constantly changing, retail-driven market. The ethnographic literature shows that this industrial flexibility can be achieved equally through the "high road" of workplace democracy as through the "low road" of casualization, intermittent layoffs, and an unraveling of workers' rights (Collins 2001; De Neve 2005; Dunn 2004; Holmström 1998; Rothstein 2005; Wright 2001). From the vantage of the shop floor, flexible production is also a complex and contested process, where day-to-day practices might look very different from the company's policies. Although there are certainly some elements of flexibility "by design" at Signature Fashions, much of the firm's ability to meet changing manufacturing requirements comes about not as a purposeful or planned response to the competitive pressures of global free trade. Instead, Signature Fashions has become a flexible factory through a complex configuration of hierarchy, authority, and discipline on the shop floor, which manages to secure flexible manufacturing operations while simultaneously denying workers' unsanctioned roles in achieving that flexibility.

Finding the Factory

The advertisement's claim that Signature Fashions clothing is made in Trinidad and Tobago is mostly true. While some of the denim jeans are now produced in China, the rest of the garments are designed and assembled in a small factory on Trinidad's Churchill-Roosevelt Highway, one mile east of Port of Spain. Here, in a plain-front building wedged between a furniture wholesaler and an industrial print shop, two designers and fifty shop-floor workers—almost all women—design, cut, stitch, serge, press, trim, fold, and package Signature's high-fashion garments for the company's stores. In contrast to the visibility of the Signature brand on its storefronts and in advertising, the factory is an anonymous building. The famed Signature logo is displayed nowhere on the front gate; the factory's only designation from the other buildings in the industrial compound is a large number 9 on its front door. With poignant if ironic juxtaposition, a twenty-foot-long billboard stood less than half a mile away on the same highway, depicting two elegantly dressed models, with the printed caption that Signature Fashions is "lovingly made" right here at home.

I was put in touch with Helene, one of the company's co-owners, by a fabric retailer I met during my first days of fieldwork. Over the telephone, Helene agreed to meet with me at her office to discuss my desire to work in her factory, unpaid, for six months.[1] When I arrived at the factory, I was greeted in the front room by a slim, smartly dressed receptionist sitting at a computer. A Signature Fashions advertisement featuring two models in knitwear rested against one of the brightly painted walls behind her. As she led me up the steel staircase to the company's offices, I realized that the wooden door opposite the stairs led to the shop floor; from behind it I could hear dozens of sewing machines clattering with productivity.

Sitting in Helene's stylish, wood-floor office, I felt like I was in a realm dedicated to fashion design rather than its industrial production. With a dressmaker's dummy and a huge drafting table, Helene's workspace seemed more like a garret atelier than the office of a factory owner. As she chatted with me across a desk strewn with fashion magazines and fabric samples, Helene's desire to talk more about the fashion elements of her company than its labor practices was evident. Breezily tossing my research proposal atop a pile of magazines, Helene began to describe what she hoped to achieve with her company: to put Trinidad on "the fashion map."

As Helene described it, the worsening position of Trinidad's garment industry was of little concern to her and her husband, Robert, when they began planning a "fashion company" in the late 1980s. They saw themselves as sharing little kinship with local bosses who for decades had run mass-production factories, churning out standard clothing like shirts, trousers, and work uniforms for export and a protected domestic market. Instead, Helene and Robert saw themselves as artists and businesspeople, devoted to the creation a new Caribbean design aesthetic—a local twist on fashions popular in metropolitan centers like New York and London. At the time of the company's founding, as today, high-fashion garments with an appealing brand name were available in few Trinidadian outlets and at an extremely high cost, partly because of the remaining 20 percent tariffs on non–Caribbean Community (CARICOM) imports.

Both Helene and Robert come from Indo-Trinidadian families[2] with a history of entrepreneurship. After marrying in 1988, the Foresters raised startup capital through their families and a bank loan. They rented a retail space in a shopping mall and initially began producing clothing in a spare bedroom at home. They decided to market their garments as "Signature Fashions," creating a logo and what Helene calls a "young, hip, and trendy image" to accompany it. At a time when many garment factories were closing down, the Foresters equipped themselves cheaply with the secondhand machines of those failed enterprises. Over the next fifteen years, the company expanded its retail space from a single shop to several stores in Trinidad's upscale shopping malls and a handful of tiny outlets in large tourist hotels. By the late 1990s, Signature Fashions was exporting its clothing to other countries in the Eastern Caribbean—including Grenada, St. Lucia, Barbados, and Dominica—where it was sold in rented stores managed by local staff in each country. Shortly before my fieldwork began in 2003, Signature Fashions moved its factory operations from a cramped, upstairs workshop in Port of Spain to a spacious industrial estate in the suburbs.

As business owners, Robert and Helene exemplify the emergence of an Indo-Trinidadian, entrepreneurial middle class, particularly in the domain of family businesses like garment manufacturing. Over the course of the twentieth century, the white elite's traditional hold on economic and political power gave way, in diverse and uneven ways, to various ethnic economic niches. Afro-Trinidadians have historically sought economic and social advancement through education and public-sector employment, while Indo-Trinidadians pursued small-scale entrepreneurialism and investment in family businesses (Henry 1993; Premdas 1993). Although early garment factories were founded by Syrian and Jewish entrepreneurs, from the mid-twentieth century Indo-Trinidadians gradually established themselves in the sector (Osirim 1997:64; Reddock 1984). Helene and Robert's position as factory owners represents a historical trend and reflects the diminution of white factory ownership described by Kevin Yelvington (1995:108) as already "anachronistic" by the late 1980s.[3]

Signature Fashions now produces three types of clothing: stylish renderings of basic garments (shirts, skirts, T-shirts, jeans, and soft-cotton track suits), touristy apparel that evokes a romantic, Caribbean aesthetic (drawstring trousers and loose-fitting "peasant" shirts), and "exclusive" designer lines (flamboyant blouses with bright embroidery, military-inspired micro-shorts, and wraparound dresses in distinctive prints). Helene and a second designer, Preston, design each of the clothing lines, which are made in the Trinidadian factory. The blue jeans that are outsourced to China are produced in standard sizes with only slight variations in cut or fabric from year to year. Having discussed outsourcing the rest of production to China, Helene and Robert determined that it would be impractical because their business relies on their ability to manufacture small runs of clothing that can be rushed to the stores in accordance with changing fashion.

For Helene and Robert, the quest to put Trinidad on the "fashion map" is not only a business strategy; it also represents a desire to transcend their territorial marginalization within global flows of culture. Brent Luvaas (2010) describes fashion designers in Indonesia who similarly assert claims to participation in a global scene by purposely addressing a real and imagined "international fashion" arena with their work, even when it will only be sold in the domestic market. Luvaas dubs this effort at self-empowerment "global repositioning" and portrays it as a strategy whereby middle-class youth assert their right to cultural production on their own terms. Demanding recognition and space in a global conversation, the Indonesian designers mixed Western fashions and corporate logos in an ironic visual commentary to critique the cultural order while attempting to widen the boundaries of international fashion from its periphery.

Helene and Robert's own attempts at global repositioning are motivated by their historical experience as members of Trinidad's "boom-time generation." Born in the 1960s, they came of age during the country's oil boom, when the government's coffers brimmed with cash, there was generous public spending, and the success of the energy sector was expected to propel Trinidad into world-class status in all things—including technology, culture, and consumption (Miller 1994a). Although the oil boom was followed by a recession from the early 1980s until the early 1990s, Trinidadians like Robert and Helene who had access to capital were able to create new businesses whose ethos remained attached to a boom-time sensibility: wealth, style, and a cosmopolitan attitude. As Robert says of their initial plans, "We wanted to move Trinidad out of this 'Third World' way of thinking and doing things."

Encapsulated in this boom-time rhetoric is a set of aesthetic, economic, and cultural yearnings to which Helene and Robert are deeply attached. These desires have profoundly shaped the kinds of bosses they would become. As Sylvia Yanagisako (2002:32) has argued, capitalist action is always "culturally produced and, therefore, always infused with cultural meaning and value." In de-emphasizing their role as factory owners in favor of an artistic self-image, Helene and Robert frequently neglect what workers perceive to be their customary and legal obligations to the workforce. Preferring to identify as fashion innovators, Helene and Robert bring to the role of factory bosses an improvisational and unencumbered approach that workers sometimes read as carelessness and indifference. These conflicting interpretations of the responsibilities of a factory boss are made manifest when workers describe labor conditions at Signature Fashions as inadequate and Helene and Robert as "uncaring." For their part, Helene and Robert at times appear frustrated and poorly equipped to address such bread-and-butter issues as working conditions and staff morale.

The alacrity with which Helene and Robert agreed to allow me to work in their factory surprised me. When I first arrived in Trinidad and began touring garment factories, it seemed evident that no firm would be willing to take me on as a participant observer and unpaid employee. Although trade unionism in the sector has been in steady decline since the 1980s, most factory owners were troubled by the idea that I might incite their workers to labor activism. As one factory owner said, "It's not anything that you would *say* to my workers that I would worry about but what the kinds of questions you would ask would start them *thinking* about that would worry me." I wondered whether Signature Fashions would prove so exemplary that it would not make a good research site. This turned out not to be the case: while other factories squeezed profitability from their workforce by casualizing labor, enacting temporary factory closures and openings, outsourcing to home workers, and paying below the legal minimum wage, Signature Fashions achieved profitability through different tactics, which nonetheless created "flexibility" in its operations. What Helene and Robert's casual acceptance of my request to do participant observation did reveal was their certitude in the virtue of their enterprise.

Hierarchy, Authority, and the Layout of the Shop Floor

The Signature Fashions factory is a large, windowless building located on a small industrial estate. There are two floors: downstairs contains the shop floor, including the stitching section, cutting room, employee toilets, and a lunchroom area. The upstairs of the factory houses the offices of the factory owners, designers, and administrators. Upstairs and downstairs contain different types of activity, which are embodied in the distinct decor and equipment found in each. Drafting tables, computers, desks, and filing cabinets comprise the open-plan workspace upstairs, where each co-owner has his or her own office with a door. Downstairs is dominated by rows of sewing machines, ironing boards, and long, high tables resting on a cement floor (see figure 2.1). The cutting room is separated from the rest of the shop floor by thin plywood walls and a wooden door. The perimeter of the cutting room, like the front of the main shop floor, is piled high with bolts of cloth wrapped in plastic and covered in dust. Rows and rows of fluorescent lights illuminate the factory.

The life of a Signature Fashions garment begins upstairs, where Helene and Preston draft sketches for new clothing by hand. This process often brings them downstairs into the cutting room, where they study the available cloth for inspiration. The cloth has been selected by Helene for its color, pattern, and fabric, either during a biennial trip to China or from the large fabric retailers in Port of Spain. Completed designs are constructed with the aid of a computer-assisted design (CAD) program, which also transforms designs into printable patterns of various sizes. These patterns, or "marks," are printed on long reels of paper, which are collected from upstairs and carried to the cutting room by one of its workers.

In the cutting room, two workers unfurl bolts of cloth back and forth across a long, wide table, creating a stack of fabric "lays." The mark is placed atop the stacked fabric and pinned into place by hand. The fabric is then cut along the pattern using a hand-operated cutter that slides along the tabletop.

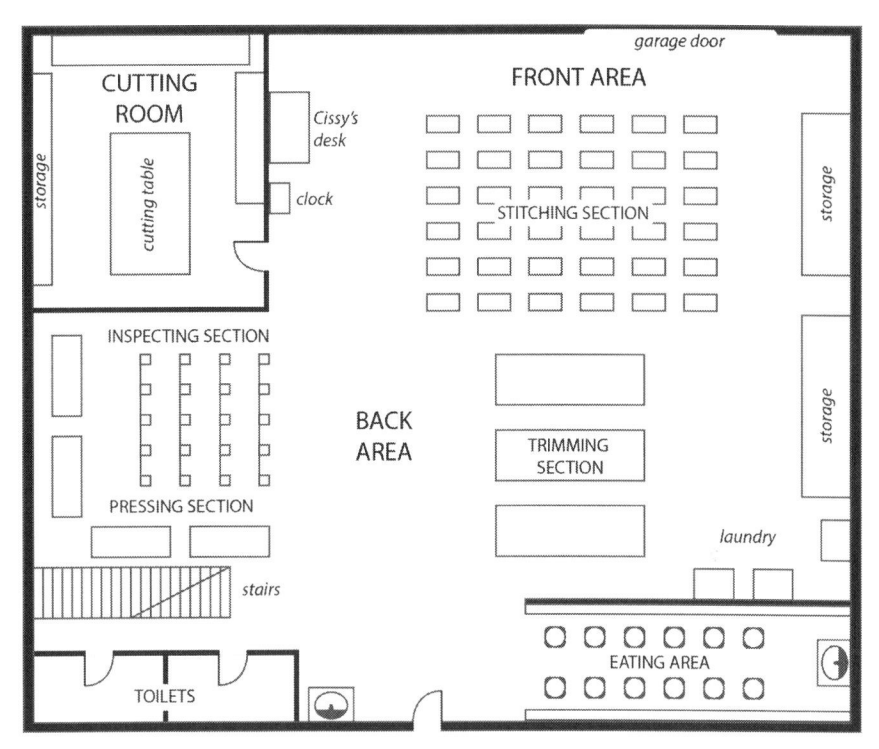

FIGURE 2.1. Layout of the shop floor at Signature Fashions (drawn by Adam Howse)

Cut cloth is bundled into parcels and tagged according to batch, lot, size, and color. These bundles are stored in the cutting room until they are carried to the main shop floor by the stitching supervisor, Brenda. Using the "progressive bundle system," a method of allocating work to stationary operators that gained popularity in the garment industry after World War II (Collins 2003:31), Brenda distributes the bundles to stitchers.

Each stitcher has two horses (low metal racks), positioned on either side of her chair. Brenda places the bundles on the horse to the left of each stitcher. The stitcher opens two of the bundles allocated to her, sews the constituent pieces together, and then re-ties the pieces into a new bundle that is placed on the second horse. From there, Brenda collects and redistributes the bundles to the next operator down the line. When the stitching operations are complete, Brenda carries bundles of garments to the back area of the factory, which includes a trimming section and a pressing section. Bundles of garments are piled on long tables in the trimming section. Trimmers stand at the tables, pluck a garment from the pile, and use spring-action scissors ("nippers") to trim excess thread along its seam lines, hems, and buttonholes.

From the trimming section, the back-area supervisor, Lystra, carries the garments to the pressing section. Workers use steam irons to press the garments by hand, operating foot levers to suction steam through the garment as it is ironed. Pressed garments are placed on plastic hangers and hung on nearby racks. Each garment is then inspected and sent back to the stitching section "to fix" if there are any problems with the stitching, then it is finally tagged for sale (although prices are not written on the tags until the garments reach the stores). Once a sufficient number of garments in a line have been produced, the garments are carried by a deliveryman from the factory to the company van and taken to Signature's retail outlets, where clothes are placed on wooden hangers and displayed under the direction of the store's manager. Stock going to the foreign stores will be packed into boxes and shipped; small lines of garments may be taken by the chief retail administrator to stores in other parts of the Caribbean by commercial airline.

Management at Signature Fashions describes the factory's work organization with reference to two spatial tropes: the supervisory pyramid and the moving assembly line. The pyramid structure of industrial organization depicts a descending hierarchy of supervision that extends from the factory owners (Helene and Robert) to the production manager (Cissy) to the two section supervisors (Brenda and Lystra) to the workers on the shop floor. Managers are positioned above workers in a scalar hierarchy of authority. Supervision should flow down the pyramid in branching fashion, while problems flow up along a chain of accountability. At Signature Fashions, this pyramidal structure of industrial organization complements a vision of the factory as a moving assembly line. Each worker is considered a fixed and autonomous operator, who must simply perform routine tasks on bundles of garments brought to her work station by her supervisor. Within this structure, workers need only "know" the task placed before them. As Cissy describes it, "You see the garments come along, and each person has their part [to do], just one thing after another."

The supervisory pyramid and the assembly line are the preeminent organizational structures of Fordism, suiting the mass production of standard goods by narrowly specialized workers. Yet, theorists of "flexible specialization" have argued that Fordist paradigms are ill-equipped to achieve the type of flexibility required to produce quickly changing, design-adaptive products for a late capitalist consumer market (Sabel 1994; Harvey 1990). Manufacturing high-end garments might be better accomplished with decentralized supervision and decision making, respect for the autonomy and skills of a well-trained workforce, and less-hierarchical management styles (Holmström 1998:17; Collins 2001:169). Signature Fashions, then, has a fundamental contradiction within its factory: the apparent incompatibility of a rigid manufacturing process and "flexible" product. As I describe later, this paradox of flexibility is worked out in many formal and informal ways on the shop floor. Signature Fashions may be organized as a Fordist factory, but it does not operate as one.

Shop-floor workers at Signature Fashions are paid an hourly wage. When I began fieldwork, this was the statutory minimum of TT$8 (US$1.33) an hour, although workers were assessed four months later and given differential wages based on performance.[4] Paying hourly sets Signature Fashions apart from most other garment factories in Trinidad, just as its high-fashion clothing lines depart from the staple items produced by mass-production factories. By paying hourly instead of by the piece, management ensures that workers can shift between different operations throughout the day without needing to administer a complex and time-consuming schematic of by-the-piece payment. It is easier, Cissy says, to "stitch it in one." Helene and Cissy also subscribe to the view that hourly payment ensures quality stitching, based on the belief that employees on a piece rate will do quick and careless work.

Helene and Robert rarely spend time on the shop floor. Cissy, the production manager, represents their authority and is responsible for the day-to-day factory operations. A former stitcher, Cissy was promoted first to stitching supervisor and later to production manager. As an Indo-Trinidadian woman from central Trinidad, Cissy shares friendship or kinship linkages with some of the Indo-Trinidadian workers; some Afro-Trinidadian workers complain that she is racially "biased" in her disciplinary tactics. When workers complain about the informalism of the Signature Fashions factory—including the lack of a clock with which to punch in and uncertainty over when pay will be disbursed on Fridays—they often do so because these things are seen as consolidating Cissy's power to make capricious judgments.

Helene and Robert's vision of themselves as artistic people, promoting a new Caribbean fashion sensibility, powerfully shapes life on the shop floor. By focusing on the design and marketing aspects of their business, they continually de-emphasize their role as factory owners. Workers at Signature Fashions often complained that the company does not do things "by the book." Those who had worked in the large-scale unionized factories during the 1980s were particularly displeased by late pay, unpredictability regarding when overtime would be required, and uncertainty over how much production was expected of them from day to day. Workers are paid on Fridays, although depending on when Robert visits the bank, pay might be disbursed at lunchtime, at the end of the workday, or after the workday has officially ended. The few workers who do not rely on their wages for the weekend's expenses always leave at the end of the day on Fridays. Most workers depend on their wages and stand at the factory gates, waiting for Robert to bring money from the bank. When I once suggested to one of the stitchers, Lata, that it was illegal for Robert to disburse payment long after the workday had ended, she yelped with laughter, "In *Trinidad?*" Many workers believed that only trade-union representation would standardize and formalize industrial relations in the factory (as a worker named Jean said, unionized factories "have to stick to the letter of the law"); yet the workers also believed that unionization is impossible at Signature Fashions. Not only were trade unions clearly uninterested in organizing the shrinking garment sector, but workers themselves were averse to collective action, having been burned by factories shutting down after successful unionization drives in the past.

Although the hierarchical, pyramidal structure of supervision at Signature Fashions seems to reproduce the rigidities of classic Fordism, there is no doubt that this factory operates "flexibly." The payment of an hourly wage, for instance, increases the ease with which workers can shift between different tasks, based on varying production demands. Yet it would be wrong to assume that industrial flexibility at Signature Fashions is achieved solely by design. Instead, workers, managers, and owners bring into the factory competing sets of desires, projects, and goals. Turning to their very different experiences of the factory as a workplace, I show that these desires, projects, and goals fall into and out of alignment at different times, sometimes finding unexpected (and productive) harmony. My approach reveals how industrial flexibility is constituted through relations *in* production (Burawoy

1979) among different categories of workers distributed across the shop floor. Although a couple of workers readily embrace Helene and Robert's vision of the factory as a "fashion company," most reject it. The labor power of those workers is secured through coercion as well as consent.

"We Deal with Helene Directly": The Cutting Room

Although the rest of the shop floor is an open plan, the cutting section is housed in a small room separated from the rest of the shop floor by its plywood walls. The room is dominated by a large table, about 14 feet long and 7 feet wide, with 3 or 4 feet between the table and the walls on three sides. The room also serves as a storage area for bolts of uncut cloth, as well as cloth that has been cut into patterns and bundled into parcels waiting to be taken to the stitching section.

The walls that separate the cutting room from the rest of the shop floor create a protected, privileged space within which the two cutting-room workers ("cutters"), Ram and Peggy, do their work. The cutters stack cloth into piles and pin the mark into place on top of the stacked cloth, then Ram cuts out the patterns with a hand-operated cutting machine. Because they are responsible for the first set of manufacturing operations after the garments have been designed, Ram and Peggy work closely with Helene and Preston, who make frequent visits from their offices upstairs to consult with the cutters on the size, quantity, and quality of the available cloth. Helene may come down to the cutting room to find out how much linen fabric is available for a line of dresses that require two yards of fabric each; Preston might ask Ram how he should plot a pattern on the computer to use the cloth available most economically.

The cutting room therefore represents a crossroads within the Signature Fashions factory, where two minimum-wage workers work in frequent and intimate contact with the company designers. Peggy, a slim, Afro-Trinidadian woman who looks far younger than her forty-two years, also serves as the ad hoc model for the clothing, wriggling into design samples so Helene and Preston can observe what they look like on the human form. With the ability to work at their own pace, listen to a small radio, and eat snacks throughout the day, Ram and Peggy have more freedom than the rest of the factory workers. The stitching of a garment takes longer than its cutting, evidenced by the bundles of cut fabric accumulating on the cutting-room shelves, waiting to be taken to the shop floor. As Peggy observes, "We don't have to hustle."

Although Cissy, as production manager, is Ram and Peggy's direct supervisor, her interactions with them are qualitatively different from those she has with the rest of the workforce. Cissy's demeanor toward the rest of the workers is authoritarian—scolding, cajoling, and raising her hand to compel them to work harder—yet she extends a quiet professionalism to Ram and Peggy. Whenever Cissy comes into the cutting room, she simply asks how the work is coming along. She never tells Ram or Peggy to work faster, even though their conversations visibly slow the pace of production. The walls that surround the cutting room create an interior space into which Cissy herself can retreat and rest, away from the gaze of the shop-floor employees. Once or twice a day, she might come into the cutting room and sit down on a chair, staring into space—allowing the mask of being "in charge" to slip for a few moments.

Given their exclusive position in the factory, it is not surprising that Ram and Peggy revel in the artistic ethos of Signature Fashions. Their representations of shop-floor life are unlike the narratives of other workers and instead resemble those of Helene and Robert. Ram told me that Signature Fashions is not really a garment factory; instead, "it really is more of a fashion house, fashion company." When I asked why, Peggy responded, "Helene don't like to see plenty people in the same thing all over Trinidad, in the same style." Ram and Peggy delight in their proximity to the designers and in the professionalism they are accorded in the cutting room. As Ram told me, "We deal with Helene directly."

The privileged nature of Ram and Peggy's work is made evident when workers from other areas of the shop floor are brought into the cutting room to do the heavy labor. For instance, in the weeks leading up to Christmas and Carnival, the most popular items are "Signature jerseys," which are T-shirts emblazoned with the company logo. Selling at TT$60 (US$10) each, jerseys are the least expensive of Signature's clothing; they make popular Christmas gifts and fashionable items to wear during pre-Carnival fetes (for which Helene works hard to ensure that the jerseys have an appealing cut and color to suit the season's tastes). Because of the imperative to produce hundreds of jerseys by the end of the year, from mid-November until January, four workers from the "back area" (Carmela, Josephine, Tina, and me) were directed to work in the cutting room, to lay and stack the fabric so it could be quickly cut and delivered to stitchers on the shop floor.

Laying the jersey fabric was exhausting work. With only a half-hour break for lunch at 11:30 a.m. and a ten-minute break at 2:30 p.m., I found myself on my feet for ten hours a day, lifting, folding, stacking, and bundling the cloth. The work was made more difficult by the fact that the cutting room is warmer and dustier than the rest of the factory. As we worked, the incongruity of our sweaty physical labor was set beside the relaxed bodily postures of the designers and cutters who leaned against the edge of the table, sketching design ideas and talking about fabric length while the rest of us lifted, stretched, and stacked the cloth over and over again.

The labor power of the cutters is secured through their eager participation in the rhetoric of the "fashion company" Helene and Robert promote. The nature of their work separates cutters from the rest of the shop-floor workers, just as the walls surrounding the cutting room create a distinct and independent space in which they operate. The cutting room plays an important role in the flexible production of Signature Fashions' garments because of its proximity to and relationship with the work of design. As Peggy said, the cutting room is not a place where workers "hustle"; hustling and an authoritarian disciplinary regime are reserved instead for the stitching and finishing sections at the "front" and "back" of the factory.

"Them Want It Now for Now!": The Stitching Section

The stitching section is the heart of the factory. Managers talk about the stitchers as if they are the emblematic Signature Fashions workers, sitting all day and guiding fabric under the needles of their sewing machines. The modes of supervision and discipline in the stitching section relate to the nature of this work. With frequent pattern changes and short production cycles, stitchers must be able to respond to a varying array of production demands. One week they might be making military-style trousers with straps and buckles and the next week sewing dresses in gossamer fabrics with frills and beading. Signature's stitchers are highly skilled and adaptive: able to stitch complex designs, skill up for new tasks, learn new machines, and endure the uncertainties of what will be required of them from day to day (figure 2.2).

As the stitching supervisor, Brenda's primary responsibility is managing the flow of work across this section of the factory by delivering bundles of garments to workers. Although she consults with Cissy on the progress of the day's work, Brenda's main job is to judge how long it will take each worker to complete her operations so she can allocate tasks. Consistent with the Taylorist principles of the progressive bundle system (Collins 2001:188), no garment should be slowed in its progress for lack of a stitcher to complete it, and no worker should sit unoccupied for want of available stitching. An Indo-Trinidadian woman who came up through the ranks as a stitcher herself, Brenda is sometimes awkwardly positioned between management and the stitchers, trying to assert her authority among her former co-workers. As Jaesok Kim (2013:10) reminds us, factory managers legitimize their authority in part by establishing social and spatial distinctions between themselves and shop-floor workers. Yet securing authority through distinction can be difficult for low-level supervisors when they share social histories and class affiliation with the workers they are supposed to oversee (De Neve 2001:142–44). Perhaps for this reason, Cissy takes greater responsibility for shop-floor discipline while Brenda dedicates herself to the procedural construction of the garments, drawing on her expertise as a seamstress to solve technical problems when they arise.

Paying an hourly wage rather than by the piece orchestrates the mode of discipline on the shop floor. For both Brenda and Cissy, the most important disciplinary tasks are to prevent workers from talking, working slowly ("skylarking"), and taking breaks (such as making multiple trips to the bathroom). Because workers do not receive incentive pay on the amount of items they produce, the managerial imperative is to keep workers operating quickly by other means. Cissy's tactics to prevent workers from talking include staring at individual workers across the room ("watching them hard"), shouting at them ("Shirley, pull your hand! Antoinette, pull your hand!"), and walking over to workers and slapping them on the back or the arm. When Cissy smacks a worker it is always with a smile on her face, although few workers share in the joke. As Glenda once told me, "I don't like the hitting. Cissy say it's a joke, but I don't like it." When I pointed out that I had never seen Cissy try to hit *her*, she said, "I put on a serious face *one time* [i.e., right away]. I don't like the hitting." Central to this disciplinary approach is a hierarchical division between mental and manual labor. Managers plan and anticipate;

FIGURE 2.2. At work in the stitching section (photo by author)

workers need only complete the work in front of them. It is inappropriate (or *fas*, a local term that connotes being uppity or bold) for workers to ask about production targets, for that knowledge is reserved for managers.

Stitchers grumble about not knowing what work is coming down the line, but this is expressed as annoyance with how "disorganized" management appears to be, not as a worker's neglected right to knowledge of work patterns. Donna described it this way: "[Managers] are more tough here. Elsewhere, they know they have the piece rate, people are working. At other places, they are looking at the calendar, they know if they have an order for more work, they plan it out on the calendar instead of harassing the workers. Here they say they starting overtime *now* for *now*. They are over-pressuring the workers." When Donna describes overtime being allocated "now for now," she draws attention to the fact that workers are given little sense of the shape and content of work as it comes down the line, including when overtime will be required.[5] Rumors circulated for weeks in November, speculating when mandatory overtime would begin and end in the run-up to Christmas. Workers may be given as little as a day's notice of overtime or Saturday work during busy production periods, and the year before my fieldwork they were required to work on Christmas Eve.

Although Donna portrays it as mere disorganization, "now for now" is actually a central facet of flexible production in the factory. The manufacturing of Signature Fashions apparel is intimately tied to its retailing. Helene and Preston carefully scrutinize what is selling in Signature's shops. They also generate design ideas by observing what Trinidadians are already wearing and international trends portrayed in films and magazines and on cable television. This retail-driven approach requires spontaneous, just-in-time production and a manufacturing system that can cope with contingency. While asserting that workers should be working with sustained effort *all* the time, managers can vary disciplinary rhythms to match fluctuating demand by urging workers to quicken the pace at key moments, otherwise leaving them to operate at a less regulated tempo. The demand for flexible production is not communicated by sharing plans, issuing quotas, or announcing goals but instead through enforced ignorance and punitive discipline. Workers describe the relentless rhythms of "now for now" as the "slave-driver situation." Shirley, a thirty-nine-year-old stitcher, commented: "Working in a factory come like they bring you back to a slave-driver situation, you know.

Because if you really pay attention to what going on in Signature: 'Pull your hand! No talking! Do your work!' And you know, like someone whipping you over your head, 'Do your work! Pull your hand! Do dis, do dis!' You sick, and you still here, you ehnt get paid! So it comes like you back in them kinda days." In addition to the "slave-driver situation," workers also described being subjected to Cissy's disciplinary tactics as making them feel "like a little girl in school." When I asked each worker how Signature Fashions could change to make her happier, the most common reply was of the kind, "They could learn how to talk to people."

Although workers experience the "slave-driver situation," "over-pressure," and "harassment" as symptoms of operational disorganization, these dynamics are actually a function of the paradoxical pairing of an adaptive, consumption-driven product and a rigid mode of production. Flexible production at Signature Fashions is achieved not through continuous innovation and an emphasis on learning but instead through a system of authoritarian hierarchy, forcing workers to cope in a pressured and bewildering environment in which mental work and manual work are strictly separated and unequally valued. When Donna contrasts other factory managers' "looking at the calendar" with the "now for now" approach at Signature Fashions, she expresses a frustration with uncertainty. From the point of view of workers, the slave-driver situation is so unnerving because intensified work rhythms feel arbitrarily imposed.

Workers do not simply accept the "disorganized," "now for now" ethos at Signature Fashions. Rather, they attempt to escape from pounding production demands by establishing control over the pace and progress of their work rather than having the assembly line impose its rhythms on them. Workers guess and discuss among themselves what amount and type of production might be required. They also attempt to psychologically and physically order their day by temporarily trading work with each other so they can move "up the line" and complete their tasks at a pace that suits them. Many workers like to "hustle" in the morning and try to "relax a bit" in the afternoon. Having friends among their co-workers helps them set a comfortable pace. For instance, one morning while I was helping out in the stitching section, Kimberly asked me to pass her a pile of the camisole tops Donna was working on. She wanted me to pick up one of the piles Donna had not yet sewn and give it to her so she could conduct her operation on the pieces first. Donna smarted at this, saying to Kimberly, "What are you doing with my things? Them don't have darts on them yet."

Kimberly replied, "I could bind them before you put [in] the darts."

Donna said, "You could wait."

Kimberly replied, "I'm on green [thread], I want to finish it out." To no one in particular, she added as she continued stitching, "I want to finish this out. I want to finish this and do the red skirts. I don't want to hustle this Friday. I don't want them telling me is Antoinette needing work. So I want to finish out this green and then do the red skirts. It won't need work for Antoinette. I ehnt able hustling this afternoon."

Donna allowed me to pick up the camisole tops she had not yet darted and pass them to Kimberly so she could run binding through them. The exchange happened quickly and evaded the attention of Cissy and Brenda. Because they are friends and because it seemed like a reasonable request, Donna helped Kimberly gain control over the sequence of her work, helping her avoid the potential hustle that would be imposed on her if she fell behind. So, despite management's insistence that workers be fixed and atomized, workers move along the assembly line by manipulating the spatial and temporal order of their day-to-day tasks. Workers outwardly acquiesce to management's rules by making no outright challenge to the system while covertly pursuing their own rhythms.[6]

In spite of management's insistence that talk on the shop floor is counterproductive, negotiations like the one described earlier are better understood as "productive sociality," shop-floor talk that facilitates rather than disrupts the manufacturing process. Workers often expressed frustration about the fact that, at Signature Fashions, a worker can never "set she hand" to one task. Working in a fast-paced company on a constantly changing product means that workers often make mistakes. If a worker on the binding machine stitches up the waistbands on a dozen pairs of shorts before remembering that she was supposed to stitch the care tag into the back of each one, she may turn to a nearby worker operating a straight-stitch sewing machine using the same color thread and quickly ask for "a stitch just so" to tack the forgotten care tags neatly into place without attracting Brenda's attention.

Although it is illicit, productive sociality is important to the very structure of factory life at Signature Fashions. It not only helps workers cope with tedium by allowing them to manage their own work rhythms, it also underpins the flexible production process by providing a means through which workers can create on-the-fly solutions to the problems arising in a fast-changing manufacturing process. Although many theorists have suggested that producing for a high-end, retail-driven market requires more "flexibility" in manufacturing operations than a Fordist regime can provide, ethnographers like Jane Collins (2001) have shown that flexibility can in fact be achieved through "hyper-Taylorist" methods that separate mental from manual labor and leave workers little choice but to comply with managerial directives in a highly orchestrated manner. But Signature Fashions workers do not simply impute flexibility into the system through their vulnerability to exploitation but also through their own agency. Thus, it is not Foucault's panopticon—an all-seeing and regulating eye of management—that secures flexible production from stitchers at Signature Fashions. A more apt theoretical framework is Foucault's concept of "governmentality," the large and small ways workers individually and collectively conform to an internalized sense of management's tacit goals (Foucault 1991).

"Real Pressure": The Back Area

The "back area" of the factory—composed of the trimming, pressing, and inspecting sections—is the last place garments are worked on before being sent to the stores. Lystra, an Afro-Trinidadian former stitcher, is the back-area supervisor, responsible for managing these three sections. Unlike the stitching section, where bundles of garments are swiftly transported from station to station, here garments are heaped in large piles on high tables, giving the impression of an endless mass of work to be done.

Because trimming and pressing are the final operations performed on a garment before it is sent to the stores, back-area workers claim they feel the most "heat" and "pressure" when finished products are urgently required. Said Audra, a forty-year-old presser, "When there's pressure for work, they pressure us, but when there is no pressure, it is easy sailing." The frustration for workers in this section, as in the stitching section, is that they cannot anticipate when such pressure will be levied. She continued: "If they were more organized, they wouldn't always be rushing, but it is always a rush to get the clothes [sewn] and then a rush to press it. Because it's the last step. The pressing comes like, 'Oh, it's just to press,' like it shouldn't take any time. But it *does* take time." Signature Fashions has become successful in manufacturing up-to-the-minute apparel that can be quickly produced and delivered to the stores. Thus, for a presser in the back area, work oscillates between "real pressure" and "easy sailing" based on how urgently the garments are needed.

Like the stitchers, back workers complain about the "now for now" ethos at Signature Fashions, which they insist is the result of lack of planning. As Tina, one of the trimmers, said to me: "They could do, like, you know you want a certain amount of work [out] for this week, then start it earlier, like last week, so you know that for sure you'll get it in. [Instead] they put it *now for now* and say, 'I want everything for this week.' And have everybody pushing work, it does be real stressful on everybody. You feeling tired, and then you have to go do work at home." Tina said that "too much work" and "hustling, last-minute work" caused the most conflicts on the shop floor. As another back worker named Bernice said, "All this 'GET THIS OUT TODAY'? *Nah*, I ehnt able with that." Yet, Signature Fashions has been able to operate as a flexible factory despite its Fordist rigidities precisely through this periodic intensification of production.

Trimmers, like the pressers, feel the urgency of their work waxing and waning along with management's cues and, like the pressers, become frustrated by the lack of transparency about when such pressure will be exerted. This is most often expressed as resentment toward how they are treated. To raise production speeds, Cissy stands over workers and shouts at them to work harder. Lystra, a mild-mannered supervisor, is more likely to plead with workers to quicken their pace, telling them, "Cissy wanting the work [done]." Rhonda, a thirty-eight-year-old back-area worker who trims and runs the buttonhole machine, told me, "It's just that sometimes the way how they does speak to you at times . . . You know, but sometimes you does just prefer the day to be done, sometimes when you see that sign and you just [*laughs*] pray that the day finished, and you go home and you relax and you make up your mind to take it again when you come in."

Management at Signature Fashions has been successful in procuring speedy work in the back area not only through shouting, urging, and cajoling (the "slave-driver situation") but also through more subtle tactics that link the goals of management with those of the workers. For example, Robert attempted to introduce a labor-saving trimming machine into the back area. He entered the trimming section one morning, dragging a small machine that he claimed, as he set up the machine on a low table, could "do the work of three trimmers." The machine had a small motor and an extended arm with a recessed blade on the end of it, like an electric beard trimmer. Attached to the arm was a rubber hose, extending down to a small bucket on the ground. Workers who trim ("trimmers") usually cut excess thread away from the garments by hand using a small set of spring-action scissors called nippers. The trimming machine Robert brought to the shop floor was intended to be a labor-saving device because the blades would rapidly cut excess threads while the internal vacuum sucked them away.

Tina was the first trimmer to try out the machine and, because the other workers seemed uninterested in it, quickly became its sole operator. (A fifty-six-year-old trimmer named Bernice muttered when the machine appeared in the section, "That machine couldn't work. I use that machine in 1976, it no good.") Despite Robert's boast that the machine would revolutionize production and could "do the work of three trimmers," it soon became obvious, to the workers' relief, that the machine could trim no faster than they could by hand. The suction was not strong enough to pull all the threads in, and the machine's blades were either not sharp enough or too recessed to gain purchase on them. Although Robert had instructed Tina to merely hold the garment up to the machine and "let it do the work," to actually get the job done, Tina would trim the garments the same way she always had, with a nipper in the palm of her hand. The only difference was that after she snipped the thread, she would hold the garment up so the machine could suck the threads away rather than letting them fall to the floor.

In the weeks that followed, Tina continued working the trimming machine each day, and it came to be known as Tina's machine. Tina set up her things on the machine's table: a cloth bag with her toilet paper in it and the plastic bags of peanuts she sells to other workers. Whenever Robert visited the shop floor, Tina toiled to maintain the illusion that she was trimming quicker than ever. Tina told Robert that it was "much faster" to work on the machine than trimming by hand and that it was a "good machine." Robert smiled and replied that this was good news: "That's progress. We don't want stagnation here, we want progress."

Tina and Robert constructed a shared representation of the machine as working well, although the other employees in the back area were not fooled. The effect was that Tina gained something of value to her: a chair to sit on rather than having to stand, the small increase in status that comes from working on a machine, and a dedicated place to store her belongings. Perhaps remembering Robert's words about working "three times as fast," Tina seemed determined to make it so. Cissy made a point of carrying huge piles of untrimmed garments directly to Tina, heaping them in a plastic laundry basket at her feet, which Tina completed as quickly as she could. In the case of the electric trimmer, Tina's and Robert's divergent goals found themselves in harmony, with the effect that the trimming machine undoubtedly increased Tina's rate of production; she worked vigorously to make it so.

This story illustrates the day-to-day relations in production at Signature Fashions. No one, including Cissy, challenged Robert's declaration that the machine trimmed garments faster than could be done by hand. For many workers, the presence of the electric trimmer in the back area exemplified Robert's obstinacy and detachment from shop-floor life and their own, cheeky knowingness. When some workers grumbled that the machine was too noisy and therefore "should throw in the garbage," a worker named Glenda declared, "But if Robert pay for it, he not going to throw it away! He want to *use* it." Workers privately criticize but publically acquiesce to management's demands. Because Tina's desires aligned with Robert's, her labor power was secured for reasons other than an untarnished acceptance of his authority. Although the introduction of an electric trimmer to the back area worked out contrary to Robert's expectations, its effects nonetheless supported his interests.

Conclusions

An ethnographic approach to factory life shows the indivisibility of economic and non-economic motivations for both workers and employers. Sylvia Yanagisako (2001:21) has argued for a "cultural theory of economic action" that would interpret all action as "constituted by both deliberate, rational calculation and by sentiments and desires: in other words, as cultural practices." Writing about how a diverse entrepreneurial class in the Italian silk industry reproduces itself over several generations, Yanagisako demonstrates that sentiments, emotions, and affect are forces of production because they "incite" capitalists to pursue particular kinds of goals that are irreducible to instrumental profit-seeking (ibid.:32).

Cynthia Enloe (1989:16–17) identifies similar social mechanisms at work among the laboring classes, describing women workers on the global assembly line as motivated not simply by wages but also by a range of "needs, values and worries" that compel their participation in the labor market. As Mary Beth Mills (1997:39) has argued in relation to Thai migrant workers, these needs, values, and worries can be composed of "traditional" obligations to community and family as well as newer desires to experience modernity through work, travel, and consumption. Capital is adept at manipulating these sentiments and using them to cheapen the value of women's labor by restricting their agency, often while appearing to expand it.

The insistence that sentiment is a force of production is confirmed at Signature Fashions, although here we see the interplay between the needs, values, and desires of factory owners and those of workers in relation to each other, as they fall into and out of alignment. On a lively shop floor, management's interests and workers' interests collide; workers acquiesce to management's demands in overt ways but also seek out individual and collective autonomy as they go about their jobs. Workers variously embrace and reject management's ethos, conforming to employer demands and also quietly subverting them. In each of these ways, workers participate in the formation of their own subjectivities, which are dynamic and enterprising. Signature Fashions workers do the work they are assigned but also quietly depart from their supervisor's instructions. Despite their employer's expectations of obedience, workers internalize more complex subjectivities that respond to both the formal and tacit demands of management.

Signature Fashions' reliance on hidden registers of production to achieve flexibility suggests that factory owners do not always know their own interests. Helene and Robert subscribe to a vision of their employees as fixed and atomized, needing only to "know" what work is put in front of them. Workers defy this vision as they go about their work, and as Glenda says in the epigraph to this chapter, they "do it our *own* style." Indeed, at Signature Fashions, flexible production relies in large measure on workers' unrecognized and uncompensated success at bridging the inadequacies of formal systems to meet the tacit expectation that they will find a way to get the job done. The aims of the factory owners, supervisors, and shop-floor employees are not the same, but at times their competing aims can find themselves in harmony. Formal and informal registers of production are mutually dependent, even though this interdependence remains unacknowledged by actors in the system.

Notes

1. I asked Helene if I could work at Signature Fashions for six months but ended up working there for nine months.

2. While both Helene and Robert say they identify as "Indo-Trinidadian," they also claim mixed heritage, including European and Chinese descent.

3. The economic ascendancy of an Indo-Trinidadian merchant and business class has been recently matched by a political ascendancy as well (see chapters 3 and 7).

4. All dollar amounts are in Trinidad and Tobago dollars unless otherwise noted. At the time of fieldwork, TT$1 was equivalent to US$0.16.

5. The phrase *now for now* can also be used in the Trinidadian context to connote a cavalier attitude of living for the moment (Birth 1999:39).

6. The fact that workers like Kimberly prefer to hustle in the morning and relax in the afternoon accounts in part for workers' nostalgic recollections of piecework. I incorrectly assumed that garment workers would prefer an hourly wage because it might allow them to slack off more than they could on a piece rate. Instead, workers said just the opposite, that with the piece rate you can set your own pace of work rather than having it imposed on you by management. Donna described working in another factory: "Piece rate was real cool, at least you are making money, and by the time you sit down [at] lunchtime, you know you make your money already. So in the afternoon, you're working for the next day." Many of the older Signature Fashions workers said they had preferred piece rate in their younger days; as they aged, they were happier working on an hourly wage. As Gita said, "I ehnt able with piece rate again, that's young people['s] thing." (For similar worker accounts of piece-rate payment, see O'Malley 1992; Thompson 1967; Salzinger 1997:565; Westwood 1984:43–45).

3

Raced and Emplaced

Signature Fashions Workers

> Global assembly lines are as much about the production of people and identities as they are about restructuring labor and capital.
> – Carla Freeman, *High Tech and High Heels in the Global Economy*

While I was working on the shop floor of Signature Fashions, my co-workers often asked whether I considered myself more of a "front" worker or a "back" worker. The shop floor is occupationally and spatially divided into two areas: the front, where stitching is done, and the back, where stitched garments are trimmed of excess thread, pressed, and packaged for sale. As an unpaid employee, I had wide-ranging access to the factory and, unlike other workers, the ability to try out different types of work. At first, I assumed that workers' questions about whether I considered myself "front" or "back" represented a context-specific way of assessing my impressions of their workplace and my own estimation of where I best fit in. Did I enjoy sitting down and stitching on a machine in the quietly humming area of the stitching section—the front of the factory? Or did I enjoy myself more "to the back," standing at my work, with the ability to move my whole body, engaging in the physical labor that "back work" implies?

Yet as time went on, I began to see how the terms *front* and *back* structured production in the Signature Fashions factory into an implicitly racialized geography. Workers "to the back" were almost entirely Afro-Trinidadian, mostly from densely populated urban neighborhoods in East Port of Spain. Front workers might be either Indo-Trinidadian or Afro-Trinidadian, although the workers who sat at the "front front" of the shop floor on the newest and most high-tech sewing machines were Indo-Trinidadian women from traditionally "Indian" towns like Chaguanas, San Juan, or Aranguez. Some of these workers shared kinship or friendship links with Cissy, the production manager, who lived in Chaguanas and was an active member of her Hindu temple in Aranguez. Although the categories *front* and *back* referred to the spatial arrangement of production, the terms also operated as a proxy language of race. When workers asked me whether I preferred the "front" or "back" of the factory, I was being asked to name a group allegiance.

A long tradition of labor scholarship demonstrates that social categories like race, ethnicity, caste, and gender are frequently manipulated to segment the labor market and divide workers' common interests (Bourgois 1988; Chakrabarty 2000; Ortiz 2002). Indeed, as Eric Wolf (1982:380) notes, categories like "Negro" and "Indian" were specifically created to enact these kinds of exclusions, making such "racial designations" a product not only of the colonial encounter but also of the mercantile capitalism of its day. In Trinidad as throughout the Caribbean, the brutal exigencies of the plantation system required subjects that were both "raced" and "emplaced" (Carnegie 2002:137); assigned to a specific location and role within the racial and class matrices of the colonial order, no one could be "without" race (Munasinghe 2001; Yelvington 1993). Recognizing the economic and political origins of racial categories helps us shed a view of race or ethnicity as pre-capitalist "primordial" attachments by repositioning them within the history of labor.

The construction and mobilization of social categories in the service of capital does not end with labor recruitment or at the factory gates. As Kevin Yelvington (1995:3) has shown, ethnic and gender differences are used to structure the organization of production; therefore, the shop floor becomes a site "where the meanings of ethnicity, class, and gender are constructed, contested, and consented to." One way this occurs is through techniques of management, whereby workers come to see themselves reflected in the ways they are labeled and addressed by their employers. Identity in this sense originates not in the person but is constructed through social relations (Salzinger 2003:176). Leela Fernandes (1997) draws attention to the processes of boundary making that enclose these social categories and how the alliances that are formed within them make certain kinds of political projects, struggles, and sympathies possible while shutting out others.

At Signature Fashions, "front" and "back" are categories through which workers learn to see themselves and others and come to form part of the logic workers use to explain their pay, treatment, and working conditions in relation to their co-workers. Even though the categories index race in ways recognizable to all, their use disavows the racial organization of production because racial categories are replaced with spatial ones. The Signature Fashions factory is a social and material field in which workers undertake various types of projects. By looking at the formation of subjects and subjectivities, we can see how workers are simultaneously constituted *within* and *by* their environment, even as they strategize to exploit it for their own ends. What makes a "worker" is not predetermined but rather open to struggles, contestations, and redefinitions.

COMMUNITY, PLACE, AND THE FORMATION OF SUBJECTS

Trinidad, it has often been noted, is a country where class and ethnicity are mapped onto the landscape (Munasinghe 2001:3; Mycoo 2006:135). Histories of slavery, emancipation, indentureship, intra-island migration, and differential occupational and educational opportunities have produced diverse geographies of settlement and residence. Kevin Yelvington (1995:102) argues that Trinidadians' traditional segregation along the lines of ethnicity and status has been increasingly replaced by residential patterns based on income, education levels, and professional class. Despite new demographic configurations, neighborhoods and regions may retain their historical associations with particular ethnic groups in the public imaginary. For example, the central sugar-refining town of Chaguanas is so associated with Indo-Trinidadians that it is perceived to be "a kind of alternative ethnic capital of Trinidad," despite the fact that its actual population is now more than 30 percent Afro-Trinidadian (Miller 1994a:27).

Approximately half of the Signature Fashions workers might be described as Indo-Trinidadian (claiming descent primarily or exclusively from South

Asian indentured laborers) and half as Afro-Trinidadian (claiming descent primarily or exclusively from African slaves or settlers). The shop floor therefore reflects the demographic profile of the country as a whole, where Indo-Trinidadians and Afro-Trinidadians each comprise roughly 40 percent of the population (CSO 2007).[1] As Viranjini Munasinghe (2001:7) has argued, the opposition of these two groups constitutes a "structural dichotomy" in Trinidad, an enduring feature of a colonial system that purposely recruited Indian indentured laborers after the abolition of slavery to drive down labor costs on the sugar plantations.

What continues to give these categories such salience in contemporary Trinidad is how party politics is ethnicized and therefore ethnicity is politicized (Khan 2004:11–18; Yelvington 1993). As one trade unionist commented to me, "Trinidad has a race-based political system, not a class-based politics." Despite numerical parity between Indo-Trinidadians and Afro-Trinidadians, electoral politics has been historically dominated by a party associated with Afro-Trinidadians. The People's National Movement (PNM) was founded in the 1950s by middle-class "colored" intellectuals with support from the urban black poor; it remains the party most supported by Afro-Trinidadians today (Ryan 1997:153). From 1995 to 2001, an (unofficially) Indo-Trinidadian political party, United National Congress (UNC), held power under the leadership of Basdeo Panday. After many years of political marginalization and attempts at multiethnic governance, the success of the UNC represented a new confidence among Indo-Trinidadians at the national level and a symbolic challenge to Afro-Trinidadian authority in state affairs. The PNM returned to power after a "deadlock" election in 2001. Memories of UNC rule were still fresh when my fieldwork began in 2003, as was a continuing sense of competition between two political parties defined on ethnic terms: "Afro" and "Indo" (Khan 2004:16; Ryan 2003).

Most of the Afro-Trinidadian workers at Signature Fashions live in areas traditionally associated with the black working class, such as East Port of Spain and the East-West Corridor running between Port of Spain and Arima. Indo-Trinidadian workers generally live in Chaguanas and its environs. East Port of Spain and Chaguanas not only represent the residential base of most Signature Fashions workers but also have two strong and opposing reputations that derive from the historical legacies of their settlement and the interethnic competition that still characterizes electoral politics.

The "Baaaaad Area": Laventille and East Port of Spain

Most Signature Fashions workers of African descent come from East Port of Spain, a collection of densely populated, economically depressed neighborhoods clustered around a hilly range flanking the Beetham Highway. These areas—Laventille, Morvant, Belmont, Gonzales, and East Dry River—are considered by many to be the "heart" of working-class Afro-Trinidad (Lieber 1981:23), with the neighborhood of Laventille serving as the symbolic center of East Port of Spain itself (Ryan, McCree, and St Bernard 1997). Small houses made of wood or concrete breeze blocks stand side by side along steep, winding streets. Running water is sometimes scarce, with frequent shortages, so many residents collect and store water in large plastic barrels outside their homes.[2] Garbage collection is notoriously infrequent.

Laventille, although it contained cocoa and coffee estates during the early eighteenth century, became known as "a haven for landless ex-slaves coming into Port of Spain from the rural estates" following Emancipation (Lee 1997:75); it was also a primary settlement area for free blacks who migrated to Trinidad from other Eastern Caribbean islands during the post-Emancipation period (Brereton 1981:70, 80). Laventille's reputation as an impoverished area endured throughout the twentieth century, although its status in the national imagination improved over time. Laventille gained fame and preeminence as the location where steelpan music first originated in the 1930s and 1940s (Stuempfle 1995). Beginning in the 1950s, colored and black nationalists drew upon components of the urban Afro-Trinidadian experience such as calypso, steelband, and Carnival to furnish the nationalist project with cultural symbols that would be read as uniquely Trinidadian, thereby validating the claim to a nation. Munasinghe reminds us that recasting the Afro-Trinidadian experience as authentically Trinidadian was central to the invention of the post-colonial "creole" nation but that it marginalized Indo-Trinidadians' contributions to a visibly national culture and claims to belonging (Munasinghe 2001, 2002, 2006).

Laventille has long been seen as "the political heartland of the People's National Movement," a political party created in the 1950s by the educated, colored middle classes, which has been the foremost party supported by Afro-Trinidadians (Ryan 1997:153).[3] Trinidad's first prime minister, Eric Williams, actively cultivated the support of Laventille in his electoral campaigns (Ryan 1997). Laventille was also the stomping ground of the militant black nationalist organizations that led general strikes during the 1970 Black Power revolt. Accusations of political patronage have been directed at the Laventille-PNM nexus, particularly in the operation of unemployment relief programs. During the oil boom (1973–81), Laventille was seen as a primary recipient of government largesse through public works projects, which were plagued by rumors of fraud and overpayment (ibid.:161; cf. Craig 1975:184).

In recent years, the dominant image of Laventille in the Trinidadian media is as a place of lawlessness, gang violence, and street crime, particularly murder (Ryan, McCree, and St Bernard 1997; Brewster 2004; Lord 2004). Laventille is also known for its high unemployment rates and the ubiquity of short-term government-backed programs like the Community-Based Environmental Protection and Enhancement Programme (CEPEP, pronounced "see-pep"). Founded in 2002, CEPEP is an unemployment relief program that organizes gangs of workers to do basic conservation work, like clearing "bush" from the roadsides. Created by the PNM, CEPEP has been criticized as a mechanism to deliver patronage to the party's traditional base: poor Afro-Trinidadians in East Port of Spain and along the East-West Corridor. CEPEP is frequently charged with corruption and overspending by its detractors (Meighoo 2004; O'Connor 2007; *Trinidad Guardian* 2005; but see *Trinidad Guardian* 2007). Laventille is also a large community of working-class families, dotted with storefront Pentecostal churches, schools, and lively panyards where steelpan music is practiced in preparation for the national competitions held during Carnival season (figure 3.1).

Workers at Signature Fashions who live in Laventille, like Josephine, Kellisha, and Veronica, and those who live in East Port of Spain more generally, like Jean, Donna, and Audra, are well aware of Laventille's negative reputation. As Josephine said when we first met and I asked where she was from: "Laventille, the *baaaaad* area." Rhonda told me that it is wise to disguise the fact that you live in Laventille when applying for a job: "They don't want to see Laventille on the form. Put your auntie, put someone up in Diego Martin. Don't put Laventille, or what? They [think they will] get a bullet in the eye?" Residents of the *"baaaaad* area" attempt to overcome the stigma attached to their community by differentiating a law-abiding "us" from a criminal "them" when speaking to outsiders, echoing the kinds of internal classifications

FIGURE 3.1. Houses in Laventille as seen from Picton Road (courtesy of Alamy)

identified by Elijah Anderson (2001) in his ethnographic account of social relations among poor African American families in inner-city Philadelphia. One Sunday, while visiting Josephine's home, she told me that on her street, people took care of one another. She said, "We cool. We were always cool. There are people who don't want to work, so they do crime and shoot each other up. That is not *us*." Josephine's sister-in-law concurred, adding, "The people who do the shooting here, they just killing their own. They know who they killing. Now innocent people may get caught in the middle, caught in the way." Given the dangers of stray bullets and robbery, Josephine insisted that it was not safe to walk the streets after dark. She would not permit me to be in her home after dark because she did not want to leave the house and walk me back to the taxi stand, and she could not have me walking alone.

Some of the Signature Fashions workers who lived in East Port of Spain were eager to move out of the area. Donna and her common-law husband (a skilled construction worker) often spoke of their plan to buy land outside of Chaguanas and build a new home for themselves. Donna said she was "tired" of the "bacchanal" in Belmont: petty feuds between neighbors that easily erupted in such a densely populated area. Donna often told me that it must be nice to live in England, where she imagined "you don't even know your neighbors at all." Although Belmont (where I lived during fieldwork) is still seen as a neighborhood of "lower middle-class and 'respectable' working-class people" (Lieber 1981:24), many of its residents now insist that the area has declined. "Burglar-proofing" (bars on the windows) of most houses indicates residents' unease about crime and attempt to fortify their homes against theft.

"Indian" Country: Chaguanas and Central Trinidad

While East Port of Spain represents the home of most of the Afro-Trinidadians at Signature Fashions, Chaguanas and its environs constitute the main area where the factory's Indo-Trinidadian workers live. Chaguanas is a busy market town in the west-central district of Caroni, located alongside the Uriah Butler Highway that runs north to Port of Spain and south to San Fernando. Caroni District, in which Chaguanas is situated, was predominantly rural up until the 1970s, when it was radically transformed by the "burst of industrialization" made possible by the oil boom and the associated decline in agriculture, especially sugar cultivation (Munasinghe 2001:99). Fifteen miles southeast of Port of Spain—a distance that can take half an hour to drive on traffic-choked roads—Chaguanas is flanked by older Indo-Trinidadian settlements such as Felicity, Charlieville, and Sou Sou Village, as well as newer housing developments like Enterprise Village (figure 3.2).[4]

During indentureship, workers from India were confined to sugar-cane plantations in central and southern Trinidad. These areas of the country later saw the establishment of smallholdings by formerly indentured workers and their growing families (Munasinghe 2001:90–91). The indelible association between central Trinidad and the Indo-Trinidadian population has been memorialized by the novelists V. S. Naipaul (2001) and Harold Sonny Ladoo (1972), who describe the Indian experience on plantations around Chaguanas, where Naipaul was born. Caroni Ltd., a sugar-producing firm that was owned by the British company Tate and Lyle until it was nationalized in 1970, is the island's dominant sugar interest, once producing 90 percent of Trinidad's sugar (Brereton 1981:217, in Munasinghe 2001:103). In the years since the oil boom, Caroni's productivity and capital worth have declined considerably, in part because of the vagaries of the world trade in sugar and in part as a result of state neglect (Pollard 1985). In 2003 the government announced its plan to disinvest from Caroni Ltd., leading to mass unemployment in the sugar-producing region (IMF 2004).

The town of Caroni serves as headquarters for the once-powerful All Trinidad Sugar and General Workers' Trade Union, formerly headed by Basdeo Panday. Panday went on to lead the UNC into power, serving as the prime minister of Trinidad and Tobago from 1995 to 2001 (at the time of fieldwork, the UNC was still led by Panday as the main opposition party in Parliament). In contrast to Laventille, with its deep support for the PNM, Chaguanas and the smaller settlements surrounding it are "UNC country," benefiting from its political patronage. Veena, a stitcher at Signature Fashions, described how her family had to collect water from a standpipe outside their home, until "when UNC came in, you get water going to *every house* in this area."

Felicity Village, where three Signature Fashions workers lived, is composed of small two-story houses on separate plots of land along well-ordered streets. Felicity and neighboring Charlieville are popular locations for Diwali festivities and "Ramleela," a public performance of the Hindu epic *Ramayana* staged throughout Trinidad during September or October each year. Veena lives in a small house with her sister, her sister's husband, and their two sons. They sleep in the front bedroom and Veena occupies the smaller back bedroom, containing a wardrobe, bed, television set, and sewing machine. The house has a large kitchen, a bathroom with shower, and a paved back yard. The property is rented, and the family is saving for their own home. They have also discussed moving to the United States if they could somehow procure visas. Veena's childhood home, two streets away, is now occupied by her brother and his family. Their house represents the common style of older Caroni houses, a two-story construction joined by an external staircase, with family bedrooms upstairs and cooking facilities downstairs.

Indo-Trinidadians who live in Chaguanas and the Central region more generally are perceived to be far more cosmopolitan in "dress, comportment, [and] manner of speech" than Indo-Trinidadians in South Trinidad, with its image of entrenched rural-ness (Munasinghe 2001:106; also see Khan 2004:72). Yet urbanized Indo-Trinidadians "from Central" are careful to distance themselves from the perceived criminality and indiscipline they claim is widespread in Afro-Trinidadian neighborhoods. As Veena's sister said to me, "I like Central because it have Indians. You see, where

FIGURE 3.2. Bungalow-style houses in a Chaguanas suburb (courtesy of Shawn Baldeosingh)

it have Indians you don't get so much of crime. It's Negroes who do the crime, most crimes. Like in Laventille and these places. That's what has the most crime." Veena did not echo her sister's sentiments, perhaps because while her sister is a homemaker living in an Indo-Trinidadian village, Veena works alongside and has formed friendships with women who live in Laventille. Or, perhaps Veena did not echo her sister's words because she suspected that I would disapprove. Laventille and Chaguanas are important locations at Signature Fashions, not simply because they are the home communities of the majority of its workforce but because they serve as the symbolic content with which the shop floor is organized. With an electoral system governed by the politics of ethnicity instead of a politics of class, "Laventille" and "Chaguanas" signal the kinds of allegiances among workers that may foreclose other types of solidarity.

Spatial Hierarchies and Shop-Floor Discipline

Although "front" and "back" specify places of shop-floor production (see figure 3.3), at Signature Fashions they also signify different categories of workers. Stitchers have higher status than the back workers who trim and press

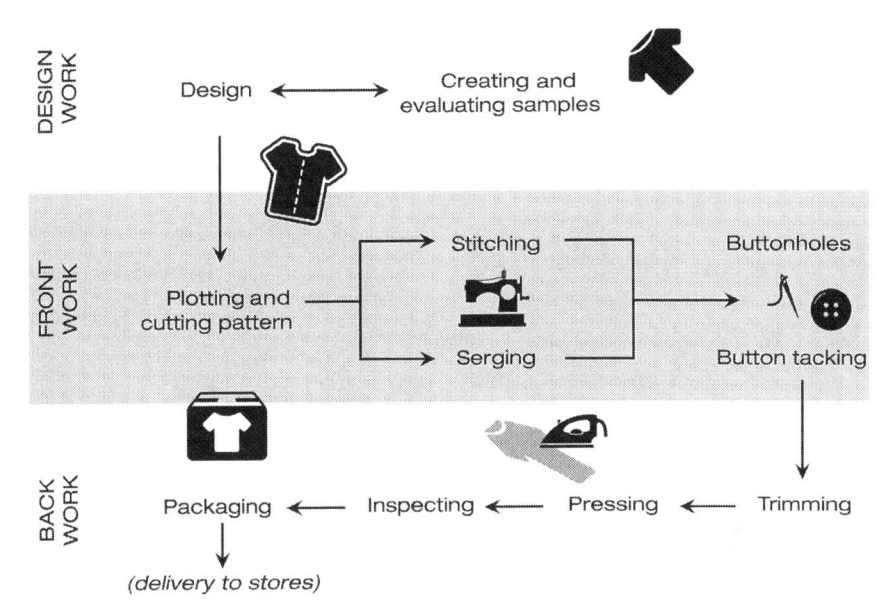

FIGURE 3.3. Production sequence at Signature Fashions (by Adam Howse)

garments. "Front work" involves operating a sewing machine, which equates with skilled labor. "Back work" is considered physical labor because workers in this area remain on their feet. Pressing garments, for example, is perceived to be difficult and physically taxing, though "unskilled."

Back workers have a reputation for being "rough" and "rude." This fact was exemplified to me one morning when Shirley called my name for help on her machine. "Wha—?" I asked, as I approached her.

She looked at me, surprised, and said, *"Can I help you?"* as if prompting me to say it.

I replied with a mischievous smile, *"Can I help you*, I said?" Shirley laughed and smacked my bottom, saying, "Yuh *real* get on like a back worker."

The antagonism between front and back workers pervades workplace identity at Signature Fashions. Stitchers say back workers just "stand up and talk." Their seemingly relaxed postures as they move through space throughout the workday are interpreted as indicating their lack of seriousness and commitment to their jobs. While stitchers are the emblematic Signature Fashions workers, sitting down and independently working at their machines, back workers crowd at the trimming tables to take up their piles of garments and stand, pace, or sway as they trim. Although workers in both groups socialize, stitchers use their machines to justify their shop-floor conversations. As Antoinette told me, "Like I could sit down whole day and talk, but my machine *running*." For management, the trimmers' embodied work practices are seen as a problem to control. They are not fixed in space but instead move through their section to gather, lay out, and trim or press garments. Like the stitchers, trimmers and pressers are left to work at their own pace much of the time but are also suddenly compelled to speed up when supervisors shout at them to do so.

At Signature Fashions, the categories of "front" and "back" are not only designative but also generative of identity. When Brenda—the front-area supervisor, responsible for the stitching section—suggested that a Christmas party should be held at lunchtime for the front workers, she and Cissy coordinated who would bring what foods for them to share on the designated day. On the day of the party, the disgruntled back workers protested that "all is Signature" and that "if it *keeping something* [i.e., having a party], it should be all ah we." While the front workers enjoyed their potluck food inside the factory during lunchtime, some back workers stayed inside to watch as they ate their own homemade lunches. Other back workers retreated outside the compound, grumbling that the party should have been for all workers or for none. Carmela said, "If it go have 'front' and 'back,' I find that is wrong. I find we is *all* Signature, and all Signature should be together." Jean, an Afro-Trinidadian front worker who, like many back workers, lives in East Port of Spain, refused to join the party. While eating her own food outside the factory with me she said, "Everybody supposed to be one, so they causing a division . . . I find they should keep for everyone or not at all."

In the instance of the Christmas party, the back workers constituted the excluded category, so it is not surprising that they would promote the idea that "all ah we" should be "one."[5] In response to exclusions of this kind, back workers construct a distinct and oppositional identity with which they form group solidarity. During an incident in which Rhonda was accused of having a bad "attitude" (see chapter 6), she took refuge in the fact that "all the workers and them all to the back" regularly praised her work ethic. Once, while Jean was being scolded by Cissy, she responded by sitting quietly and praying.

Later that day, when Cissy and Brenda started quarrelling, the back workers asked Jean with delighted astonishment whether her prayers had conjured the discord between them ("Jean, what you do? You pray on their head?"). Although she worked as a stitcher, Jean frequently sought the emotional support of the back workers from her neighborhood, who shared her feelings of mistreatment.

Spatial relations in the factory materialize a managerial ideology that workers must be assigned to different areas of the shop floor and that the work performed there is not of equal value. As Lisa Rofel (1992:103; emphasis mine) reminds us, "Factory spatial relations are not just the *setting* for disciplinary actions, but are themselves part of the same mode of power and authority." The phrase *back workers* implicitly references an Afro-Trinidadian woman undertaking arduous but perhaps untechnical work, while *front worker* evokes rows of Indo-Trinidadian women, who may have personal linkages with middle management, seated in skilled pursuit. The presence of several Afro-Trinidadian stitchers has not destabilized the equating of front work with Indo-Trinidadians. How has the geography of the factory become so racialized, and why does it persist?

For one, the racial valence of "front" and "back" is created and recreated through hiring practices. Workers generally enter the factory through someone they know. Although the front gate of the Signature Fashions factory displays a sign "STITCHERS WANTED," it rarely drew applicants to the factory door. Helene and Cissy insist that it is better to hire workers already known to existing employees, who can vouch for an applicant's character. Helene told me, "From the beginning, we'd get the first people and ask the staff if they have any friends."

Recruiting workers through the recommendations of current employees contributes to the racialized geography of the shop floor. Back workers doing heavy jobs like pressing garments bring in friends and neighbors interested in similar work. Skilled stitchers "to the front" of the factory similarly bring in friends, neighbors, and former co-workers also known to do that job well. Kavita, a fifty-one-year-old stitcher, described Signature Fashions' means of recruitment and its effects on the organization of labor:

> Now the stitchers in front, well, when we come for work, now I hear, inside here, you don't get through like that, you don't just come and say "I come for

work." Somebody have to know you! Know your background, know what you could do, before you get through [with a job] here, right? . . . So that is how, apparently, everybody started coming, alright? So, I wouldn't know if anybody in the back just come and they put them to iron, you know, but I doubt it. Because anybody you see come who does come with somebody, or something like that, apparently, is like, if they need an ironer, one of them ironers will tell them, "Well, look . . ." she have a friend who iron good. Cissy will tell her to bring her, and so . . . they would come. So that's how this front-and-back thing come about, basically, that is it.

Kavita demonstrated a keen interest in the organization of production; as a former stitching supervisor at another factory, she frequently reflected on the relations in production at Signature Fashions and shared her insights with me. Yet her assessment that the racialized geography of the shop floor replicates itself through recruiting practices alone is not true. Although Kavita said "I wouldn't know if anybody in the back just come and they put them to iron . . . but I doubt it," this is what happens. Take the case of Annie, a thirty-six-year-old grandmother from Laventille. Annie visited the Signature Fashions factory one day to inquire about a job as a stitcher. She had worked in the garment industry for fifteen years and could operate both a straight-stitch sewing machine and a serger (a sewing machine that uses five spools of thread to stitch the inner seams of garments with interlocking stitches). She heard about the factory from Josephine, a back worker who lives in Annie's neighborhood. After Cissy tried her out on the various machines, she was offered a job as a serger in the stitching section.

Annie was a large, wisecracking woman, with a loud laugh and a penchant for off-color humor. She did not get along with many of the workers at Signature Fashions because she "carries herself too rough and rude," in the words of Jean. While some workers—like Amanda and Josephine, who knew Annie from Laventille—claimed she could "push work" as well as anyone in the stitching section, whenever production needs abated, Annie was sent to the back to help with the trimming. Five weeks after Annie's hiring, another serger was hired, an Indo-Trinidadian woman named Devi—an acquaintance of Cissy and cousin of another front worker named Nalini. Once Devi was installed as a serger, Annie's position in the trimming section was made final, and she was permanently reassigned to the back area.

Annie did not stay in the back area long. Within two months of her hiring, she was suspected of having stolen three garments from the assembly line and was fired soon after (see chapter 4). Many workers told me they were happy to see Annie go because her coarse manner was out of keeping with Signature Fashions' reputation as a prestige brand, which as employees they were keen to protect. When rumors later circulated that Annie was planting trees and collecting garbage by the roadside for the unemployment relief program known as CEPEP, a front worker named Lata said, "That good, she'll fit in better there."

Annie is not the only Afro-Trinidadian who entered the factory as a front worker but later became a back worker. Both Josephine and Rhonda began working at the Signature Fashions factory as stitchers and were later relegated to back work. Josephine was told that her stitching was slow and of poor quality; Rhonda simply found herself increasingly assigned to buttonholing and button tacking until she was no longer working on a straight-stitch sewing machine in the front area. After I left the field, Jean was also asked to move from her job as a serger in the front of the factory to a pressing job in the back; I heard from another worker that she refused her new allocation and quit.

Physical discipline was not uncommon at Signature Fashions. Cissy slapped and pinched workers who talked back to her, though always in a jocular manner. What workers actually found most bothersome was her incessant shouting to work faster, to stop talking, and to "pull your hand." This style of discipline, which workers occasionally likened to "the slave-driver situation" (see chapter 2), was seen as unnecessarily severe. Given this context, I interpreted the jokey hitting and pinching of workers not as playful fun; the workers themselves rarely took it to be so, unless they were being purposely "bold" and cheekily inviting rebuke. The notion of Cissy's conduct as aggression masked as play was drawn out by Jean, who said, "Cissy now come at you in play form because she know if she come [at you] serious, something could happen."

Afro-Trinidadians from East Port of Spain, like Jean, believed they were targets of Cissy's ire. These allegations were often expressed indirectly, as when Kimberly was scolded for starting a new bundle of work before she had been told to and Antoinette commented, "Your hair have to be *straight* [to do so]," meaning that only an Indo-Trinidadian worker would be permitted to take such liberties. As Antoinette described it:

The production manager—I'm not lying to tell you—you never work hard enough, and you're never good enough. If you observe, I mean you here for a while and you observe, you will see the people that she like. They could give her how much trouble that they want, you know she will boil down. But, should I stop for *one* minute to tell somebody something, "PULL YOUR HAND I EHNT GIVE YUH ENOUGH WORK?" You know? I mean it has been going on ever since [I started working here]. You know, sometimes I wonder if it is because I am black, I am African, or what. What, I mean, how much more could you want from one person?

In my interviews with workers, those who identified themselves as Indian were less likely to describe Cissy's disciplinary tactics in negative terms than were those who described themselves as black or African. This is reflected in the words of Aparna, a forty-year-old Indo-Trinidadian woman from San Juan, who works as a stitcher in the "front front" of the shop floor. She said, "You see here [at Signature Fashions] . . . the supervisor and the production manager and things . . . it's not racial. I find myself cool here." Aparna contrasted Signature Fashions' "not racial" character with the anti-Indian taunts she had faced in another factory, where "they always talking about Indian coolie, and, you know, racist talk . . . I don't like that. I like everybody to be one." What Indo-Trinidadian workers appreciated about Signature Fashions was that they did not feel singled out as Indian but instead were treated simply as "workers." It was the Afro-Trinidadian workers who in this instance felt marked as racialized others.

When front workers conceded that Cissy shouted at Afro-Trinidadian workers more frequently, they were likely to note bad behavior of these "other" workers that had attracted criticism. For example, when I asked Kavita if there was a "racial" cast to the discipline at Signature Fashions, she agreed that many workers find it so. She offered her interpretation: "But what I believe, some of them inside here, they might say okay, if we come late one day, Cissy mightn't quarrel with *us*. Them say it because we are the same race. But check it—*them* coming late every day! You understand, *we* may come late only if it have an accident or something on the highway for us not to reach on time. Because we always on time." Kavita refuses to specify "we" and "them" on the assumption that I would understand to whom she was referring. She claims that Afro-Trinidadian workers might perceive a "racial" element to discipline at Signature Fashions but rationalizes their treatment as a result of their own behavior. She says *"we* may come late only if it have an accident or something" as if "we" are the more constant and trustworthy workers, while "they" come to work late and act unprofessionally.

Race enters official discourses on discipline in the factory, but only rarely is it articulated using racial terminology. When Cissy once complained to me about how hard her job was, she said it was because workers "only want to come in in the morning, *then* they talking to each other, and *then* they think about work." She said that the "mentality" of many of the workers is "not to work": "They don't feel the urgency to get the job done. They don't say to theyselves, I have to get *this* done today and go do it. I don't know why that is . . . this a Trinidad thing. Nobody work until they see me get vex." Helene attributed different work ethics to different racial groups in an interview with me, which reflects widespread beliefs rarely stated so openly: "The pattern of work is different between Negroes and Indians, you know. This is a general observation, not racism. Negro people are generally harder to motivate. Their productivity is lower. I don't know where that comes from, but that's what I see. Indians . . . they work harder. It comes from the family. There are some Indian workers who are inefficient, too. But they have a stronger family background than the blacks." Helene was quick to add, "It never comes to me when I'm hiring workers . . . if they are suitable, we hire. But that's just an observation about the difference."

Discussions about the "Trinidad thing" of work avoidance are rooted in colonial racial ideologies that generated discrete and stereotyped characters such as the "lazy African" and the "industrious Indian" (Puri 1999). Viranjini Munasinghe (2001:50–66) reminds us that the opposing stereotypes of African versus Indian workers were created by nineteenth-century advocates for the indenture system, notably sugar plantation owners who would profit from bonded labor in the years following the abolition of slavery. A discourse of workers of African descent "as free-spending, luxury loving, and improvident, in contrast to the industrious, diligent, self-sacrificing East Indian" supported the case for indentureship and created mutual antipathy "even before the two groups encountered each other" (ibid.:64, xi). As Daniel Segal (1994:223) has observed, the image of "Europeans" as masters, "Africans" as slaves, and "East Indians" as indentured laborers endures in contemporary Trinidad because the occupational niches into which each of these populations was inserted in the plantation economy serve as a wellspring from which future understandings of racial difference have been drawn. The plantation thus operates as master symbol structuring contemporary Trinidadian understandings of ethnic and racial difference into self-evident categories.

Because ethnic and racial designations in Trinidad historically emerged as categories of labor, their meanings obtain not from a primordial past but instead from occupational activity. Although this might imply that defying occupational expectations could therefore rework "race"—revealing its invented and contradictory nature—the attribution of race limits occupational imaginaries, as brilliantly captured by V. S. Naipaul in his 1967 short story, "The Baker's Story."[6] It is the tale of a "black black" baker in Trinidad whose delicious bread would not sell until he placed a young Chinese man at the front counter of his shop, confined his own movements to the back kitchen, and hung a Chinese-style sign on his storefront: "Yung Man Bakery."

Naipaul describes the baker's realization that his business was unsuccessful not because of the quality of its bread but instead as a result of the inconceivability that a "black black" man could run a quality bakery:

> Well, it had this coconut cart in the old square and I stop by it. It was a damn funny thing to see. The seller was a black feller. And you wouldn't know how funny this was, unless you know that every coconut seller in the island is an Indian. They have this way of handling the cutlass that black people don't have. Coconut in left hand; with right hand bam, bam, bam with cutlass, and coconut cut open, ready to drink. I ain't never see a coconut seller chop his hand. And here was this black feller doing this bam-bam business on a coconut with a cutlass. It was as funny as seeing a black man wearing dhoti and turban. (Naipaul 1967:143)

By self-assuredly enacting the coconut seller's habitus, the "black feller" cuts an unsettling figure. Because his body is raced as "black," it is freighted with occupational expectations that are incongruous with his convincing performance with the cutlass. The baker muses to himself, "And then I see that though Trinidad have every race and every color, every race have to do special things" (ibid.:145). Rather than challenge this view, the baker grows rich by capitalizing on it.

Turning back to the Signature Fashions factory, we find that attributions of skill, like the taste of the baker's bread in Naipaul's story, are constituted not by what is objectively evident but instead by what is comprehensible in light of preexisting concepts of appropriate conduct for each group. Workers are constructed into type and then appear to "naturally" inhabit the categories preferred to them. Annie became a back worker not because she was naturally inclined toward heavy, non-technical labor; nor was she simply channeled toward back work because of her race and home neighborhood. Rather, she became a back worker because her body and comportment appear to "fit in" there, and so she both becomes and reproduces the category *back worker* through her assignment to it.

Workers at Signature Fashions are addressed by management and each other through spatial rather than racial categories. This language reflects the kinds of linguistic moves that are necessary to operationalize race in a context where direct talk of race may be considered unacceptably divisive (cf. Munasinghe 2001:242–43). Yet when Afro-Trinidadian workers say that "if it keeping something, it should be all ah we," "it is them causing a division," and "they say your hair have to be straight so," they place at the center of their ire the other workers and sometimes Cissy in claiming that individuals are dividing the workforce and preventing unity among them. This is an example of how what is essentially a managerial strategy—the layout and operation of the shop floor—becomes experienced as a horizontal conflict between workers themselves (cf. Burawoy 1979:67).

Just as Kevin Yelvington found in a Trinidadian factory in the 1980s, workers at Signature Fashions are divided and addressed by management in ways that align occupational categories with particular social categories. Yelvington (1995) argued convincingly that class, ethnicity, and gender operate not as ancillary to production but in fact as part of it because they become the means through which labor is organized, disciplined, and experienced. The social processes through which workers end up in different areas of the factory are naturalized because they comport with workers' unspoken sense of inevitability in the relationship between occupation and race. At Signature Fashions, these processes are potentially more insidious because they are masked by the seemingly neutral categories of "front" and "back."

While many workers see Signature Fashions as a highly "racial" factory, they sometimes defy its raced and emplaced logics in their relationships with each other. For example, Veena and Veronica—two of the younger stitchers, who do not have children—share a workplace friendship, often talking about their aspirations to "get my own place," marry, pursue further education, and travel. While Veronica and Veena have very different social backgrounds—Veena is an Indo-Trinidadian Hindu from central Trinidad, while Veronica is an Afro-Trinidadian Catholic from Laventille—they are workplace friends, eating lunch together and talking about their future plans. Workers with a mutual desire to discuss the latest plot twists of *The Bold and the Beautiful* may be drawn together, as might those eager to discuss family problems (especially worries about teenage children). While the factory relies on a racial organization of production that coheres with naturalizing ideologies of the fitness of distinct groups for different types of work, workers are not only subject to discourses that "make" them in the factory, they are also actors who can navigate and resist those categories. Groups of workers who eat lunch together may confound the antimonies of "front" and "back" without dismissing them entirely.

From Laboring Subjects to Entrepreneurial Selves

On a typical day, I left my house shortly before 7:00 a.m. and walked along the narrow, densely populated streets in hilly Belmont until I reached the Circular Road. Donna lived nearby and often joined me at the corner. Although she was a stitcher at Signature Fashions, with her leather handbag and shoes, Donna often looked like she could be a schoolteacher or heading to an office job. We waited for one of the route taxis (private cars that ferry passengers along a fixed journey) to take us down the hill to Port of Spain. Even in the early morning, newspaper sellers and fruit vendors would be out in force, and the commercial streets downtown were choked with people and cars heading in various directions. Before the stores opened at 9:00 a.m., suitcase traders would sit with dozens of American basketball jerseys hanging from storefront security grilles. Our taxi dropped us off on Charlotte Street, and we would walk across Independence Square and down Broadway.

At Broadway, we waited for another taxi to take us to the factory, calling "highway? highway?" at every car that rolled past. Sometimes it was hard to find a taxi to take us along the highway that did not demand the full fare to Chaguanas. Donna could also be picky, insisting that we stand on the corner and wait for a "good" car. She often said, "I don't want they mashed-up old vehicles, the ones with the tail pipe *dragging*. It makes no sense I pay three dollars to go to the highway with tail pipe dragging." When we finally got in our taxi, we "took a drop" at the industrial compound and walked up a narrow footpath to the factory. By the time we arrived, the sun would already be hot, and we walked through the gates as slowly as we could without arriving late.

Donna and I were lucky; our transportation to and from the factory cost us "only" TT$11.50 (US$1.85) and took about forty-five minutes. Carmela, who lived in Arima, spent TT$16 dollars on her daily commute, while workers like Dolores, Tina, Veena, and Kavita spent TT$18 dollars going from and to Chaguanas—a staggering sum that consumed more than a quarter of their yearly wages. Travel costs in Trinidad are high as a result of the paucity of public transportation. In this oil-producing country, the primary means of transit are the car, route taxis, and maxi-taxis (vans that ply a fixed route). The international rise in gas prices meant higher costs of transportation for Trinidadians, even though their country is an energy producer.

Although all workers travel some distance, sometimes at great expense, to work in the Signature Fashions factory, the meaning of their work and significance of their wages is not the same for all. The anthropology of labor has long demonstrated that there are complex, locally variable reasons why people work. Ethnography allows us to look beyond the push-pull factors of dry economism to the wants, needs, passions, and plans that motivate participation in the labor force. Workers are not simply rational actors striving for economic maximization but rather emotional, bodily beings who may be compelled to enter even grossly exploitative employment not just for money but also to pursue goals like independence and companionship and even to escape from home (Lynch 2007; Mills 1999; Shah 2006). Factories are not simply places of employment; they are sites where people attempt to enact many types of projects.

Sitting on wooden crates stacked outside the factory one morning, I chatted to Glenda about my research while waiting for the gates to open. When I told her that I wanted to understand the experiences of garment workers like her, she stopped me and said, "I wouldn't say *garment worker*, you know. I am into the sewing, but I would not say 'I am a garment worker.' Me, I could do my little things, I could help myself." I was so stunned by Glenda's assertion that I asked no follow-up questions at the time. But over the weeks and months to come, I learned that although "garment worker" might be an occupational category recognized by Trinidad's national census, it conveyed an image of deskilled factory employee that many of my informants rejected. Women like Glenda, who have toiled in the industry over many years and possess the skills to create entire garments from scratch, more readily describe themselves as "into the sewing." The phrase not only implies a commitment to making a living through the production of clothing (whether in factories, small workshops, or at home sewing for private clients) but also evokes the pleasures of working with cloth as a knowledgeable agent. Being "into the sewing" means loving to sew and as such is less an occupational description than an assertion of cherished expertise. The phrase conveys the ideals of choice and professionalism to which workers aspired even when they seemed impossible to achieve in monotonous, poorly paid factory jobs. By proclaiming "I could help myself," Glenda emphasized that her sewing skills afford her a sense of self-sufficiency, helping her cobble together a livelihood through employment as well as own-account work in the informal sector.

All of the fifty or so Signature Fashions workers are women, with the exception of Ram, a twenty-seven-year-old man who works in the cutting room. With an average age of thirty-nine, most workers are Afro-Trinidadian and Indo-Trinidadian women ages thirty-five to fifty-five. This demographic profile marks a contrast between Trinidadian garment workers and the young women in many other parts of the world who, over the past four decades, have been recruited into export-oriented garment work along the "global assembly line" (Elson and Pearson 1981; Fuentes and Ehrenreich 1983; Hale and Wills 2005; Caraway 2007). Factory employers in Trinidad—like the transnational Barbadian data-entry firms described by Carla Freeman (2000)—see older women with their own families as the most constant and able workers.

Trinidadian garment workers are not new entrants into the paid labor force; they are long-standing members of the urban or rural proletariat with histories of employment. Garment work for these women represents neither a rupture from previous modes of livelihood nor a challenge to patriarchal relations in the home (cf. Cairoli 2011; Mills 1999; Ong 1987a; D. Wolf 1992). Instead, both the skill of sewing garments and participation in industrial production are part of a historical tradition of female waged labor. A recognition of the relationship between older and more recent forms of employment helps us understand, as Alisa Garni argues, how contemporary women's work can be simultaneously continuous with and a break from previous forms of income generation, social relations, and gendered relations (Garni 2014; cf. Masi de Casanova 2011).

Because Signature Fashions workers have usually worked in garment production for more than twenty years, they have experienced firsthand the changing fortunes of Trinidad's garment industry: from its national expansion in the 1960s and 1970s (Greaves 1974:14) to its shrinking during a national recession in the 1980s, followed by the industry's decimation under the competitive pressures of free trade since the early 1990s (Singh 2004). All of the shop-floor workers at Signature Fashions began waged work during their teenage years; many of the stitchers have held several factory jobs before working at the Signature factory in careers punctuated by layoffs, childbirth, and periods of sewing at home for private clients. Women who identify as "into the sewing" are drawn to the work as much out of the pleasure of making garments and their identity as seamstresses as by bare economic calculation, which is why they continue to seek jobs in this sector even as those jobs disappear and working conditions deteriorate.

Workers at Signature Fashions rarely have more than a secondary school education; many completed only primary school. Working-class Trinidadian families have long perceived garment production to be a suitable and achievable occupation for their daughters. Although it is low-paid, garment work represents a desirable alternative to the agricultural labor traditionally performed by Indo-Trinidadians or employment in other types of factories (e.g., food processing) that might be perceived as an option for urban, working-class Afro-Trinidadians.

Although all the Signature Fashions workers gather outside the compound at 7:30 every morning and work in the factory all day, employment does not have the same meaning for each of them. Workers do not share the same interpretation of the significance of their job within their broader life projects, nor do they necessarily share a commitment to being "into the sewing" and remaining in the industry. The three biographies that follow show that although the factory addresses women as laboring subjects, Signature Fashions workers experience their jobs not simply as employees but also as active agents, seeking and exploiting opportunities for themselves.

A Stitcher's Story: Kimberly

Kimberly is a stitcher at Signature Fashions, where she has been working for three years. She is thirty-seven years old, and when asked about her "race," she describes herself as of "African descent, though I have mixed family, we mixed between something there." Kimberly lives in St. Joseph, a small town located on the densely populated East-West Corridor between Port of Spain and Arima. Although her parents had eleven children, Kimberly alone continues to reside in her parents' house in St. Joseph after having lived intermittently with the two fathers of her three school-age children. The wooden house in which Kimberly lives with her parents and her children was built by her father little by little, on land he bought when Kimberly was a child.

Kimberly has worked in the garment industry for twenty years. She completed schooling at age thirteen and began taking sewing classes with a local seamstress in her neighborhood. She learned to draft and cut patterns "freehand," which entails resting a garment of the desired size onto uncut cloth, tracing its shape with tailor's chalk, and then cutting out the pattern with a seam allowance on all sides. Although derided by professional seamstresses and tailors as imprecise and amateurish, such opinions underrate the considerable skill required to do freehand work well.

When she turned fifteen, Kimberly entered a local trade school where she spent three years learning dressmaking and tailoring. By the time she completed the course, Kimberly was sufficiently "into the sewing" to create women's garments in precise measurements entirely from scratch, so she began sewing clothing for herself and her sisters. She said, "I get fed up [sewing at home] and I say let me try something different. So I went to my first garment factory, to really know how to hustle work and *push* work." Kimberly began her first waged employment at age seventeen in a garment factory producing men's and women's apparel. There, she learned the discipline of sewing on a piece rate:

> I was just sewing the fly. They didn't start me on piece rate at first because I was still young and I didn't know about hustling the machines yet. The fly is hard, with the curve to go around. When you're young, you're thinking about the money, I used to cry trying to do that fly . . . I cried and cried and then I got it perfect . . . I could push work, [on] piece rate I could make *real* money.

They called me in the office, they give me a promotion and wanted to give me a flat salary, so whenever someone stay home, I could do their work. I didn't want to do it. I prefer to do my piece rate. So I decided not to do it, and I get fed up after a while and I just leave.

During Kimberly's early years of employment, despite the national recession, garment factories were still a ready source of work for women "into the sewing" because of state policies to stimulate the industry by banning the importation of foreign apparel, removing the purchasing tax on locally made garments, increasing the distribution of textile import licenses for local manufacturers, and clamping down on the illegal importation of clothing (Chouthi 1988; Monsegue 1989; Trinidad and Tobago Express 1987). With her skills in dressmaking, Kimberly never struggled to find a job. Before being hired by Signature Fashions, Kimberly had already worked in seven different factories. Her decision to leave a particular factory was usually driven by discontent with its working conditions. In describing her career biography, she used phrases like "I get fed up after a while and I just leave," "I get fed up again and look for a next factory," and "I said to myself, *anything* to get me out of there." One of the factories where Kimberly worked shut down after a successful unionization drive in the late 1980s, and as a result, "I try not to get involved in all of that [trade unionism]." Although she noted that the unionized factories she worked in were often the "best" because "there you get your benefits" (such as cost-of-living allowance, a pension plan, sick leave, and vacation leave), she felt trade unions possessed insufficient clout to change the industry now.

Kimberly's entrances and exits from the garment sector over the past twenty years have been punctuated by her relationships with the two fathers of her children, who provided a place to live and helped her with money, particularly when she was pregnant. She often chose to stay home when she was living with a male partner because nourishing a relationship with a stable breadwinner could see potentially greater returns than hustling to make money on her own. In this respect, romantic relationships do not belong to some internal and non-monetized private domain to be set against the public arena of work. Instead, they form part of an integrated economic complex for sustaining life, which is not at odds with the genuine feelings workers like Kimberly expressed for the male partners who were intermittently part of their households.

A friend told Kimberly that Signature Fashions was a good place to work, and when the factory she was employed in three years ago seemed heading toward bankruptcy, Kimberly approached Signature Fashions and asked for a job. Kimberly loves to sew and is considered one of the most skilled stitchers in the factory. Although she usually operates a straight-stitch sewing machine, she may also be called to operate a wide variety of specialized equipment: hemmer, binder, double-needle, overlock, or fellar. She often is asked to stitch up samples of clothing for Helene.

During my fieldwork, Kimberly's mother died. The death of her mother was a terrible blow, and Kimberly worried openly about how she would make do without her help. Although Kimberly's relationship with her mother was sometimes strained because her mother had converted to Pentecostalism some years before and disapproved of Kimberly's "making a child" without being married to the father, her mother had proven to be a huge help. Kimberly said: "Since I came home with my baby, she used to bathe my child, she was there all the way helping me. She helped me so much. She used to help me plenty. I would organize their lunches and go on my way, and now I have to get them out of the house, so that's a bigger stress." Although Kimberly receives money from her children's fathers, she struggles to find someone to look after them when she is at work and they are out of school. With her mother gone, Kimberly must manage all of the domestic chores on her own, a substantial burden after working all day in the factory.

The poignancy of struggling as a single mother without one's own mother to help is echoed in Kellisha, a trimmer in the back area of the factory. Kellisha lives with her seven-year-old daughter in a small two-room flat beneath her father's house in Laventille. Because Kellisha's mother died ten years before and she does not have sisters, she feels a keen sense of vulnerability without the company and aid of other women. She has a distant and adversarial relationship with her father, preferring for the most part to stay out of his way (although her flat does not have running water, so she must collect buckets of water from his house for cooking and washing). Like Kimberly, Kellisha is dependent on her meager wages, struggling to even find taxi fare to do grocery shopping.

Kimberly and Kellisha consider Signature Fashions a good place to work because employment there is stable, if not highly paid. But Kimberly says she must constantly "hustle" to find additional income to help her make do "because the cost of living is always going up, and now you pushing plenty work for very little money." Kimberly says she wants her children to have the opportunity to go to university but that it seems a remote possibility. To improve her financial situation, Kimberly has recently expanded her sewing for friends and neighbors at home. While Kimberly takes pleasure in being "into the sewing," she does not like the burden of sewing at home for clients after work, preferring instead to restrict this off-the-books economic activity to Christmastime. "Dressing the house" at Christmas is a time-honored practice, and each December Trinidadians of all faiths and income levels spend a considerable amount of money purchasing new draperies and cushion covers for the front room of the home.

As a mother struggling to get by on factory wages of TT$320 (US$53) a week and the additional contributions of her children's fathers, Kimberly sees sewing at home as the easiest way to increase her income. Kimberly participates in the *sou sou*, an informal savings group among Signature Fashions workers that is a long-standing tradition in Trinidadian society (cf. Mose Brown 2011:119–30; Senior 1991; Yelvington 1995:117). Each member pays TT$50 or TT$100 a week and after ten weeks receives a lump sum of TT$500 or TT$1,000. Kimberly intends to use her savings to buy a better sewing machine—one that does embroidery—so she can offer more styles to her clients.

A Serger's Story: Nancy

Nancy did not want to be a seamstress. A self-described "tomboy," when Nancy was in secondary school she desperately wanted to learn welding, woodworking, or masonry. Places in those courses were usually allocated to boys, and Nancy found herself assigned to dressmaking instead. She left school at age seventeen without completing her diploma and began working at a local garment factory. (She later completed a dressmaking course under the Youth Training and Employment Partnership Programme, a World Bank–funded government program to train young people in a trade.) After her first employment at Fancy World, she worked at a string of different factories, including Universal Uniforms, where she spent several years before being hired by Signature Fashions at age twenty-eight.

Nancy loved working at Universal Uniforms. Although she was employed as a stitcher, she also taught herself how to fix the sewing machines, becoming the de facto factory mechanic. Nancy enjoyed being called upon to tune up any machine that was "giving trouble," which provided an opportunity for the self-proclaimed tomboy in her to gain expression. Nancy worked as the assistant supervisor of the stitching section but left Universal Uniforms because she felt disrespected when her request for a raise was turned down. Nancy approached Signature Fashions, and after Cissy tested her skills, she was offered a job working the serger.

Although Nancy was firm in her decision to leave Universal Uniforms, where she felt she had been exploited, she missed the freedom and authority she had there and seemed frustrated by her low status at Signature Fashions, where she worked to build a reputation for herself from scratch: "I feel uncomfortable that I am on a serger alone now because I get accustomed moving all around . . . when you one place, you feel like you stagnant, you ehnt moving nowhere at all."

Like more than a third of the workers at Signature Fashions, Nancy is married (a group that includes several women in "common-law," cohabiting unions). She and her husband wed shortly after the birth of their daughter, six years previous. Because her husband's employment in construction, house painting, and food service is irregular and intermittent, Nancy's factory wages are essential to their small household.

Among the married women at Signature Fashions, the significance of their income to the household budget varies considerably. While some workers, like Nancy, depend on their wages to "make groceries" and buy other necessities, there are other workers for whom factory wages can be used to purchase less essential items. Shirley is one worker rumored not to "need" her job. At age thirty-nine, she has two small children and a grown son from a previous relationship. Her husband, who has a well-paid unionized job with the national electricity corporation, did not like her working outside the home. As Shirley explained to me, "He feels his money is enough for us, and he finds I should be home looking after the children." Shirley worked as a stitcher at Signature Fashions for five years but stopped working shortly before I left the field. Her eldest daughter was starting primary school, and Shirley agreed to quit her job "so I can take her to her school in the morning, them kinda things." Many workers teased Shirley for her sassy attitude and propensity to argue with her supervisor. They said of her, by way of explanation, "Shirley doesn't need the work."

For other married women, their financial situation is much less felicitous. Bernice, a trimmer in the back area of the factory, lives behind a television-repair shop run (but not owned) by her common-law husband in Port of Spain. With three teenage children, all in secondary education, Bernice constantly worries about money. At fifty-six years old, she believes she will not readily find employment should she lose her job at Signature Fashions. Although Bernice describes her husband as "mean," she is dependent on him for their shared home. For the last two years, she has been waiting on the government register for subsidized housing for herself and her children. Her dream is for one of them to successfully migrate to the United States or Canada and send remittances to provide for her in older age. Both of Bernice's sisters have attained higher class positions in Trinidad through work and marriage, but she says it would "shame" her to go to them for financial assistance. Even though Bernice's wages are essential, she often spoke about how she "enjoys" coming out to the factory rather than staying at home all day with her husband working nearby. Because it gives her the opportunity to escape her house for several hours a day, Bernice experienced her participation in the public world of waged labor as a haven from home life.

Nancy says it is important for women to have their own income, but she is also proud to have a husband who contributes to the household budget. She said to me, "I don't wait for my husband to give me money to go and make groceries. What I do is I make groceries, and when I reach home, he will just give me money as well, like for groceries and to buy for this and buy for that." Nancy cherishes the sense of achievement her work confers upon her and calls herself an "independent woman" because she does not rely on a man:

> Most women like to hold their own responsibilities and be independent. You know? But most women you'll find dependent on men is like them *young* generations, who are men doing drugs and stuff, and they have fast money. They want style, brands, they want different things, you know? Longtime some husbands never used to allow their wives to work. They would stay home and cook, clean, do everything. And then the husband bring home the money. But now it's different, you see, it have independent women now, in this time. They aren't waiting and being dependent, just stay home and cook and wash and t'ing. They want their own money in their pocket.

Despite her skills and achievements in the industry, Nancy hoped to escape from the garment sector and pursue a different type of employment: "Because you see right now in Trinidad, women doing men job . . . they're doing tiling, they're doing different kind of things." Shortly before giving birth to her son, Nancy said: "You see after [I have] my baby, I might not come back. I get fed up of sewing. I want to go do a course . . . I had my goals to be a firewoman or an officer—the men's work, nah? You find you didn't get through, and people down-courage you, saying you can't do this, you can't do this, and this is not for you. But that's what I wanted to do." While Nancy strained against the gendered expectations that shaped much of her working life, today she finds herself excited by the idea that women no longer have to work solely in traditionally female occupations. Indeed, the government of Trinidad and Tobago now encourages women to enter nontraditional fields such as masonry and welding through government programs and an expanded school curriculum (Drosdoff 2004; Hosein 2006:30). Nancy hoped to do a course in tiling or masonry after the birth of her son, but I do not know whether she pursued it.

A Trimmer's Story: Tina

Tina is thirty-nine years old and works as a trimmer in the back area of the factory. She is the only Indo-Trinidadian in the trimming section; all of the other back workers are Afro-Trinidadian. Raised a Muslim, Tina says she "more carr[ies] on like a Christian" now. Although she lives in the traditionally Indo-Trinidadian town of Chaguanas, she is married to an Afro-Trinidadian man who sells bags of peanuts on the highway.

Tina did not finish secondary school; she was forced to drop out when her stepmother became ill. At age sixteen, Tina learned to sew from "a lady down by me." She says at the time, "I wasn't thinking about a job, I was only thinking about helping myself. You're home at the time, you want to learn to sew. I decide to take a little course." Tina says that while she "cannot really cut [patterns] perfect on my own, I have ideas where I can help myself." She sews herself skirts to wear to work, as well as bed linens and curtains for herself and others.

As Patricia Mohammed (1989:37) notes, up through the 1960s a large proportion of both working-class and middle-class Indo-Trinidadian women were "housewives" (excluding women working in agriculture and family businesses or those pushed into wage labor by poverty). Beginning in the 1970s, greater educational opportunities and changing social norms led increasing numbers of Indo-Trinidadian women to work outside the home, reconfiguring gender relations across the economic classes.

Tina's first paid job was in housekeeping, which she did for several years, cleaning houses with two other women. She found the work grueling and so wanted to "look for a betterment." Employment in a garment factory seemed both accessible and agreeable: "I liked sewing, and I always want to be in something that was, like, you know, I would learn more, I would gain more experience, so that I could do something on my own. Sewing is the onliest thing I could think of. Sewing is the only thing I have on my mind, really." Tina's first garment factory job was at Excellent Apparel in Port of Spain. She did some stitching but found it difficult to get up to speed in the piece-rate factory and was allocated trimming instead. Tina then worked as a trimmer in two other factories, each of which closed down. She learned about the availability of jobs at Signature Fashions from Donna, whom she knew from Excellent Apparel. At the time of my fieldwork, they had both worked at Signature for four years.

While trimming is often considered low-skilled work, Tina identifies as being "into the sewing" by emphasizing her ability to trim well: "That is my field of working in, trimming. I know about trimming." While back workers have a reputation for being unruly, Tina is quick to point out her professionalism and industriousness: "I like my supervisor to say, 'She's a good worker.' I like to hear those things about myself. And for myself, I like to know that I *am* a good worker."

Tina was raised in a conservative Muslim household and fell out with her father when she chose to marry an Afro-Trinidadian Christian. She said: "And me and my father never really get along because of that. Because he always feel, you know, that I shouldn't marry to a Negro, I should marry to somebody of my own race. But it is not the *race*, it is how a person treats you. That is all that matters. It is not the hair, the color, it is how a person treats you. No matter if somebody of your own race." Tina talked about her frustrations over the fact that when her father died, neither her brother nor she inherited property or money; all of his assets went to their stepmother, with whom they have a strained relationship. Tina spoke about how she and her husband were trying to save up for a home of their own, lamenting their difficulties in simply paying rent with their small salaries: "Buying food alone is so much, so you hardly have [enough] to put away for a home, to purchase a home. Everything is so expensive."

Tina says that as a child, her parents were "very strict. So all we wearing is like head-covering and long clothes. You have yourself covered." Tina contrasts this style of dress with the way she dresses now: "I didn't know anything like being 'in style.' So now, you're on your own, you learn for yourself, you learn what is in style, what is not in style. You could wear that now, but long ago, you wear at that time what your parents told you to wear." Coming out to work and having opportunities to experiment with being "in style" is important to Tina; she buys factory rejects from Signature Fashions when they are available and also "thiefs a chance" to make garments with the help of fellow workers. For Tina, then, employment and consumption are entwined, and both are important elements in fashioning her independent and adult identity. Tina's forging of a selfhood concerned with being in style represents for her a break from a past she now sees as confining and even wrong in its intolerance for people of African descent. As Carla Freeman (1993, 2000) has argued, issues of style and dress may not be secondary or tangential for working-class Caribbean women but instead constitutive of a gendered work identity that is actively cultivated and invested with meaning. The pleasures of dress are important to Tina, and being a "good worker" engaged in the production of fashionable clothing gives her a feeling of pride.

The stories of Kimberly, Nancy, and Tina suggest diversity and differentiation within the Signature Fashions workforce and the impossibility of simple categorization into interest groups along lines of ethnicity, age, marital status, class, or occupation. While nearly half of the Signature Fashions workers are single mothers and more than a third live with long-term partners (whether married or not), these categories on their own provide little explanation for the meaning or importance of waged work to individual women. Similarly, "ethnic" differences (such as the experiences of Afro-Trinidadians compared with Indo-Trinidadians) do not uniformly influence women's motivations in pursuing factory employment. For women "into the sewing," the ways they navigate factory work depend in large measure on the alternatives available. Decisions to forms alliances with co-workers, to resist factory discipline in illicit ways, or to simply walk away from a job if it becomes intolerable are shaped by the wider dimensions of a worker's life—including familial responsibilities and sources of additional income—located outside the factory context. In this respect, women workers are never free "agents" but are instead located in relationships and obligations that shape and constrain them.

Conclusions

Signature Fashions is a place of subjectification and a place of opportunity. It demands a mode of inquiry that encompasses both. In theorizing how anthropology might approach these kinds of dynamics, Sherry Ortner cautions against making the individual actor the unit of analysis for its tendency toward either culpability or victim-hood. Ortner (1996) proposes that we should analyze instead the field of action—which she dubs "the game"— rather than simply the choices of individual actors located within it. Doing so allows us to see a factory like Signature Fashions as a place where people come to enact certain kinds of projects (which are open to adaptation and can be marked by ambivalence), at the same time as they are shaped by what happens to them there. Signature Fashions workers "make" the factory work, but they are also made by it.

By examining the categories of "front" and "back" in the factory, my aim has been to show how spatial practices instill social hierarchies on the shop floor. Building on Kevin Yelvington's insight that rather than a one-way process whereby ethnicity dictates occupation, Trinidadian ethnic categories are also an effect of production, I show how associations between ethnicity and occupation are not simply deployed on the shop floor but also find themselves reproduced there. Despite the everyday ways in which Signature Fashions workers constantly reappraise, subvert, and rework racial categories, "front" and "back" constitute a powerful discourse with important effects. Because of the use of spatial categories rather than racial ones, the use of race at Signature Fashions is more subtle and potentially more insidious than in the factory Yelvington (1995) describes, where white and Indo-Trinidadian men supervised women of African and Indian descent. Working bodies are assessed, classified, labeled, and inserted into production in ways that make some kinds of future more possible than others for each worker in the system. On issues of health and crime (chapters 6 and 7, respectively), we will see how "front" and "back" influence the ways workers are treated and the kinds of entitlements—material and symbolic—they can successfully claim. Workers at Signature Fashions constantly blame one another for the "disunity" among them, pointing to the bad behavior of the "back workers" or the self-satisfaction of the "front workers" as culprits undermining their common interests.

Signature Fashions is an uneven, ideological field, in which workers' opportunities are not all the same. *This* is the field in which they strategize and actively cultivate their own projects. An examination of workers' illicit activities in chapter 4 will allow us to drill down into the shop-floor "structures" to reveal the extent to which they are open to manipulation. This manipulation, I argue, transforms the labor process in ways that are hidden to the actors inside it.

Notes

1. Trinidad and Tobago's Central Statistics Office lists the country's population as 1.3 million, composed of "40.3% of East Indian descent, 39.5% African, 18.4% Mixed, 0.6% European, and 1.2% Chinese and 'Other'" (CSO 2007). However, rather than accept the fixity, validity, and transparency of ethnic categorization contained in such statistics, we must be aware of the ideological and strategic uses of ethnic labeling. As Aisha Khan (1998:500) notes, "When asking what identity categories mean, we must always also ask to whom, as well as when and why they are constructed, and whether they are constructed strategically." Daniel Miller (1994a:52) notes, for example, how the seemingly stable numbers of the "mixed" population in Trinidad over recent decades can be explained in part by the rejection of the category *dougla*—which locally signifies "mixed-race" individuals of both Indian and African heritage—by individuals of that heritage who for reasons of kinship or identity choose to attach themselves to either the Indo-Trinidadian or the Afro-Trinidadian population rather than to both.

2. Although is not uncommon for Trinidadian homes to have plastic water barrels outside, in middle-class homes they are self-replenishing because they are connected to the main water supply, while water barrels in Laventille usually stand alone. Michelle Mycoo (2006:137) describes the requirement for such barrels as "state failure to perform basic state functions."

3. The PNM formed the government in Trinidad and Tobago during the years 1956–86, 1991–95, and 2001–10. Although the "colored" middle classes of the Independence era distanced themselves from the "black" working class, the PNM

from its earliest years was able to create an alliance between the two groups while also gaining votes from the "white" minority (Rodman 1971:25–26). In the public imaginary the PNM remains an Afro-Trinidadian party, although as Don Robotham (2003) cautions, "Afro-Trinidadian" is an internally differentiated category that cannot be set unproblematically against "Indo-Trinidadian."

4. Daniel Miller's excellent ethnography of Chaguanas provides detailed though anonymized portraits of its various settlements (Miller 1994a:24–57).

5. The sentiment that "all ah we" should be "one" resonates with a popular ideal of the Trinidadian nation as both culturally diverse and harmonious, as captured in the National Anthem (Birth 2008:77–82). Kevin Birth (ibid.:66–67) reminds us that such unifying rhetoric was central to both the PNM's election strategy in 1956 and that of the National Alliance for Reconciliation (NAR) thirty years later but that by the 1990s party politics were defined largely along ethnic lines.

6. I am grateful to Viranjini Munasinghe for introducing me to this story.

4

"Is We *Own* Factory"

Thiefing a Chance on the Shop Floor

> We must develop a nuanced analysis that clarifies the ways people manipulate and take advantage of the structures of opportunity surrounding them—sometimes transforming and sometimes reproducing relations of power and inequality—rather than positioning people either as duped or as powerless to resist, reinvent, or renovate.
> – *Deborah Thomas, Modern Blackness*

Thiefing a chance is a term workers use to refer to a wide range of illicit practices they undertake during the workday, from stitching little items for themselves using company materials and machines to trying out a new sewing machine without managerial permission. Many of the workers maintained their own home businesses in the evening, designing and stitching low-cost clothing for friends and neighbors. Sewing at home helps workers augment the minimum wage they earn at Signature Fashions and gives them a certain stature in their home communities. Workers would bring these "private jobs" into the factory and sneakily hem a dress or serge its seams on the industry-grade machines to give their homemade garments a more professional look. The production manager would leave a box of fabric scraps in the lunch area. Too small to be used in the manufacturing process, these scraps were ostensibly to be taken home to be used as tea towels or rags. Workers would use them instead to stitch up small things for themselves: patchwork aprons and cotton dust masks for use in the factory or cloth bags and dolls' clothes to take home. Workers might describe *any* of these activities as "thiefing me little chance," which simply means taking advantage of the brief time when supervisors are distracted or absent from the shop floor to steal a moment's work on other projects. Like *la perruque*, described by Michel de Certeau (1984:25), or the factory-made "homers" described by Michel Anteby (2008), these small acts redirected hourly-paid workers' time and use of factory equipment toward personal projects; nothing material was taken except a trivial amount of thread.

Despite my knowledge of such everyday acts of copying and pilfering, as well as the informal networks of mutual aid that I call "productive sociality" (see chapter 2), workers were reluctant to talk about them, usually shrugging off my questions on the subject. All of this changed after six months of working in the factory, when I came to realize that thiefing a chance not only meant sneakily stitching or trying out new machines; in fact, workers operated a covert assembly line, furtively producing duplicates of Signature Fashions garments for themselves. *This* type of thiefing didn't become known to me until I became complicit in it, largely by accident, when I asked a worker to thief a chance for me.

That week, we were making camisole tops out of stretch-cotton cloth. Shirley was working on the binding machine, attaching straps to each of the garments. One morning while I was helping her cut the straps as they came out of her machine, she said casually, "You could ask Kimberly to cut you a camisole, and I'll stitch it up for you." Kimberly, it was widely known, was always "cutting." She had the ability to look at a piece of fabric, put a pair of scissors to it, and—just by sight—cut out a pattern for a pair of trousers, a shirt, or a skirt in the correct size. The joke was that Kimberly cut so much fabric while sitting at her sewing machine that her skirts were full of little holes where she had hurriedly cut through the fabric on her lap and her own clothes, too.

I had noticed Kimberly cutting camisoles with what I assumed to be scraps of discarded cloth. A little while later I approached her and asked quietly, "If I get some jersey fabric from Peggy, you could cut a camisole for me?" She nodded slightly. I didn't think much more of it. I had worked with Peggy in the cutting room for a few weeks during the Christmas rush. I would ask her if she had any scraps of cloth, deliver them to Kimberly, and have her cut a camisole shape for me at lunchtime. Shirley had already volunteered to stitch it up. It didn't seem like too big a deal. More than really wanting the camisole, I was curious to see if Kimberly would actually cut me one.

After finishing my work with Shirley, I joined Glenda at a side table to cut and turn collars. A little while later I heard Antoinette hissing to get my attention. I could not see her mouth, which was hidden behind her dust mask, but her eyes were smiling. She beckoned me over. Pretending to cut some threads for her, I came and stood next to her machine.

She whispered, "You ask Kimberly to cut you a camisole?" I said yes. She slapped my leg and giggled, looking around the room to make sure Cissy, the production manager, was out of sight. "I thought you would *never* ask!" She started laughing again, turning her head left and right every couple of seconds to make sure no one was coming. She said, "We go make you a whole *closetful* of Signature clothes. You ehnt know how *long* I wanted to make something for you. But I didn't know how you would be about it. I didn't know if you would think it was stealing. I wanted to make Michael a jersey; I wanted to make you so many jerseys. And now, girl, we go make you some *real* clothes!"

Antoinette's excited chatter about thiefing a chance and her sudden willingness to describe its material practices and moral logics marked a deep contrast from her tight-lipped responses to my earlier questions. I quickly realized that in simply asking Kimberly to cut me a camisole, I had unwittingly nominated myself as an eager participant in the process. In the time that followed, I came to learn a great deal about the complex practices of thiefing. The first and most obvious challenge to my prior view of shop-floor life was that workers did not just use scraps of cloth to make simple garments for themselves but instead cut cloth intended for legitimate production to create precise duplicates of the designer clothing the factory produced.

I tell this story because it recounts the moment when I first learned that in addition to the workers' many unofficial activities in the factory, they operated a second assembly line to generate Signature Fashions clothing for themselves. This moment represents a qualitative shift in my interpretation of the factory as both a site of production and a social world, thereby coloring my perception of everything I observed afterward. Because "thiefing" was so neatly incorporated into everyday factory processes, I had been unable to distinguish it from the various other forms of unofficial activity commonly taking place. Once I learned how sophisticated and coordinated workers' illicit practices really were, I struggled to make sense of their meaning. Was this a covert form of everyday resistance (Scott 1985), a subversion of the employers' appropriation of the workers' labor? How might thiefing a chance as a coordinated, collective enterprise relate to other forms of communal activity, such as labor activism? What moral logics underpin this practice? Is thiefing limited to the Signature Fashions factory, or is it widespread across the industry?

In this chapter, I present a detailed ethnographic account of the exchanges, conflicts, and relationships involved in thiefing a chance at Signature Fashions. Although "thiefing" is a broad category and takes many forms, I focus on workers' production of precise duplicates of the factory's own products. I examine the intense social negotiations involved in these processes, arguing that the criteria by which workers justify, define, and defend thiefing provide an interpretive window onto their understanding of the opportunities represented by the factory and the moral landscape in which they are embedded. Thiefing a chance is the expression of an individualistic, enterprising subjectivity. Workers talk about thiefing as a daring enterprise through which they create "we own factory." Yet rather than uncritically accepting these triumphal narratives of risk rewarded, I investigate the ways thiefing both subverts *and* confirms modes of discipline in this flexible firm. By analyzing a second meaning of the phrase *thiefing a chance* (trying out a machine the worker has not been trained to use), I demonstrate that despite its contestatory appearance, thiefing often works in the service of capital, providing workers with opportunities and incentives for self-skilling.

Thiefing a Chance at Signature Fashions

At Signature Fashions, workers' covert production of garments takes place alongside the main production of the factory but is conceptually and materially separated from it. While the factory's "real work" (a term workers used) comes through official channels and is delivered in bundles to the shop floor by supervisors, thiefed work is initiated by individuals, who manage the production process themselves by asking others to work on their garments. Mutual aid is already commonplace because workers rely on one another to help them correct mistakes, create "flow" (see Chapter 6), and make the workday more tolerable. The negotiations involved in thiefing a chance are enmeshed within the same factory processes that require mutual aid, but they exist in a parallel plane to the primary work of the factory. Although "real" garments and their thiefed copies are materially identical, they have distinct "social lives" (Appadurai 1986) because their production is facilitated by horizontal relationships of exchange, reciprocity, and trust that are different from the hierarchical workplace relations of capitalist wage labor.

A thiefed garment always began with a worker "begging" Peggy, who worked in the cutting room, for cloth. She could ask either for cut cloth, which Peggy would cut into the same patterns as the real work (sometimes by laying an extra length of fabric to the pre-cut stack), or plain cloth, which the worker who requested it would have to cut by hand herself. Peggy might furtively hand the extra cloth to workers or attach it to a bundle of real work going to the shop floor. For her work in the cutting room and her access to cloth, Peggy was central to the process of thiefing a chance. Although Peggy did not work on a sewing machine, she was known to have in her closet a whole range of clothes—"*all* Signature and in every color," in the words of one worker—other workers had stitched for her. Workers who thiefed a chance had to be sure to "go down good" with Peggy and be careful not to be so *fas* (bold or uppity) as to demand too much of her.

The distinct social life of thiefed clothing begins the moment scissors are put to cloth to cut a pattern into it. Even when Peggy placed extra lays of fabric on top of the official count—so the material for thiefed garments could be cut alongside legitimate fabric—the thiefed cloth was always tied in such a way that it could be distinguished from real work, forcing a spatial separation between the two even within the same bundle. This allowed workers not interested in thiefing a chance to simply pass the item along. Thus, materially identical pieces of fabric were never perceived to be so by workers on the shop floor: the separation between "real" and "thiefed" work was always meticulously upheld.

While almost all workers at Signature Fashions participated in thiefing at some time or another (either managing the production of their own garments or providing stitches to others), those most involved in it were workers on specialized machines whose operations were necessary to complete most garments. Operators of these machines—like Shirley, Kimberly, and Antoinette—had the greatest capacity to enlist the aid of others in making their own garments in return. These workers may thief as many as fifteen items in a year; most other workers would thief far fewer. Because thiefing mostly requires stitching, back workers had little to trade on and therefore fewer opportunities than front workers to thief a chance.

When supervisors participated in thiefing a chance, workers often grumbled that these requests were the "worst" because of the pressure of having to sew quickly under direct supervision. Yet even though workers thiefed a chance for their supervisors, their own thiefing practices had to be scrupulously hidden from view. This concealment upholds the distinction between official and unofficial work. When one worker, Lata, was discovered with a half-finished shirt on her sewing table, she was reprimanded for her carelessness, yet she was not sent home. Although managers and workers share complicity, vigorous effort on all sides renders such work invisible, in the guise of being labor for the factory itself (cf. de Certeau 1984:25).

Not every kind of garment coming down the line would be thiefed. Garments that required extensive work, like ruffles, might be deemed too complex to bother trying to copy. Also, Peggy would not provide costly fabric, and workers did not ask her for it. Thiefed garments are usually of simple construction and standard fabrics rather than those used in the "exclusive" lines.

Just as workers have to be careful not to ask too much of Peggy, they also must be careful not to ask too much of each other. Annoyed by what she perceived to be Lata's excessive thiefing, Donna commented to me that Lata had "sat down whole day to make jerseys for she whole family: she brothers, she cousin, she niece, *everyone.*" Lata was making the clothes as gifts for her family members following the birth of a niece. Donna wondered, "If she brother have a new child, she couldn't go and buy some nice little thing? Instead she have to make *all* that work for everybody." Similarly, Libby had a reputation for being "too bold" in asking for many items of thiefed clothing, and workers regularly accused each other of asking for too much.

Garments have use value; they also have symbolic value. Many of the most enthusiastic participants in thiefing a chance at Signature Fashions are single mothers with little disposable income to deal with issues of style for themselves and, importantly, for their daughters. Others may have more household income because they are married or cohabiting. By thiefing clothes for themselves, workers gain access to symbols of wealth, success, and fashion in a context where such symbols are important. Daniel Miller (1994a:223) has noted, for example, that in Trinidad many women duly expect the giving of clothing in a romantic relationship. By creating and wearing high-status garments themselves, Signature Fashions workers are able to play with the ambiguous signification of their dress in social gatherings outside of work, by disguising or leaving open to speculation where their clothing came from. When attending parties with various workers, I observed how a "Signature" garment might become a point of intrigue with a member of the opposite sex. At my going-away lime, one man asked Antoinette where she got her "Signature" top. She replied sassily, "I buy it my*self*," then broke into a flirtatious smile.

Thiefing clothing also contributes to a worker's status among her peers in the factory, since workers curry favor with those who can help them thief. But thiefing a chance also contains the simple pleasure of breaking from workplace monotony and the enjoyment of a good ruse. One afternoon, Shirley roared with laughter at Aparna, who watched nervously as Shirley quickly hemmed a T-shirt for her, calling out, "She frighten and is *I* taking risk!" Thiefing certainly contains some risk, which may itself be a source of excitement and fun.

As thiefed work threads its way through the shop floor, it is stitched up in a materially overlapping but conceptually separate space from the real work of the factory. Both real work and thiefed work are the products of managed negotiations between workers on the shop floor, with the sometime intervention of supervisors; both types of work involve social agendas, obligation to others, and ideas of reciprocity and trust. Both activities form part of the day-to-day world of Signature Fashions, a "flexible factory." Yet despite these similarities in the sphere of production, real work and thiefed work bear a crucial distinction: workers believe thiefed clothes can be justly smuggled out of the factory; legitimate factory work cannot. This distinction points to the interpretive criteria through which workers classify thiefing as a moral practice.

A Collective Activity or an Individual Enterprise?

"I didn't know if you would think it was stealing," Antoinette had said to me with relief after I first asked Kimberly to thief a chance for me. Thiefing is always haunted by its possible interpretation as "stealing," a position the factory owners might take. I was often told by workers not to bring to work photographs of parties we had attended together in which someone was wearing a thiefed Signature item. When Shirley turned up to work one morning in a shirt she had thiefed, workers teased her for her "boldness" because if asked about the shirt, she would have to lie and say she had bought it at one of the stores in town. After growing tired of her co-workers poking fun at her during lunch, Shirley announced, "If God say that it wrong, I go say to he, 'I very sorry, I didn't realize,' and that will be that." When I asked her if thiefing a chance is stealing, she quipped, "I don't think it stealing because we does do it *quick.*"

The similarities between thiefing and stealing generate humorous banter. "All these Christians in here? Check they wardrobes," Antoinette once said, though I could not be sure if she was using their participation in thiefing as evidence that it was not stealing or as commentary on the moral laxity of Signature's Christians. Nonetheless, Glenda, the most visible Christian in the factory because of her frequent attempts to convert other workers to her newly found faith, commented to me, "Stealing is wrong, eh? But the only reason I don't thief chance here is I wear these long skirts. You could do it, though, you wear them kind of things."

The few workers at Signature who took no part in thiefing seemed to think it was not worth the hassle of sneaking stitches and carrying the items out of the factory. Donna described the first time she smuggled a skirt home in her handbag as an "awful" experience. She said, "My heart was beating *whomp, whomp, whomp,* and I was so *worried* I was going to get caught." While Donna still might "make up a little thing" in the factory for her daughter and freely assists other workers, she determined that thiefing for herself was barely worth her effort: "I does find them clothes ehnt worth so much so."[1]

The five or six workers who never take part in thiefing a chance tend to sit toward the front of the shop floor. These "front front" workers rarely relied on any form of mutual aid to complete their work, instead priding themselves on their self-reliance and openly competing with one another (though in a joking way) for the yearly "best worker" award. Usually a paperweight or a clock, this award is presented to a worker chosen for her punctuality, efficiency, cheerfulness, and skill over the previous year. While these workers were criticized by others for being "stale" and "boring," they rarely responded with a direct critique of thiefing. Veena pointedly said during a visit to my home, "[Thiefing] is stealing, and I would not take a pin from that factory, not a *pin.*"

While such assertions seem to challenge the boundary between thiefing and stealing, all Signature Fashions workers actually draw a sharp distinction between thiefing garments in the factory and stealing them outright. When three completed shirts (real work) went missing from the assembly line during my fieldwork, Annie, who had been working at Signature Fashions for just two months, was dismissed from her job the next time she was late to work. The official reason for her dismissal was "lateness," but it was well-known that management suspected her of having stolen the shirts.[2] Workers assumed that only someone who had been at Signature a short time could have stolen the shirts; any other worker would know how to thief them. Annie's dismissal saddened those who knew her well and vigorously proclaimed her innocence. Among other workers, the incident gave rise to jokes about Annie's foolishness and arrogance in stealing from the factory.

The fact that everyone considers stealing a serious offense demonstrates its conceptual separation from the day-to-day thiefing that is tacitly allowed to flourish. This is an instructive distinction because it goes to the heart of how thiefed clothes are morally interpreted vis-à-vis the legitimate work of the factory. Real work, thiefed work, and stealing are best understood as positions along a continuum. Real work is situated at one end of the spectrum: the work of the factory that people are paid to do. Real work is owned and authored by the factory itself, and although workers may rely on mutual aid to complete this work, they principally labor over it dispassionately, for a wage. Stealing is located at the opposite end of the spectrum and also represents a fixed moral position: taking the real work of the factory from the assembly line is clearly an offense. Stolen items are always seen as the property of the factory, and workers say that to steal "just so" is wrong.

Yet in between the fixed points of "real work" and "stealing" lies what Michel Anteby (2008) would call a "moral gray zone" in which thiefing is conducted and defended. For workers at Signature Fashions, the moral acceptability of thiefing hinges on the question of ownership. Veena claimed that thiefing is stealing because materials are taken, declaring her refusal to take even a pin from the factory. Most other workers interpret thiefing differently, distinguishing between the materials used in the factory's main production and those used in thiefing. When workers speak of "thiefing a *chance*," they allude not to the taking of an object but to the taking of a risk. By begging Peggy to find and cut some cloth for them, they engage in social action to claim the items as their own. The rest of the process similarly requires risk taking and social efficacy: each constituent part of the garment must be obtained and stitched through careful negotiation with other workers. Because individual workers entirely manage this process themselves, thiefing is placed in an interpretive category similar to that of their own work (like sewing at home or sneakily stitching for their clients on factory machines) for which they assume responsibility and ownership.

In the act of thiefing, workers almost always recreate and wear the exact styles produced for the stores (and they never sell thiefed garments), not only because copies are easy to produce but also because of the singular allure of owning an *actual* Signature Fashions garment. Yet by pilfering patterns as well, workers can make well-designed outfits at home in the bright silks and soft satins they prefer rather than the linen and brushed-cotton earth tones Signature produces for Caribbean elites and foreign tourists. In making stylistic choices about the production of quasi-Signature garments at home, even the thiefed factory items come to be seen as initiated and authored by workers themselves and therefore rightfully theirs.

In his ethnography of side production in a French aeronautics plant, Anteby (ibid.) shows that craftsmen on the shop floor make an important distinction between theft as the taking of new materials and "homer"-making, which required the creative transformation of factory scraps into small tools and decorative items. Echoing the kinds of moral distinctions workers at Signature Fashions made between "thiefing" and "theft," the craftsmen in Anteby's account emphasized that they primarily used unwanted materials, they transformed those materials through their skilled labor, and the items they made would be kept or traded but rarely profited from (ibid.:83).

The workers at Signature Fashions sometimes refer to thiefing a chance as "we own factory." The phrase has an intentional double meaning. In Trinidadian English, "we own factory" could be taken to mean two things: "*our* own factory" or "we *own* the factory."[3] The use of the phrase highlights workers' reconceptualization of the relationship between themselves and their workplace. The factory is described as a space in which they can undertake their own projects (*our* own factory), asserting possession of the space itself (we *own* [the] factory). The factory thus becomes a resource for workers, containing materials, machines, and ideas, all of which the daring person uses for her own purposes.

Thiefing is given individual, not collective, justification. The "wickedness" (miserliness) of the factory bosses was a constant topic of worker discussion, but it was rarely used as a justification for thiefing a chance. Workers sometimes said they deserved "a little jersey or two" because unlike other garment factories, Signature Fashions did not give each worker a T-shirt at Christmas. Yet such compensatory justifications for thiefing were generally muted; workers did not use the language of *lagniappe*—a local phrase denoting the "little extra" given by a fruit-and-vegetable seller to a loyal customer—in their narratives of thiefing as moral practice (cf. Thompson 1958:175). Workers never collectively represented their actions as defying management, possibly because their shop-floor supervisors were complicit in the practice and the factory owners were so remote.

During my first conversation with Antoinette about thiefing, she told me she would make me a shirt, adding "because I feel you should be getting something, a stipend. You working here every day, and that wicked." The fact of my working at the factory for no pay (a situation the workers found scandalous) was sometimes proffered to me as an explanation for why my thiefed items were well deserved. Antoinette indicated that by "doing something" for me, she could better the "worthless" factory owners by suitably compensating a foreign guest laboring in her midst. (To be fair, Helene and Cissy did present me with two Signature Fashions T-shirts at Christmastime and two more shortly before I left Trinidad the following November.)

The interpretation of thiefing a chance as individual risk taking rather than a collective endeavor is demonstrated by the debates that arose after Lata was caught thiefing. When Cissy discovered the half-finished shirt resting on her sewing table, she immediately demanded to know for whom it was being made. Lata said truthfully that it was for Kimberly. When questioned by Cissy, Kimberly said, "I don't know nothing about that." Lata's naming of Kimberly, and Kimberly's subsequent silence in response to Cissy's questions, instantly became a raucous topic of lunchtime gossip among workers.

Workers agreed that Lata had been reckless in leaving the shirt exposed, although they were divided over whether she was wise to identify Kimberly as the shirt's owner. Some workers argued that she should not have named Kimberly, if only to protect her own interests. Carmela said, "Who go help she [thief a chance] now?" Other workers insisted that because it was

Kimberly's shirt, Lata need not risk a scolding or dismissal for illicitly working on an item that was not her own. Devi said, "If I thiefing for Kimberly and I get caught? I go *say* it for she." Antoinette concurred, adding, "At least if I go lose my [job], it go be because I thiefing chance for *myself*" rather than accepting dismissal for participating in somebody else's scheme.

Workers universally applauded Kimberly's silence, maintaining that she was not obliged to furnish the truth to anyone. As a strategy to avoid punishment, Kimberly's unresponsiveness succeeded. Cissy scolded Lata and Antoinette (who had obviously serged the garment's inner seams) and then stormed off with the shirt in hand. In all the debates that circulated around this incident, workers never suggested that they should, on principle, protect one another collectively. Lata's words and Kimberly's silence were assessed as personal, rather than collective, strategies. Despite the huge coordination involved in thiefing a chance, it is conceptualized as an interconnected series of individual enterprises, which is why Lata was not condemned for identifying Kimberly. While it was deemed too risky to thief a chance with her for a few weeks, Lata was not ostracized by the group.

Although there is a diversity of worker perspectives on thiefing, what is universal is the unwillingness to conceptualize thiefing as a cooperative endeavor, despite the fact that it is an intimately and extensively coordinated activity. Thiefing is described in individualistic terms, as a calculated practice in which some choose to engage while others do not. Thiefing is not positioned as ideologically or materially opposed to the aims of factory owners. Workers use a language of "opportunity" to describe thiefing, not the language of resistance.

Beyond Resistance and Accommodation

Laying bare the provisional moralities that operate on the shop floor offers an interpretive window onto workers' intentions, motivations, and assessments of thiefing. Such moral frameworks are shaped not by the factory context alone but also by cultural values widely discernible in Trinidadian life.

Anthropologists have long recognized the existence of multiple value systems at work within West Indian culture. Peter Wilson famously asserted that West Indians are oriented, at different times, to two ideological systems: Euro-centric colonial ideologies, which focus on social hierarchy and "respectability," and a locally based "creole" value system characterized by egalitarianism, communitas, and status competitions to build a streetwise "reputation" (Wilson 1969, 1973; see also Besson 1993; Freeman 2000; Sutton 1974; Yelvington 1995). The coexistence of these two frameworks points to dual aspirations among West Indian people: to the "transient" pleasures associated with short-lived status contests and to the "transcendent" moral virtues of stability and domesticity (Miller 1994a). Thomas Eriksen (1990:31–32) argues that these two value orientations encapsulate different moral valences. As in the case of the workers who compete for Signature's "best worker" award and those who pursue instead the material bounty that thiefing provides, people may gravitate to one value orientation or another "based on the rewards a person is seeking" (Browne 2004:96).

The idiom of thiefing a chance relates to the reputation/transient moral framework in which illicit activities and informal labor are prized within a creole cultural schema that celebrates cunning, resourcefulness, and self-reliance. As Katherine Browne (ibid.) reveals in her work on the informal economy in Martinique, the values embodied in practices like thiefing do not just celebrate cleverness and style; they also extol a past and present ability to flourish in a context of economic vulnerability. She calls these practices "creole economics," which refers to the culturally patterned ways illicit earning is practiced and rendered moral in the Caribbean context. The values of bravery, guile, and opportunism that are central to creole economics were born in the slavery experience. Being cunning not only increased a slave's chance of survival but also extended a sense of dignity and self-determination (ibid.:209). Browne shows how these ideas about personal autonomy and the will to survive become encoded in trickster tales and everyday speech, later materializing themselves in the widespread practices of off-the-books earning in contemporary Martinique. Trinidadian garment workers engage these same moral discourses when they describe thiefing a chance as an individual initiative. They present thiefing as the lone exploits of the enterprising few rather than collective theft by many.

Anthropological engagements with workplace pilfering and theft suggest that such activities not only serve workers' short-term material needs but can also be ideologically oppositional acts in a context of workplace hegemony. As Robin Cohen (1980:21) writes, theft can be seen "as a form of labour protest which has the effect of reducing the rate of exploitation of the workers by an informal wage supplement . . . 'theft' becomes an act of recovering some 'surplus value,' which would otherwise be appropriated by the employer." Analyzing shop-floor theft as "a form of labor protest" evokes the material returns of illicit practices and their symbolic significance within the politics of labor. Instead of relegating such actions to the immaturity of an unformed class consciousness, scholars have begun to give theoretical weight to hidden, covert acts that affirm workers' sense of personhood (Ong 1991; Ngai 2005).

Yet in contrast to the examples of "everyday resistance" described by James Scott (1985), whereby Malaysian peasants covertly undermined the material and ideological interests of landowners through gossip, filching, and evasion, workers at Signature Fashions put effort into symbolically and materially *separating* thiefed and non-thiefed clothing. Maintaining a boundary between the two types of clothing is a necessary part of making thiefing a chance morally acceptable. Signature Fashions workers do not fantasize about thiefing as revenge (cf. Scott 1990:28) and rarely portray it as a form of redistributive justice—a way of recuperating the value their skill and diligence have infused into garments priced far beyond what they can afford. Thiefing a chance is consistently described as exploiting an opportunity rather than taking from factory owners. This spirit of entrepreneurialism drains thiefing of any counterhegemonic power.

John W. Roberts's treatment of the New World trickster as black folk hero provides a historical lens onto the moral economy of American slavery, revealing that notions of "taking" were complex and varied in slave communities in the southern United States, particularly with regard to the property of the slave master (Roberts 1978, 1989; cf. Mintz 1976). Frederick Olmstead observed the following on early-nineteenth-century Virginian slave plantations: "Everywhere on the plantations, the agrarian notion has become a fixed point of the negro system of ethics: that the result of labor belongs of right to the laborer, and on this ground, even the religious feel justified in using 'Massa's' property for their own temporal benefit. This they term 'taking,' and is never admitted to be a reproach to a man among them that he is charged with it, though 'stealing,' or taking from another than their master, and particularly from one another, is so" (Olmstead 1856:117, in Levine 1977:124–25). Like Katherine Browne, Roberts and Levine tie their discussions of slave codes to contemporary practices. Each of these scholars points to a reading of ownership that is historically contingent but culturally continuous. I take these accounts not as evidence of an unbroken line between slave codes in nineteenth-century Virginia and the activities of Trinidadians (of both African and Indian descent) in a present-day garment factory. Instead, I read them as a reminder that all practices contain cultural legacies. Thiefing a chance must be analyzed in reference to the highly developed discourse of "taking" that developed in Caribbean societies (Genovese 1976:603), whereby seizing an opportunity is not the same as stealing a thing.

Worker narratives of thiefing contain a deep strain of individualism and resourcefulness. While Deborah Thomas (2004:231) warns against uncritical repetition of "timeworn tropes about black vernacular culture," like the notion of "duplicity," what is interesting is how such negative portrayals of cunning self-reliance have become decisively reworked in the neoliberal era as positive characteristics of the successful economic self. Carla Freeman (2005:3) notes this trend in Barbados, arguing, "The primacy of market rationality and the emphasis on entrepreneurial individualism are now simultaneously hailed by the state as part of a global neoliberal agenda, and re-interpreted as 'native' qualities of the Afro-Barbadian majority, celebrated . . . for their predisposition toward multiplicity and flexibility." This convergence between Caribbean cultural dispositions of flexibility, creativity, and self-reliance and the emerging neoliberal insistence on adaptability, entrepreneurialism, and resourcefulness shows how long-standing cultural forms have been refashioned for new economic imperatives (Freeman 2007; Heron 2011).

Workers do not conceptualize thiefing a chance as oppositional to the aims of factory owners; workers also do not account for thiefing as a means of reappropriating surplus value. Instead, thiefing a chance is seen as a reward for those individuals daring enough to play the "game" of creative production on the shop floor. The explanatory logic of resistance, grounded as it is in oppositional class politics, must be rejected on two grounds: first, because workers themselves insist on a depoliticized interpretation of thiefing and second, because of its ambiguous effects (both symbolic and material) on the labor process. Thiefing is not ideologically driven and can work in the service of capital. Although workers thief a chance to make the most of their situation, in doing so they may contribute to the "flexible" character of the shop floor. By turning to the secondary meaning of "thiefing a chance" (a worker's trying out a machine she has been neither trained on nor authorized to use), we can probe the hidden relationship between these illicit activities and formal production in the factory.

Thiefing Skills

While most Trinidadian garment workers are first taught to sew by female kin or a local seamstress, the skills needed in an industrial factory are different from what one would learn in a home-based trade. Operating a heavy-duty machine and keeping up with fast-paced, piece-rate work cannot be learned until one enters the factory. During an industry boom in the 1970s and early 1980s, new employees might have been trained on the job. Yet given the abundance of skilled stitchers in Trinidad and a shrinking industry, factory bosses—including the owners of Signature Fashions—simply refuse to train workers who cannot do work as assigned (cf. Jayasinghe 2001:74).

The lack of training at Signature Fashions seems curious in a factory that relies on workers' expertise and adaptability to meet the flexible demands of production. Helene worried that if she formally trained workers, they would be "snatched by other factories offering more money." Workers therefore have to seize opportunities to procure skills for themselves. This situation was described with surprising frankness by Bernard, owner of a notorious local sweatshop: "Most of [my employees] would have been people who couldn't really sew, but they would have eased their way into it. Sometimes you would have given them little chores to do around, and they would have wanted to learn to do something. So every time that they had a slight moment, they would jump on a machine and ask somebody how to operate it. Because they would have want to be stitchers. Once they get the first break, they would eventually hurdle that dilemma." This kind of thiefing a chance on the shop floor has long been a means through which factory women self-train; I encountered many personal stories of this type in my interviews with garment workers. As one Signature Fashions worker, Aparna, said of her first job in a garment factory, "I had to lie and say that I could work that [industry-grade] machine." Although her lack of skill was immediately obvious to her supervisors, Aparna was allowed to stay on, learning as she worked. In talking about these acts of duplicity in attaining their first factory job, many workers play with culturally valorized discourses of cunning individualism.

For Aparna, the sweetness in recounting her story derives in part from her boldness in taking a chance.

This narrative exaltation of thiefing as a survival strategy in a tough and unstable industry is best conveyed in a quotation from Antoinette:

ANTOINETTE: I went [to my first factory] as a trimmer, really.

REBECCA: Did you know how to sew on a machine at that point?

ANTOINETTE: No, I did not. I really worked as a trimmer, just like trimming thread and stuff [by hand], and while I was there now, I used to thief chance and go on the machine, the serger, because I was just, this machine fascinated me when I saw it, nah.

REBECCA: So you would ask people, "Can I go on this?"

ANTOINETTE: No, well, I would just like, when the boss was to the front, I would run [*claps hands*] on the machine, and I would try to learn to thread it and, you know, thief me little chances, and people encourage me, you know? But I learned—there you learned to iron, you learned to cover buttons, you learned to tack, but you wasn't allowed to go on the machine. But I thief chance to go on the machine. And then one day he come out and he saw me, and he start to cuss and, oh, you know, start to get on ridiculous, nah? And then, 'bout two or three months after, the person for the machine didn't come to work, and he had a wedding to do. And he didn't have a choice but to put me on that machine! [*Laughs.*] And that's why I will always take chances, and I go, yeah, do me little things, nah?

Antoinette's quotation ends with the statement "And that's why I will always take chances, and I go, yeah, do me little things, nah?" By playfully evoking the various meanings of thiefing a chance, Antoinette morally validates her copying garments at Signature Fashions by drawing attention to her earlier success in learning how to sew through similar acts of personal daring. In an economic sphere where training is not found easily, such skills may be seized by a worker who insists on having them.

Thiefing a chance by slyly trying out a new machine becomes one way for workers to "skill up" for new tasks. By refusing to train, employers have managed to cast skill acquisition as the personal ambition of employees rather than the formal obligation of employers. It is workers, as self-motivated, self-responsible agents, who must procure their own skills to participate in wage employment, even though such skills are a fundamental requirement for the manufacturing process. Factory owners have thus successfully *individualized* skill, recasting it as the business of workers—for their own self-improvement and vocational advantage—thereby externalizing the cost of maintaining their workforce by relegating skill acquisition to the home, the neighborhood, or the interstices of formal production (see chapter 5). Yet in contrast to the hidden, suppressed quality of thiefing factory-made garments, thiefing a chance on a sewing machine is a public, almost scripted act.

Carmela, a back worker at Signature Fashions who does not sew, stood at a high table all day, trimming, pinning pockets, and marking where buttons should go. She had worked at Signature Fashions for more than seven years. One afternoon I was sitting in the back area with Rhonda, putting eyelets on men's shirts using a hand crank. Kimberly had been using the binding machine to stitch binding onto the sleeves of T-shirts all morning. She ran out of binding, so she sat down in front of the binding cutter to prepare more material for herself. While Kimberly was busy with the binding cutter, I watched Carmela cast an eye to the front door (through which Cissy, the production manager, had just exited) and, with a mischievous grin, slip into the seat in front of the binding machine. She turned on the machine and took a little scrap of jersey cloth from the front of her apron. She started running the cloth through the machine, crisscrossing the fabric with the bright blue binding left on the reel. As she was doing this, Audra (another back worker) walked past slowly, eyes on Carmela, and announced to Rhonda, "What Carmela is doing?" Rhonda, not rising to Audra's attempt to "bring confusion," didn't take her eyes off her work.[4] "All Carmela could do is sit down and talk," said Rhonda dismissively.

Audra peeped an eye to the door to make sure Cissy was out of sight and called out loudly, "What? Carmela get a promotion? She machine operator now?" Rhonda and I looked over at Carmela, who was running the binding back and forth across the cloth, doing as much stitching as possible on the small scrap of spare jersey material she had in her hand. As she stitched, Carmela's mouth hung open in a loose smile, as if she were enjoying a good joke. She ran another line of binding across her cloth and cut it with scissors. She looked around the room at all the workers now watching her and called out, "Anyone want anything bind?"

Audra put a hand on her hip and called out, "Watch she doing binding now!"

"Want anything bind?" Carmela asked again, running the same piece of fabric through the binding machine and cutting the end of the binding with a flourish of her scissors. Some of the front workers turned around in their seats, laughed, and shouted joking abuse at Carmela. They soon shook their heads and settled back into their work. Seconds later, all that could be heard was the whirring of the sewing machines and the buzzing of the sergers.

Carmela remained at the chair in front of the binding machine, although once she had filled the scrap of cloth with all the practice binding that would fit on it, she went back to trimming the button-down shirt she had in her hand, remaining seated on the chair. By the time Cissy returned to the floor a couple of minutes later, Kimberly had resumed work on the binding machine, with Carmela standing nearby, trimming the garment in her hand and occasionally looking over at Kimberly's stitching with an expression of interest.

Unlike workers' imperceptible acts of thiefing a chance to produce garments for themselves, thiefing a chance on a machine to learn a new skill is always a public performance. What Carmela's story lacks but would be sure to gain in time is a moment when Cissy catches her on the machine. Like Antoinette's story of being caught thiefing a chance on a serger at her first factory job, such moments were a persistent feature of workers' narratives about gaining sewing skills and increasing the diversity of their assigned tasks in the workplace. Cissy will eventually "catch" a worker who thiefs a chance on a machine; she will scold her with exaggerated fury, waggling a finger in her face and telling her it's "not your machine to work." Cissy would sometimes pinch a worker's bottom as she made her way back to her work station, giggling. Although Cissy's ostensible reaction is anger and reprimand, a worker who has been caught thiefing a chance on a machine may indeed be called upon at a later time to operate it in earnest, if so required by the pressing demands of production.

What Carmela's story illustrates is the public function of thiefing a chance. By operating a machine one has never used before, a worker subtly presents herself as a potential learner. By thiefing a chance with humor and style, the worker can gain skills on a machine without courting derision from her co-workers for trying to "get above" or "advantage" (meaning disadvantage) them. Thiefing, then, acts simultaneously as a social leveler and a status-raiser. By good-naturedly putting herself in line for new responsibilities, a worker avoids the risk of losing face that would accompany an outright request to work the machine.

I knew that Carmela was eager to learn to sew on a machine. During an interview with her, when I asked what Signature Fashions could change to make her a happier worker, she said, "They could give us the chance to try on those machines." Carmela was a single mother struggling to raise her teenage daughter alone. Her daughter excelled at school, earning a funded place at one of the top secondary schools in Trinidad. Carmela described sitting at home in the evenings with her daughter while "she studying her books . . . and I read the newspaper." Learning to work on a machine and progress to the front section of the factory was something Carmela could not readily articulate, given her intense solidarity with the back workers over what they saw as the front workers' exclusivity and snobbery. Nonetheless, for Carmela, learning to sew on a machine would be a way of "getting on" and improving her situation, much the same way her daughter was getting on through her educational achievements.

The public drama of thiefing a chance, as well as its prevalence, makes it clear that thiefing cannot be regarded as marginal or arbitrary; instead, it requires an analysis that places it squarely within the relations in production. Although elements of thiefing may seem to constitute resistance by workers to an exploitative labor process, workers disallow this interpretation by refusing to cast thiefing as taking from their bosses. In fact, thiefing can be a means through which workers accommodate managerial demands to "flexibly" respond to the conditions they find themselves in, making the practice more amenable to their employers' interests than they realize.

Conclusions

Reflections on my participation in thiefing a chance have troubled me since leaving the field. My initial justification for accepting thiefed clothing—that as a participant observer I had license to participate in everything—seems duly problematic. I mostly wonder, in retrospect, whether workers would have gotten in trouble if they had been discovered thiefing a chance for me. The example of Lata getting caught with a thiefed shirt gives me hope that there would have been no penalty. Yet my plan to take all the blame should someone be caught thiefing a chance for me (even if it meant losing my access to the factory) seems hollow in retrospect. My access to the factory was far less important to me than the workers' access to the factory was to them. It was my field site; it was their workplace. But certainly, for a time, I was caught up in the workers' thrilling assertion that Signature Fashions was "we own factory." Participating in the rhythms of the workplace and being part of its social world, I was taken with the idea that it *was* the workers who, ultimately, "owned" the shop floor; without them, the factory was inconceivable. This view is problematic but not uncommon. As Michael Burawoy (1985) suggested, such a belief is part of the trick of management on workers: convincing them, for the most part, that the interests of the property owners are the interests of everyone, meaning that the factory (source of both profit and livelihood) "belongs" to capitalist and worker alike. Burawoy notes that this trick was what Antonio Gramsci described as hegemony: "the presentation of the interests of the dominant classes as the interests of all" (ibid.:10). Like the workers, I believed that accepting the four shirts they made for me did not constitute a financial hardship for the factory owners. However, my accepting them did represent a disloyalty to the owners, who so kindly allowed me to conduct fieldwork in their factory.

Thiefing a chance is a structuring feature of shop-floor life at Signature Fashions. Not only does it draw on, and contribute to, the "flexible" orientation of the factory—by encouraging workers to skill up for new tasks and reinforcing networks of mutual aid—it is also a day-to-day practice that contributes to workers' interpretation of factory work. The effects of these illicit practices are diverse and unpredictable, and they do not necessarily imply ideological or material opposition to the aims of factory owners. In pursuing their own projects of production and self-making, workers consistently conform to managerial demands that they respond "flexibly" to changing work conditions. In so doing, they come to embody new subjectivities associated with the neoliberal insistence on self-reliance, resourcefulness, and opportunism (Freeman 2005; Ferguson 2009), which are deeply inflected by West Indian cultural mores that celebrate cunning, creativity, and nerve (Browne 2004; Heron 2011). With their celebratory accounts of thiefing, workers valorize a particular representation of themselves as agents, maneuvering within the complex and trying conditions of garment work.

Embedded within a discourse of triumphant individualism ("we own factory"), workers depict thiefing as a daring attempt to make the most of the structural conditions in which they find themselves. Yet we must not confuse intentions and effects. As Geert De Neve (1999) has argued, within complex, locally situated relations in production, effects often diverge from what actors intend. Writing about power-loom workers in the South Indian textile industry, De Neve argues that employers' practice of giving workers cash advances (*baki*) has served its intended purpose of tying workers to their employers in relationships of patronage. It has also helped workers achieve a degree of job stability, since employers will not dismiss indolent or difficult employees who owe them large sums of money. Yet by establishing dyadic employer-worker relationships, baki has also created an individuated subjectivity among workers, steering them away from collective action and toward "more individualized strategies of negotiation, resistance or withdrawal" in the face of labor grievances (De Neve 2005:312). De Neve argues, then, that one of baki's profound effects is to have "successfully fragmented the labour force, thus preventing the rise of union activity" (ibid.:312).[5]

Recognizing the wide-ranging and unpredictable effects of baki pushes us to consider thiefing a chance more critically, particularly in relation to the issues of worker consciousness and organization. What insidious consequences lurk behind workers' celebratory narratives of thiefing? Can discourses that valorize cunning self-reliance ever accommodate collective solidarity? In chapter 6, I return to the question of thiefing a chance as it relates to individualistic forms of worker subjectivity. By examining the conditions under which workers become vulnerable to workplace injury, I consider the implications of the triumphalism contained within workers' celebratory narratives of thiefing a chance. What does the convergence of a neoliberal discourse emphasizing self-reliance and the individualizing subjectivity derived from thiefing a chance mean, ultimately, to workers' interests?

Although I have depicted thiefing a chance as a set of practices, it is also the spirit of entrepreneurialism, which pervades garment workers' livelihoods. In chapter 5 I look at how the process of achieving skills is a lifelong struggle through which workers link formal and informal sectors of the garment industry through their working bodies. Workers pursue skills not simply out of a means-ends rational calculation but because they love sewing and take pleasure in learning. To understand the effects of thiefing, we must consider not simply what workers *do* when they thief a chance but also what thiefing a chance *does* to them.

Notes

1. Donna's husband's employment in the construction sector meant that her household income was greater than that of most other Signature Fashions workers.

2. The swiftness of Annie's dismissal was partly a result of the fact that she was still within the six-month probationary period, during which time employers have more latitude to dismiss workers and fewer legal obligations in terms of severance pay (Yelvington 1995:113; ILO 2004).

3. Gayelle Television, a locally owned TV channel promoting Trinidadian arts, culture, and political debate, was launched in February 2004 under the slogan "At last, we own television" (Baldeosingh 2004).

4. "Bringing confusion," also called *commess*, means to stir up trouble and incite gossip (Mendes 1986:36).

5. Michel Anteby's (2008) analysis of side production in a French aeronautics plant comes to similar conclusions. He argues that by allowing skilled craftsmen to make small items for themselves with factory materials and tools, management diffused the craftmen's righteous anger over the devaluation and deskilling of their work and provided space in which they could practice skills and enact valued identities, which may have helped avoid direct labor confrontations (ibid.:131).

5

"Keeping Up with Style"

The Struggle for Skill

> The whole metaphor so central to modernism of the radical break seems inapposite here: be it the radical break of the migrant from rural community to urban anomie; or of the artisanal master to the routinized and de-skilled factory worker. These kinds of sweeping away of the past are by no means an imagery familiar to the pluriactive household. A more familiar image would be one of the continuity of flexibility, adaptability and transformations, alike in skills, tools and the package of household livelihoods.
> – Gavin Smith, *Confronting the Present*

Early one morning, while Antoinette was serging the sleeves onto a set of blouses, she said to me, "I go thief a pattern for this shirt." She pointed to the sample blouse hanging from a plastic coat hanger above Cissy's desk. Across the stitching section, bundles of indigo linen were piled high on the stitchers' horses, and workers throughout the area were diligently stitching the fabric into blouses. Antoinette said, "I thiefing my little t'ing."

"How?" I asked, and she pointed to a small stack of newspapers she had laid on her horse. She told me she would take each constituent piece of the blouse and create a pattern from the pieces by tracing their shapes onto newspaper. As she said this, her eyes followed Cissy's movements around the room and her hands smoothed a piece of newspaper on her lap. She placed an unstitched sleeve on the paper, sliding a couple of pins through the cloth to hold her "pattern" in place. Using a pen, Antoinette traced the sleeve's outline. When Cissy came near, Antoinette scrunched up the newspaper and wedged it onto the little shelf under her machine.

Antoinette told me quietly, "You could lose your work over it," using the common phrase workers used to refer to getting fired.

I whispered, "Are you hiding from Cissy or Brenda?"

"Cissy," Antoinette said. "Brenda would allow it. She could make little things at home [too], y'understand?" As Antoinette continued tracing, I watched Cissy's movements: standing at the front of the stitching section, entering the cutting room, then out of the cutting room to the back stairs. It occurred to me that this simple act of watching was something that only I could do without being scolded. Had Cissy noticed any other worker tracking her movements, she would have snapped at her to get back to work. Antoinette had wisely enlisted me as her lookout.

After copying the back piece, Antoinette said, "Now I need the yoke." She called out quietly to stitchers nearby, asking what parts of the garment were contained in their bundles. The other workers surreptitiously handed them over. She scribbled in pen on a corner of newspaper, "Serge back and top stitch center seam." She called out to Shirley, "What size you on?" When Shirley mumbled that the blouses she was stitching were large, Antoinette said, "I looking for medium." Over the course of the morning, Antoinette was able to copy each element of the blouse onto the newspaper, which she folded and stuffed into her apron front when she was finished. Antoinette said with a smile, "Have to keep up with style if you sew for people."

This chapter examines the relationship among skill acquisition, informal labor, and the constitution of economic selfhood by Signature Fashions workers. Workers like Antoinette who are "into the sewing" combine factory employment with cash-in-hand projects for private clients. That afternoon at lunch, Antoinette told me she was making five white shirts for a client in her neighborhood, each in a different design. The woman had recently taken a job in a Port of Spain hotel and needed clothing to wear, "all white shirts, but she still want *style*." Antoinette said she would be paid TT$200 (US$33) for the five shirts, a sum representing more than half a week's factory wages. More important, if the woman was happy with Antoinette's work, she might commission more clothing and encourage others to visit her. The client herself had been referred to Antoinette by a mutual friend.

In chapter 4 I argued that workers conceptualize the factory not only as a place of wage employment but also as a resource for acquiring designer clothing and access to new skills. But the knowledge workers retrieve from the factory is not limited to practical expertise; equally important to the independent seamstress is knowledge of the latest fashions. Antoinette said, "If you sew for people, it hard to have a new style. You [usually] just do it your way, so it's nice to have another pattern to use." Access to creative inspiration and fashionable designs holds economic importance for the independent seamstress. The democratic availability of this knowledge is in part what allows such practices to flourish; as Antoinette noted of her stitching supervisor, "Brenda could make little things at home [too]."

Antoinette's copying of a pattern in the factory to implement at home illustrates one way Signature workers' own-account sewing for private clients is tied to the formal garment sector. Trinidadians often use factory employment to create small-scale business opportunities for themselves, like cooking food at home to sell in the workplace, sewing for co-workers, or doing auto repairs for each other outside of work hours (Yelvington 1995:214–20). At Signature Fashions, this kind of petty entrepreneurialism is commonplace: Tina sells bags of peanuts to her co-workers for TT$1 each, while Shayna buys salt prunes and pepper cherries in bulk and sells them on the shop floor in small plastic bags. Veronica sells herbal remedies she obtains from a neighbor, and Kellisha cooks sweet *pons* to sell to other workers.

Yet Antoinette's act of "thiefing" a pattern demonstrates that the factory may be used by workers not only as a site for selling small items to each other but also as a source of knowledge and expertise that can be directly imputed into home-sewing enterprises, linking formal and informal sectors of the garment industry. With the post–oil-boom recession in the 1980s and the structural adjustment and trade liberalization that followed, Trinidadian women who are devoted to making a living through sewing have faced a formal sector of shrinking job opportunities and declining working conditions. To make ends meet, they increasingly rely on off-the-books enterprises, such as stitching school uniforms in August for cash-in-hand payment, sewing Carnival costumes on a part-time basis, or working days in the factory while dressmaking for private clients at home in the evenings. These jobs supply diverse sources of income while blurring the distinction between formal and informal industrial sectors; multiple types of work—some regulated, some unregulated, some taxed, some untaxed—take place in and around the same physical sites of production (cf. Bolt 2012; De Neve 2005; Mollona 2005).

By exploring how women "into the sewing" struggle for skill, this chapter examines workers' internalized sense of economic selfhood and the nature of the garment industry in which they operate. A growing body of literature on neoliberal subjectivities suggests that self-training and self-management have become imperative in a post-Fordist era of flexible production (Bourdieu 1998; Freeman 2007; Martin 1994; Molé 2010; Urciuoli 2008). Facing economic instability and precarious employment, workers must adapt to new conditions on the ground by continually seeking out opportunities to retrain. For Trinidadian garment workers, self-skilling articulates almost seamlessly with the widespread practice of pursuing multiple livelihoods, bridging a formal economy defined as wage employment and an informal economy composed of off the books, own-account work. I argue in this chapter that as garment workers struggle for skill, they inculcate themselves with a self-reliance that helps them survive the unpredictable and unforgiving environment of the contemporary garment sector. However, because the motivation to learn how to sew is driven not by bare economic calculation but instead through registers of yearning and desire, garment workers expose themselves to an intimate form of exploitation whereby their love of sewing justifies degraded work conditions and lack of formal training opportunities.

Garment Work in Trinidad: Antecedents and Opportunities

As Joycelyn Massiah (1986:177) famously asserted, "Women in the Caribbean have always worked" (cf. Bolles 1996:12). Since the earliest days of plantation slavery, through the era of indentured labor, and during early and late industrialization, women have played an active and visible role in Trinidad's workforce (Reddock 1994). However, we must be tuned to the fact that while the existence of Trinidadian women's public labor is long-standing, its meaning, location, and type have been subject to redefinition throughout history, shaped by competing gender ideologies, women's changing economic strategies, and their access to opportunities in the formal and informal sectors—each embedded within the wider context of Trinidad's relationship to the world system. Caribbean women have "always worked," often shouldering the "double shift" of domesticity and wage labor, the "triple shift" of informal labor (Freeman 1997), and even a "fourth shift" cultivating social networks of support (Yelvington 1989, 1991).

The importance of seamstressing as women's work dates back at least to the plantation era, when throughout the Caribbean domestic slaves sewed for the planter's family and other slaves (Buckridge 2004:46; Higman 1984:172–73). As Hilary Beckles (1999:140) argues, seamstressing afforded some enslaved women an opportunity to "make economic decisions as 'free' persons" by cultivating their own clients among both slave and non-slave populations, even when the practice was discouraged and outlawed by white power holders. After the full abolition of slavery in the British Caribbean in 1838, dressmaking facilitated the self-transformation of many formerly enslaved women into independent petty producers (Buckridge 2004:41; Osirim 1997:48–49). Seamstresses—much like the female "hucksters" who traded in the vegetable market—left the plantations and populated the bourgeoning Caribbean cities in astonishing numbers. By the late nineteenth century, Trinidadian women outnumbered men in Port of Spain by a ratio of 100 to 74, with seamstressing second only to domestic service in occupying urban women (Reddock 1993:249). Independent seamstresses usually worked from their homes, visiting clients to take measurements and conduct fittings; the value of their skills conferred respectability on their work despite its "outside" nature, and many Afro-Trinidadian seamstresses came to occupy the lower middle classes. Yet the informal economy of dressmaking, like that of huckstering, domestic service, and prostitution, was notoriously volatile; women working in those sectors would have been particularly susceptible to economic hardship.

By the beginning of the twentieth century, Trinidad was largely a "four-tiered," ethnically stratified society (Brereton 1993). White elites, descended from colonial officials and French and English planters, occupied the top of the socioeconomic hierarchy. A middle strata contained various racial/ethnic groups, marked by a shared marginality vis-à-vis the white elites: mixed-race, "coloured" middle classes; Venezuelan migrants and laborers; and Chinese, Portuguese, Jewish, and Syrian-Lebanese merchants and traders. The majority population of Afro-Caribbean ex-slaves and their descendants comprised the second-lowest strata of the hierarchy, with rural "East Indians" relegated to the bottom (ibid.; Crowley 1957).

The middle strata of marginal whites was heavily involved in the early garment trade, originally as middlemen selling imported fabric (Buckridge 2004:130). Although Afro-Caribbean hucksters ruled the clothing trade immediately after Emancipation, they were soon surpassed by Syrian-Lebanese Christians and European Jews, who had begun migrating to Trinidad in the late nineteenth century (Anthony 1997:344, 556). These traders established themselves first as rural cloth peddlers and later set up their own stores and garment manufacturing operations. During the first three decades of the twentieth century, small-scale, independent production by seamstresses and tailors increasingly gave way to mechanization and mass production in newly developed factories (Reddock 1993). By the mid-twentieth century, Indo-Trinidadian entrepreneurs began establishing themselves as retailers and manufacturers in the rapidly developing garment sector (Osirim 1997:64; Henry 1993:71).[1]

Sewing has two main components: drafting patterns and cutting them into cloth (both glossed as "cutting") and assembling the pieces together ("stitching"). Industrial manufacturing separates and routinizes cutting and stitching as specialist domains of activity, creating an occupational niche for "stitchers" who can operate a sewing machine but do not perceive themselves as being able to sew. As one stitcher, Veronica, said to me, "I don't even say that I know how to *sew* because I couldn't really *cut* [patterns]." The industrialization of Trinidad's garment trade began in the 1920s with a system of "putting out." Merchants distributed pre-cut fabric to stitchers, who completed the garments at home for piece-rate payment (Reddock 1984:11). This putting-out system recruited the labor not only of Afro-Trinidadian stitchers but also of Indo-Trinidadian women who until recent decades faced higher social restrictions on working outside the home (Miller 1994a:222).

By the 1960s, Trinidad's garment industry was primarily based in vertically integrated firms where cutting and stitching were performed on-site. With national independence in 1962, the government instituted policies of import substitution, such as tariff restrictions on foreign goods, alongside initiatives to promote export-led growth by stimulating investment (Osirim 1997:50; Yelvington 1995:58).[2] Beginning in 1966, consumer goods that could be manufactured locally were placed on a "negative list," restricting the importation of readymade garments into Trinidad and Tobago (Greaves 1974:8, 12). The 1970s and 1980s saw the rise in garment production for the regional market of

Caribbean Community (CARICOM) countries, in which Trinidad was a leading industrial player (Anthony 1997:366). Ronald Reagan's Caribbean Bain Initiative (1982) and 807 Provision (1987) guaranteed duty-free access to the US market for garments assembled in the Caribbean from fabric produced and cut in the United States. These policies spurred export-oriented production in Trinidad, though on a more modest scale than in nearby Jamaica, even after the creation of export-processing zones in 1988 (Dypski 2002; Griffith 1990; Ramprasad 1997; Reddock 1998).

Gavin Smith (1999) reminds us that local landscapes of garment production the world over are often remarkably heterogeneous as a result of the low barriers to entry of new producers and firms and the recent proliferation of horizontal subcontracting networks under global post-Fordism. In Trinidad, although mass production grew during the twentieth century, small-scale producers have endured, including within their ranks independent seamstresses and tailors working from their own homes and shops. With the collapse of the formal garment industry after the 1980s recession, trade liberalization in the 1990s, and the loss of preferential access to US markets with the end of the Multi-Fibre Agreement quota system, this informal sector continues to provide livelihoods for women and men "into the sewing" against the otherwise devastating currents of globalization. National development initiatives now attempt to harness the economic power of the informal sector by providing administrative and monetary assistance to seamstresses and tailors as part of an agenda to reduce poverty through micro-enterprise (ILO 1997; Karides 2010).

Home-based seamstresses are paid in cash. Clients include trusted friends and extended family members, as well as a broader network of associates and friends of friends. Because work at Signature Fashions is steady and pays at least the minimum wage, employees who are "into the sewing" tend to think of factory work as their primary occupation, with sewing for clients at home as an irregular, seasonal activity. In contrast, workers at Universal Uniforms—a factory that is open only when its owners have a contract to fill—are more likely to consider sewing at home their primary occupation and factory work a source of intermittent income. More than half of the Signature Fashions workers earn extra income by stitching clothing for friends, family, and neighbors at home, though the frequency with which they do so varies. Many more Signature workers say they worked as independent seamstresses in the past but have given up the practice for a variety of reasons, including not wanting the hassle, preferring to relax at home after work, and having fights break out with unhappy clients.

By maintaining factory jobs while also pursuing independent money-making activities, Signature Fashions workers are similar to women and men throughout the Caribbean who manage multiple income-generating pursuits at once (cf. Barrow 1986; Bolles 1996; Harrison 1998; Senior 1991). This practice of "occupational multiplicity" was defined by Lambros Comitas (1973 [1964]:157) as a livelihood strategy whereby a person is "systematically engaged in a number of gainful activities, which for him form an integrated economic complex." Observers of the region have described occupational multiplicity as an adaptive response to economic vulnerability that "often served as a type of insurance for community members, a buffer should there be a downturn in any one of their occupational sectors" (Thomas 2004:223).[3] For Trinidadian factory workers, Kevin Yelvington tells us that the imperative to cultivate livelihoods in the informal sector reflects the inadequacy of wages and therefore operates as a subsidy to businesses because workers shoulder the cost of the reproduction of the labor force (Yelvington 1995:215; cf. Portes and Walton 1981). Yet at the same time, as Katherine Browne (2004) has shown for Martinique, engaging in economic activities that are off the books and outside state regulation can be driven by complex motivations, including the desire for freedom and autonomy, as well as the enjoyment of own-account work that Trinidadian women "into the sewing" so often describe.

The Struggle for Skill

In the Anglophone Caribbean, for much of the twentieth century, learning how to sew was considered not only a life skill but also leverage for a young woman's claim on respectability because of its association with domestic competence. For many working- and middle-class girls, at least during the 1960s and 1970s, learning how to sew was fundamental to achieving a gendered respectability, like knowing how to clean one's home properly or cook a meal. Jamaica Kincaid's celebrated poem, "Girl," makes this association explicit: "this is how to sew on a button/this is how to make a buttonhole for the button you have just sewed on/this is how to hem a dress when you see the hem coming down and prevent yourself from looking like the slut you are so bent on becoming" (Kincaid 1983:3). Although these values appear to defer to European standards of social hierarchy, Daniel Miller's reappraisal of the Trinidadian domestic sphere reminds us that women's household labors advanced values of dignity, stability, and self-determination that have been vital to the anti-colonial struggle (Miller 1994b; cf. Besson 1993).

Basic skills in sewing—such as darning holes and hemming trousers with a needle and thread—afford a sense of self-sufficiency for both men and women; for this reason, sewing remains to this day part of the national primary school curriculum. Such capacities are regarded simply as being able to "do something for yourself," which can help an individual "make do" in difficult economic times (Senior 1991:129–33). As Glenda, a Signature Fashions worker, said to me: "[Sewing] is a way of independence. It's a way of not having to pay that extra money to have someone to sew for you. You could make your own clothes, you could sew your curtains and things like that. You could sew a hole in some clothing and not rely on somebody else for it."

Trinidadian women who make careers in the garment sector usually describe an early exposure to seamstressing by a mother, aunt, or sister or being sent "by a lady who sews" (to a lady who sews) in the neighborhood to learn how to cut and stitch garments to size (Reddock 1984). Although secondary schools have offered vocational training since the 1970s, garment workers rarely describe formal education as the source of their sewing skills because garment production has been taught as a general rather than a specialist subject, equipping students with broad knowledge but few practical competencies (Campbell 1997). Sending a daughter "by a lady who sews" or enrolling her in a dressmaking course is a way of equipping her with specialized training. As Dolores, a stitcher at Signature Fashions, said of her daughter: "School wasn't there for her. Like, to pick up. And she wasn't wanting to do that. So we sent her to learn how to sew."

When a child is "sent by a lady who sews," skills are sought in both cutting and stitching. Young women who demonstrated flair for designing and drafting patterns might be able to establish their own small businesses, sewing clothes, pillow covers, and drapes for individual clients in a rented commercial space or at home. Those who learned how to sew proficiently on a machine but did not excel at cutting might find employment as a factory stitcher. Yet the categories "independent seamstress" and "factory worker" are neither mutually exclusive nor absolute. Seamstresses who sew for private clients may occasionally seek employment in a factory when work is slow or simply for the adventure of coming out into the workforce. Equally, factory workers may sew at home for the love of sewing or to make ends meet.

As my sewing instructor, Donny, often said, "To really be able to cut . . . means turning a flat piece of fabric to clothe a complex figure like the human body." Drafting a pattern requires the use of an "inch tape" to "size" a person and translating those measurements onto cloth with chalk. In addition to inch tape and chalk, wooden rulers in a variety of sizes and shapes are used to plot patterns (figure 5.1). Once some basic skills in cutting have been learned, a seamstress can endlessly adapt even a relatively simple construction like a skirt into a range of different stylistic effects: pleating, flaring, flouncing, creating a "fish tail," or adding pockets, belt loops, and embroidery. My observations of sewing teachers and interviews with both teachers and learners reveal an emphasis on non-linguistic, practice-oriented instruction, with the teacher demonstrating tasks the learner is required to perform as the teacher watches. Although the learner must rehearse her teacher's way of cutting, teachers recognize that each learner will come to "have her own style" and that she must "take her time" to discover and develop her "own way." Unlike cutting, which is usually learned from an instructor, learning how to stitch on a machine requires minimal instruction and a great deal of practice. Now that pedal machines have been almost entirely replaced by electric models in both factories and homes, stitching is seen as highly skilled only when the stitcher has attained a measure of fluency and speed with a range of different procedures.

Alongside training with a neighborhood seamstress or taking a dressmaking course, a commonplace means of acquiring sewing skills is by "thiefing" them: carefully and cunningly watching a seamstress at work and later attempting the techniques oneself. Crystal, a forty-one-year-old independent seamstress in Port of Spain, described learning to sew as a child when her older sister was taking lessons. Crystal's mother's boyfriend paid for classes for her sister, but Crystal was deemed too young to attend. So she would hang around the front room of their home and watch her sister sew:

> No one ever showed me *nothing*. I watch everything my sister did do, and them didn't know it! Like this: while she sewing, I watch how she thread the

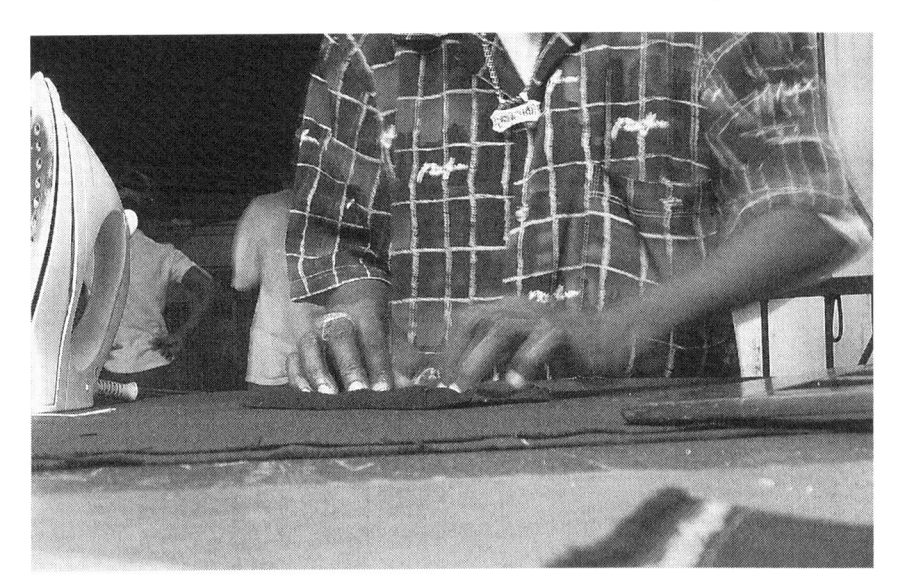

FIGURE 5.1. A tailor plots a pattern onto cloth (photo by author)

machine, I watch how she put the shuttle in. I'm watching all of this and she doesn't know that I'm watching her . . . Now, I didn't know how to cut or how to sew. So I wait 'til my sister gone. And hear this, as the end of she foot leave the house—I watching she—as the *end* of the foot leave the house and I can't see her no more, I dive on that machine!

Anthropologists have long recognized that positioning oneself (both physically and socially) in the most advantageous position to "steal" the master's skills can be an important, if unspoken, dimension of apprenticeship (Marchand 2008:252). Writing about Italian seamstresses between the two world wars, Vanessa Maher (1987:143) explains that "stealing with the eye" was imperative for novices because the apprenticeship system was structured to prevent them from "acquiring the whole trade." When expert knowledge is jealously guarded, the "crafty" apprentice must feign indifference while surreptitiously absorbing the master's know-how (Herzfeld 2004). In an environment of scarcity, where families may invest in private training for some but not all of their children, Crystal's story captures the imperative to live in the wake of another person's opportunity by "thiefing" skills not openly offered.

Alongside these neighborhood-based thiefing practices is a long tradition of thiefing skills from the factory. A Signature Fashions stitcher named Shirley recalled her first factory job: "I is a friendly person, so, you know, I talk to everybody, and everybody say 'alright.' So I say 'let me try out that machine,' and they say 'come, nah, come, come.' And then, you know, from there you learn and [my supervisor] catch me one day, 'Oh yeah yuh buggah, you want to sew? Now I put yuh on machine.' So it's these kind of t'ing that happen."

Like Crystal's description of learning to sew by secretly watching her sister at home, Shirley revels in her act of duplicity for the audacious, resilient self at its center. Given that the incident Shirley describes occurred in the early 1980s (when the industry's expansion meant that formal training in factories was still widespread), her account shows how thiefing a chance on the shop floor is an enduring rather than a new phenomenon. The experience of neoliberal globalization in Trinidad has not radically transformed local work processes, ideologies, and cultural values but rather has built on and extended the capitalist foundations already in place (Robotham 1998:308).

Working in a garment factory is perceived by many women "into the sewing" as having infused a measure of speed and professionalism into their independent vocations. Factories are considered places of discipline where one learns to do complicated tasks with extreme efficiency. Repetitive factory work helps workers accumulate "knowledge in the hands" (Merleau-Ponty 1962:144), which they describe as "setting your hand" to a task that will subsequently "come like second nature." Signature Fashions workers described learning a number of technical "tricks" at work, such as how to do a zipper fly with one, rather than two, pieces of cloth (which is quicker than the way seamstresses teach it, though clients cannot tell the difference) (see figure 5.2) or how to stitch a collar with a pointed (rather than rounded) peak. While the Signature Fashions factory—with its multi-skilled workforce, constantly changing products, and implicit inducement to "skill up"—offers exposure to many technical skills, garment workers equally describe mass-production factories as imparting know-how of this kind.

Gaining skills through factory work defies widespread perceptions of industrial factories as sites of deskilling. Authors such as Harry Braverman (1974:170–71) observe that the fragmentation of the labor process means that factory workers under a Fordist regime learn a limited repertoire of skills, which cannot be transferred in any meaningful way to livelihoods outside

FIGURE 5.2. A garment worker stitching up trouser flies (photo by author)

of capitalist wage labor. Yet this depiction of inevitable deskilling fails to account for how women "into the sewing" interpret their own expertise and neglects how skills may be accumulated over the lifespan. In the following passage, Josephine, a "back worker" at Signature Fashions, recounts the trajectory of her career in the garment industry.[4] Her biography shows the inseparability of skill acquisition from work practices and how both are greeted with alacrity by the enterprising seamstress. My aim is to draw attention to the agency and intentionality of workers "into the sewing" as they acquire skills while also revealing the emotions of pleasure, excitement, and satisfaction that animate these endeavors. Learning to sew is simultaneously an education in being a flexible economic actor in a context where such skills are not only necessary but culturally valued.

When I first met Josephine, she was thirty-six years old and had been working in the garment industry for twenty years. She lived in Laventille with two of her eight brothers, a sister-in-law, and their children in the small wooden house in which she had grown up. Josephine was raising her eight-year-old daughter, Gabby, with neither the financial nor emotional support of Gabby's father, who had returned home to Jamaica around the time of her birth. As the following passage shows, Josephine interprets skill as a field of struggle and a source of everyday pleasure. As she describes a career pursued in garment factories, on the street, and at home, Josephine demonstrates her creative capacity to "improvise a livelihood" (Gregory 2007:30) by undertaking both wage employment and own-account work while also gaining precious know-how from each of these domains:

> When I left school, I was thirteen years old, I went by a neighbor and take some sewing [lessons]. That only last for about six months. I [also] did a sewing course for two years. I did bridal, bath suits, and panties. My mom was really a cook, she didn't like much sewing. She loved to cook. That was nice for her, but I like to sew because I like to wear clothes, *nice* clothes. I started sewing for myself first, then, after the information reach out that Josephine does sew, people come. Friends and family come, and they still coming!
>
> I did pressing in my first factory. I was sixteen years old, I was home at the time, sewing for people. And I wanted to explore, so I start to look for work. I get through with a pressing job in San Juan, at Top Style Manufacturing. I start off there as an ironer, and I last for six months. And they put me to use the machines. They start me off gradually, using different machines in the factory. They trained me in the buttonhole, the button tack, and the straight stitch, putting a collar, a pocket, or a hem.
>
> They come to receivership and close down for good. I was unemployed for a while, being home, doing my own thing. After that I went to Tru-Fit Garments, in San Juan again. I spent about four months, working straight stitch, and after that I went to House of Menswear, in San Juan again. At House of Menswear, now, I went in as a serger. I serge for a while, and then I went on the buttonhole. I used to do buttonhole and straight stitch. I used to do the buttonhole on the collar. The peak of the collar, like how it has a button-down? I used to do that. But there, they don't always have work for the year. You work a six months and work slow down, so they send you home and tell you they'll call you back when they need you, so that's when I stop working there, and I end up at this Signature Fashions.
>
> [Right now] I'm still training for anything! Anything and everything. I train to cook, I train to tie-dye. I take [cake] icing courses. I train. That's what always make me want to sign up [for free government courses] and train and

hang my certificate up. People could come by me, so I could get money. I love that. One of my plans for the future: I get a serger now [sent from a brother in New York], and I want to get some cloth, and I want to come out into the streets and sell to everybody. On the street, on the weekends. I have plans.

[Having] my daughter make that more [important] because, you know, the father don't support her like he should. So I have to make the move, do things, do things to help her. I enjoy what I'm doing because I could have *real* money. Because if you could make a garment, you could make that and charge people a price. Some people would pay and some people wouldn't *like* to pay, but sometimes it's a hundred dollars, I could get a hundred dollars in my hand. I tell them it's $150 or $200. Some give me piece-piece, and some give me the money [all at once]. My friends and all come, and I make them something. I still take chances with them, and I love it. [I make the most money] at Christmas and Easter and Carnival time. And school clothes.

Well, at Signature Fashions I work as a machine operator, sewing as I said, but they say I too slow or I'm not neat, so they put me in the back to make buttonholes. And that's when I start off making buttonholes. I pin pockets, I trim, I tack buttons, I mark, I hem . . . This year make it ten years [at] Signature Fashions . . . I like my salary. Piece rate is too killing.

Josephine's narrative reveals the instability of employment in the local garment industry. Her account is peppered with factory closures and layoffs: "they come to receivership," "close down for good," "you work a six months," "they'll call you back when they need you." She chooses not to linger on moments of hardship but instead represents them as the structural conditions she must navigate to "make the move, do things" and "have real money."

One of the most important contributions of feminist scholarship to debates on skill is the recognition that women's labor becomes cheapened in the marketplace by "naturalizing" it (Chapkis and Enloe 1983; Elson 1983). Sewing is under-compensated either as an intrinsically feminine ability or as a capacity learned at home rather than in the public sphere of capitalist production (Harrington 2000:10; Collins 2003:173). As Melissa Wright (2001:370) has observed in Mexican *maquiladoras*, employers may even nurture a discourse of female workers' lack of skill because perceiving the worker as herself skilled would "undermine a system that depends upon acceptance of her cheapness and her expendability." Josephine's biography shows the undervaluation of sewing skills to be less a product of where these skills are acquired than of the extent to which the training process is visible and publicly validated. In pursuing skills over the course of her work biography, sometimes in the interstices of formal employment, the role of Josephine's labor in self-training is rendered invisible as just another form of thiefing a chance.

Josephine accords little significance to distinctions between formal and informal modes of learning, just as her career trajectory has intermittently embraced both "formal" and "informal" sources of income, ranging from a taxed hourly wage to off-the-books cash payment. Trinidadian women "into the sewing" maintain a living by cobbling together multiple opportunities; where formal-sector employment offers few compensations (such as benefits, insurance, or even a steady income), there is little incentive to classify wage employment as distinct from informal or even illicit work. Keith Hart (1973, 2010) lends support to this view in suggesting that the very notion of an "informal" economy relies in the first instance on a reliable formal economy, without which the distinction breaks down.

Josephine entered the industry in the early 1980s, when the expansion of the garment sector and nationwide labor shortages compelled factory managers to train workers on the shop floor, which contrasts with the rising importance of thiefing a chance to acquire skills in the factory today. Josephine depicts "skill" not merely as a technical set of capacities but as a cumulative project located in her own body. The factory, a sewing school, home: all are potential arenas for encountering and attaining new expertise. Even a repetitive activity like stitching pockets or buttonholes becomes a well-practiced competency. Josephine proudly lists her former factory tasks—"I used to do the buttonhole on the collar"—as evidence of the knowledge she has, quite literally, at her fingertips. In careers that span several decades, women like Josephine attempt to wrest valuable skills even from the most basic, repetitive jobs. Knowledge acquired in the factory can later be transacted for "real money" from private clients.

Accumulating know-how makes sound economic sense in a competitive environment, but Trinidadian garment workers do not simply pursue new skills out of rational calculation. Josephine's narrative reveals her desire to do work that allowed her to "explore" the outside world and her delight in work and learning: "I like to sew," "I'm still training for anything," "I enjoy what

I'm doing," "I still take chances with them, and I love it." Josephine presents skill as an embodied project of self-making through the acquisition and performance of expertise. The narratives of garment workers who are "into the sewing" emphasize the importance of curiosity and desire animating these endeavors. When Antoinette described to me how she illicitly taught herself to operate a serger at her first factory job, she said, "I used to thief chance and go on the machine, the serger, because I was just, this machine fascinated me when I saw it, nah." Her propulsion toward that machine was not generated by a calculated career strategy but instead through the medium of the sensuous, desiring body.

We know from ethnographies of craft and apprenticeship that learning skills is at the same time an education in cultural values (Argenti 2002; Dilley 1999; Marchand 2003; Simpson 2006). Pierre Bourdieu (1977) and Michael Herzfeld (2004) emphasize the tacit dimensions of this learning: how social hierarchies, gender ideologies, and other subtle "structures" become inculcated through the process of skill acquisition and are reproduced in the body of the skilled agent. If disciplining the body into a particular craft is simultaneously a process of incorporating (or "taking into the body") the ideologies of work that structure skill's meaning and practice, what kinds of ideologies are actualized within the bodies of Trinidadian garment workers in the neoliberal period? Learning to sew provides Trinidadian women with the know-how to make a living, either through employment or petty production for private clients. But because acquiring these skills requires self-motivation and even cunning, Trinidadian women "into the sewing" simultaneously learn to adopt an economic disposition of self-reliance, adaptability, and resourcefulness that has become essential to their ability to construct livelihoods in the contemporary garment sector.

Improvising Livelihoods "Into the Sewing"

The availability of work in the informal sector for women who are "into the sewing" derives from the continuing importance of neighborhood seamstresses in Trinidad, particularly for the middle- and low-income individuals seeking fashionable, one-of-a-kind outfits only local seamstresses and tailors can provide, often based on a client's own selection of fabric and sketched designs. With the increasing availability of readymade garments from abroad, the role of the neighborhood seamstress seems to be declining; still, many Trinidadians insist that to obtain a special outfit for an important social event (like a graduation or a wedding), there is no better choice than to visit a skilled and trusted seamstress.

Trinidadians place marked emphasis on the "newness" and style of their clothing (Miller 1994b:77). Secondhand clothing, with the exception of children's clothes from close kin, may be considered not simply inferior but actually repugnant. Yet the prevalence and persistence of tailors and seamstresses in places like Port of Spain are also a result of the importance of having new, distinctive clothing for the endless stream of life-cycle rituals, holidays, and "fetes." For many Trinidadians, making and wearing clothing for a particular event is an important part of the excited anticipation of the event itself. When Audra's daughter was preparing for her "graduation" celebration (a dinner and dance sponsored by her school), Audra often discussed fabric and design with other workers. She told me that her daughter had suffered the embarrassment of attending a previous graduation in a store-bought dress, only to find another girl wearing the same one. So as not to repeat the error, she was having a dress made to her own specifications.

The importance of stylish and new clothing for special events must be understood within the broader context of West Indian cultural life. As Katherine Browne (2004:16) has described for Martinique, Trinidad can be considered a "gaze-oriented social environment" in which dress plays a large role in the establishment of social identity. As Thomas Eriksen (1990:33) notes, "The aesthetic sense of Trinis naturally reaches a peak during the annual Carnival, but aesthetic judgments are also omnipresent during the remaining 363 days of the year." Style is equated with urbanity, as captured in Trinidadian novelist Earl Lovelace's famous passage about the embodied pleasures of becoming modern through rural-to-urban migration: "They come [to town] with country all over their face, their shoulders broad from cutlassing cocoa and felling mora trees, with caps on, cheap silver chains around their necks, their socks peeping out bold below the fold of their trousers, walking in a kind of slow, rolling crawl, trying to look like townmen; and a few months later, cap gone, slim, cool, matchstick in mouth, they coasting with the swing of the city, asking a man for a cigarette, shouting full-lunged to a friend across the street, moving up Calvary Hill as if they own it" (Lovelace 1998 [1979]:69). A lack of style is associated with being "from country" and even, because of the historical association of Indo-Trinidadians with agricultural labor, with being a "country Indian" (Munasinghe 2001:102; Eriksen 1990:34). Clothing is used to mark a boundary between the privacy of the home and the public world outside, with a careful presentation of the self in the public sphere and informality in dress at home. Elisa Sobo (1993:10) tells us that in rural Jamaica, though it is acceptable to wear old, worn-out, or skimpy clothing at home, "to 'walk out,' even if only to a local shop for salt pork, requires attention to appearance."

The increasing availability of readymade imported clothes, particularly with brand-name or faked brand-name logos, has not destroyed the custom-made clothing trade in Trinidad, only shifted its contours and possibilities. As Daniel Miller (1994b:77) notes, in the quest for a distinctive personal style, readymade imported clothes "work" because the difficulty and expense of acquiring them render them unique. For young people, the allure of having "brand-name" garments often outstrips the desire to have "uniquely made" clothing from a local seamstress or tailor, particularly for casual social events. Nonetheless, people of all ages still rely on tailoring and seamstressing for formal attire. Many Signature Fashions workers expressed surprise when Jean announced that her daughter wanted to order a wedding dress readymade from the United States.

By having an outfit made to order, a client not only ensures the uniqueness of her clothing; she can also participate in creating a "look" in collaboration with the seamstress. Clients generally choose and purchase their own fabrics in one of the many fabric stores in Port of Spain, San Fernando, or Chaguanas and discuss with the seamstress what they want made. Negotiations over cut and design often involve sketching ideas on a piece of paper. As the client describes how she wants the garment to "hang" and "fit," the seamstress explains what is possible given the length of fabric that has been purchased. Each seamstress will have her own approach to dressmaking and will develop the client's garment in keeping with her own sewing capabilities.

Home seamstresses must have a straight-stitch sewing machine, a long-standing fixture in the Caribbean home (Pollard 2005). Ideally, a seamstress will own a serger as well, to sew interlocking stitches along the inside seams of a garment to prevent fraying. In the absence of a serger, she might double-stitch the seams or use the "zigzag" feature found on domestic sewing machines. Sewing machines of all varieties are a common purchase with the proceeds of rotating savings groups known as *sou sous*, to which many Signature Fashions workers belong, depositing TT$100 for ten weeks in order to receive a lump sum of TT$1,000. Sewing machines also make treasured gifts, whether from local boyfriends or sent by family members who have migrated to the United States, Canada, or England.

The demand for seamstressing throughout the year rises and falls in tune with the Trinidadian calendar of life-cycle rites, national holidays, and annual festivals, as follows:

> *January–March*, when clients require fashionable clothing for the fetes and soca/calypso performances held during the weeks leading up to Carnival. Some stitchers may also find work in Carnival *mas* camps during this time, though most Carnival costumes now require little sewing and are instead made by gluing decorative elements onto readymade bikinis and shorts imported from Asia.
>
> *May–July*, when teenagers require formal clothing for "graduation" dinner-dances and clients of all ages require clothing for weddings. This period is also important for seamstresses who specialize in making "African dress" because revelers by the thousands parade through the streets of Port of Spain in African-style outfits to celebrate the emancipation of slaves in the British West Indies on August 1.
>
> *August–September*, when children require uniforms for their schools, cut and sewn to precise specifications.
>
> *October–December*, during the Diwali, Eid, and Christmas periods, clients require formal clothing. November and December are the busiest months for seamstresses who sew the draperies and cushion covers clients buy to "dress the house" at Christmas.

The ongoing, seasonal rhythm of social activity in Trinidad provides yearlong work. One Port of Spain seamstress remarked, "It don't really have a quiet time of year. I just go from one thing to the next one. Always something to do." Signature Fashions workers estimate that they could make up to TT$1,000 sewing during the busy Christmas season and much smaller amounts at other times. At Signature Fashions, the weeks leading up to Christmas require a great deal of overtime work in the factory, yet workers still try to meet demands for cushions and draperies in their home communities. As Antoinette insisted, "I doesn't really sleep at all at Christmas. Carnival neither."

Signature Fashions workers who are "into the sewing" dedicate themselves to different specialties. Some, like Brenda and Lata, specialize in making two-piece "skirt suits" for professional clients or their own co-workers, since Signature workers dress in blouses, skirts, or skirt suits and leather shoes on their way to and from the factory.[5] Other workers, like Kimberly and Peggy, sew fashionable clothing in line with the latest trends. Most common are the seamstress like Antoinette and Josephine, who produce all types of clothing, ranging from a "whole wedding" (bridal dress, bridesmaids' outfits, and even in some cases men's clothes) to stylish casual-wear, as well as soft furnishings.

I was standing in Josephine's kitchen at her home in Laventille when one of her neighbors stopped by to ask Josephine to make a dress for her. The woman nodded to me but was not introduced. She admired some of the cloth Josephine was working on, then started to describe the wedding she was planning to attend in a couple of weeks' time.

"You wear short dresses or long dresses?" Josephine asked the woman.

"I want to look *real* nice," the woman replied. During their discussions about the garment, the woman added "like a mother, because I am one."

Watching Josephine discuss the dress with her client, I began to think about the particular social interactions the production of clothing entails. A seamstress or tailor will be told about the relevant event and the kind of dress required. As the seamstress and the client sketch designs together or talk about the cut of a garment, the client's desire for a particular type of self-presentation relies on the seamstress's acuity in reading and presenting social distinction. Vanessa Maher (1987:140, 142) thus describes dressmakers as "ritual experts," who must be skilled in the manipulation of symbols to "contribute to the social and personal identity of her client." By speaking of the type of person one *is* and wants to be *seen as*—"like a mother, because I am one"—the client conveys a tacit knowledge that the seamstress must be able to recognize and implement. This skill at social discernment confers upon the seamstress a special status in her home community, which transcends mere monetary rewards.

Sewing for clients at home is not without hardships. To make enough money to survive, an independent seamstress must extend her circle of clients beyond the intimate group of friends and neighbors. Having outsiders come into one's home is seen as a risky ordeal. Erica, one of the stitchers at Signature Fashions, told me why she quit sewing for clients and decided to pursue factory work instead: "But when you take in work, it's like a *chance*. Being a seamstress, and that is too much headaches, you know? Wondering whether people be paying you or not. I always had this thing about me living alone and always having people in and out. You know? You always feel you can't know, can't be certain, who will be coming in, for what purpose they'll be coming for, you know, right? So I find it is better for me to be *outside*, and so I began working at the factory." The stature and economic freedom an independent seamstress can achieve are always shadowed by risk. The exposure to strangers with unknown intentions or the "chance" of being taken advantage of: the independent seamstress bears all of the liability should things go wrong. A seamstress's expertise does not always go uncontested, and she may find herself defending her work to an unhappy client who refuses to pay. Aparna told me that while she continues to sew clothes for herself, she rarely does so for others "because I find when you sew for people, they always like to tell yuh it ehnt fitting good and this thing? And because of that I don't like to sew for people."

Although Signature Fashions workers occasionally stitch their homemade garments on the factory machines to give their seams a more professional finish, seamstressing for private clients usually takes place at home. Wherever it is performed, seamstressing shapes the subjectivities of workers who participate in it by influencing how they see themselves as economic actors: savvy, entrepreneurial, and self-reliant. Their identities as laborers, both individually and collectively, in the Signature Fashions factory are therefore inflected with an entrepreneurial energy. This is captured in the self-designation of many workers as being "into the sewing" rather than identifying as a "garment worker." They perceive their professional identity to be tied not to employment at a factory but instead to skill and "love" of sewing, from which they believed they would always be able to make a living.

Taking Fashion, Making Style

Daniel Miller (1994b) argues that Trinidadians generally distinguish between "fashion" and "style." "Fashion" denotes the popular, ever-changing clothing trends that become widely accepted by members of the populace. To be "in fashion" means dressing in a fairly conventional, if constantly revised, repertoire recognized as being in vogue. "Style" refers to self-presentation. While the pursuit of style can draw on and even drive current notions of fashion, it is essentially an individualistic enterprise, a "personalized context for fashion" (ibid.:75). Style is not just about being up-to-date; it is about knowing and displaying one's best self through attractive, well-suited, and original clothing. Fashion's emphasis, then, is on "the dissolution of individual identity through appearance in a strictly conventional, if internally diverse, category of appearance," while style "appears as a highly personalized and self-controlled expression of particular aesthetic ability" (ibid.:74).

For the workers at Signature Fashions who sew at home in the evening, the distinction between fashion and style is important. "Style" is what clients seek when they arrange to have clothing made for them. The garments must honor the client's particular aesthetic, social identity ("like a mother because I am one"), and desire to adhere to conventional norms of taste. In contrast, "fashion" is what is sold by Signature Fashions, manufactured apparel to be bought and worn by Trinidad's economic elite and filtered down to the population-at-large by cheaper stores who copy and rework Signature's designs.[6] The knowledge that Signature's workers garner from the factory is about fashion rather than style. The independent seamstress can translate this information on cut, color, fabric, and design into garments that will suit her clients' personal projects of style. When Antoinette copied the pattern for a Signature blouse, she would not be remaking it in the stiff linen fabric of its original design but instead in a softer cotton or white satin to fulfill her client's wish for clothing that would be both appropriate to her "hospitality" job and communicative of her personal aesthetic.

A woman working as an independent seamstress needs not only technical skills but also knowledge of the latest fashions.[7] Each of the seamstress shops I visited contained a stack of well-worn "fashion books," which were shown to clients to help them communicate the kind of "look" they were after. These fashion books were actually glossy clothing catalogs, usually sent or brought back from the United States. Working in a company like Signature Fashions provides workers with exposure to information about current fashion trends. Because this information is crucial to their success in serving private clients, workers consider Signature Fashions a particularly good place to work if they also stitch at home. Yet this fashion knowledge is not uncritically accepted by workers but is instead a domain of appraisal, interpretation, and selective reproduction.

Designer clothing possesses what Arjun Appadurai (1986:38) has dubbed "semiotic virtuosity," meaning the ability to convey complex social messages. Some commentators portray these messages as an instrument of social hierarchy, a "system of social differentiation" that must be constantly reinvented as old fashion symbols become diffused throughout the population (Maher 1987:144). Yet Trinidadian fashion does not move from "the elite" to "the masses" in a unidirectional manner. Trinidadian fashion emerges instead from various social contexts and actors, stratified not only by class, ethnicity, and gender but also by more subtle determinations of taste. Moreover, Trinidad—a diverse, multiethnic, and arguably "transnational" context (because of the prevalence of migratory and consumption circuits into and out of the country)—simply does not have a single, univocal social hierarchy at work. Criteria for judging the beauty, desirability, and social inflection of dress are commonly contested; both wearing clothing and judging the clothing of others reveal one's status and position within this vast web of signification.

Although Signature Fashions represents an authority on fashion that workers can retrieve and use for their own purposes, workers do not uncritically accept every item of Signature clothing as equally appealing. The factory does not simply represent a domain of authoritative "fashion knowledge" that workers capture, rework, and "translate" to their clients at home. Fashion is itself a domain of discursive struggle, in which workers articulate very different systems of value and aesthetic judgment from those of Signature's designers. As Signature Fashions clothing passes through the hands of workers, the garments represent an invitation to reflexivity. The materiality of the garments inspires spirited conversations about their style, quality, and worth. This commentary might emerge from technical frustrations, as when Veena complained to her supervisor that the flimsy gossamer fabric for the blouses she was stitching was "rampling up so," adding under her breath, "I don't see why somebody want to show their bra and t'ing [through their clothing] anyway." The designer lines of clothing garnered the liveliest discussion among workers, in appreciation or criticism. A deliberately crumpled men's shirt trimmed in gold piping, for example, might elicit from workers a *steups* (the sound of sucking air through the teeth in disapproval) and the dismissive phrase, "*Some*body go buy it." When we were trimming a set of red trousers with a series of strings hanging off the waistband, Glenda plucked at the strings and commented, "I'd *never* wear that—someone could grab me on the street." Other distinctive styles will generate commentaries of desire: "If you see how *sweet* this one looking, straps go flush against the back and all."

What makes these discussions about the clothing significant at Signature Fashions is that these are not the conversations of interlopers examining products destined for other people. Unlike workers in Mexican maquiladoras, who cannot afford the blue jeans they produce (Peña 1997), or South Asian garment workers stitching clothes for Western consumers (Lessinger 2002; Lynch 2007), Signature Fashions workers might create exact replicas of factory clothing or copy patterns to be remade in different fabrics at home. A statement about "how *sweet* this one looking" might be followed up by "begging" some cloth from Peggy or scrutinizing other workers to detect whether anyone is thiefing a chance to copy the garment. The workers' gaze is selective, not simply evaluative.

Rather than accept the fashionableness of the clothing they produce, Signature workers constantly discuss its significations. Tight-fitting, white-cotton trousers were deemed vulgar, particularly by the older workers. Said Bernice, a fifty-six-year-old Signature Fashions worker: "Waist so low and belly way out, navel showing, nah! Why you want to be exposing that? These shirts, they cost $100, did you know that? One-quarter yard of cloth and belly hanging out. Tight waist. Tight-tight on the sides. We used to wear our clothes to suit. If you going out you dress *different*. Not always tight-tight." Although Bernice's criticism of the shirts was ridiculed by some of the younger workers, many agreed that such clothing would appeal to consumers who are "worthless," a local term connoting moral laxity (Mendes 1986:165). Similarly, clothing in outrageous styles, particularly for men, was deemed ridiculous and worthy only of a mindless pursuer of "fashion." These discourses reveal the workers' positionalities in relation to Signature's intended consumers. Workers often took the clothing as emblematic of elite persons whom they occasionally emulated but often disparaged. Special condemnation was reserved for clothing deemed transgressive of the gender boundary: "mannish" clothing for women or "faggoty" clothing for men. Such styles were taken as evidence of frivolity and the moral degradation of the elite, who were seen to have lost sight of essential community values invested in a traditional gender order. Workers' aesthetic judgments communicated a sense of moral superiority over wealthy consumers, for whom it was believed money could not buy good sense:

> "This shirt is a man's shirt or for a woman?" asked Shirley. Preston has brought her a sample T-shirt for her to stitch up for an upcoming fashion show. The shirt was lime green, light blue, and had a white string, similar to a shoelace, running down the front of it.
> "It for a man," said Preston, smiling and then looking at me. Preston is one of the designers at Signature.
> "Well, I does find it look faggoty for a man," said Shirley. She looked over at me. "Ehnt? Ehnt it look womanish?"

Preston's shirt never did make it into the fashion show; however, Shirley later "thiefed" one of the men's shirts derived from Preston's original design and began wearing it herself. She said its sleeveless look was too feminine for a man and better suited a woman.

Lively discussions about the quality and beauty of the clothing sometimes convey a class critique. As a stitcher named Nalini observed, "Shopping at Signature is for big shots." Amanda, a back worker, said to me, "Signature have their class of people [who buy the clothes], certain type of people." When I asked her who the Signature Fashions clothes are really "for," she replied, "Bankers. A lot of bank people love Signature clothes." She recounted a story of visiting her bank on personal business and being asked by an employee whether she could get her a discount on Signature Fashions clothing.

Workers' assessments of the Signature Fashions clothing not only pertained to specific styles as they circulated through the shop floor; they also addressed the monetary value of the garments themselves. Positioned as hourly wage workers in the production of expensive garments, workers have an ambivalent relationship to the "value" of the items they produce. On the one hand, they perceive the high cost of Signature clothing as evidence of their own skills and diligence, which create a "good fit" and "nice style." These discourses penetrate the wage labor system, as workers conclude that there is an unfair disproportionality between their wages and the price the clothing earns in Signature's stores. As Jean once said to me, "Plenty people see how much [Signature Fashions clothing] does cost, so they think we [workers] must be making [a lot of money], too."

Workers also frequently say that Signature Fashions clothing is expensive for "no reason" or "for that logo alone." More than one worker told me never to waste sixty dollars buying a Signature T-shirt, since it is nothing more than a normal T-shirt with the "Signature Fashions" logo printed across the front. As Glenda warned me, lest I be taken in: "Don't let me catch you in a Signature store. You could buy that same shirt on Charlotte Street[8] for ten dollars. It the same; the only thing different is the label on it." In critiquing the clothing in this way, workers are commenting less on the quality of the products they make than on the virtues of imagined customers who pay top dollar for them. The bright-red trousers that had attracted such derision sold for more than TT$269, an exorbitant sum of money to Signature Fashions workers, nearly equal to a week's wages. Customers are imagined as silly-minded and naive—purchasing clothing of dubious fashion simply because the "Signature" logo is attached to it. Workers assert themselves as prudent shoppers who know the difference between a bargain and a rip-off.

Even though workers sometimes mock the consumers who pay for Signature Fashions clothing, they are well aware that the garments confer social status on the wearer. The popularity of Signature Fashions garments is sustained in part by the fact that local celebrities—calypso stars and television personalities—wear Signature clothing and attend the company's fashion shows. The distinction afforded by the Signature Fashions label signifies its high cost. Workers believe the discrepancy between the material worth of the garment—based on the components of its production (including labor)—and its market value is bridged by the logo attached to it; this value discrepancy is what workers virulently critique, even as they thief Signature Fashions clothing to access some modes of distinction themselves.

When working as independent seamstresses or simply selecting and producing clothing for themselves, Signature Fashions workers may use factory designs but revise them in keeping with alternate conceptions of fashion. When Signature began producing a line of "sweat suits" with contrasting colors of piping on the cuffs, seamstresses reworked these baggy, comfortable clothes for a closer fit, with piping added to the trouser legs to emulate more accurately the styles worn by American hip-hop artists on cable television.[9]

Gita described to me how she "watched the style" of the V-neck jerseys Signature was producing and then reworked it at home: "I like how they does do the V-neck, but then I think I like how they does do it, but I wouldn't want it to be tacked; just having it hang kinda loose is nice." Studying how it is done in the factory allows workers to copy the technique and experiment with the fashion at home.

For workers, then, Signature Fashions exists not as a source of authoritative fashion knowledge but instead as a highly situated reference point: garments that are produced to appeal to Caribbean elites and foreign tourists. Workers understand Signature Fashions' aesthetics to be positioned within particular matrices of class and race from which they are purposely excluded as low-wage workers. Rather than uncritically accept these garments as fashionable and therefore alluring, workers assessed them from their own situated locations, choosing at times to align themselves with different aesthetic judgments than those of the Signature Fashions designers. These actions exemplify the process of objectification Daniel Miller (1992:165) has identified in Trinidad in relation to the consumption of "foreign" commodities, which Trinidadians do not "merely accept, reject or transform" but also make, remake, and actively construct in the project of expressively making themselves.

Academic research too often encounters economic subjects either as laborers governed by factory control (Lynch 2007; Ngai 2005) or entrepreneurial selves making their own living in the informal sector (Stoller 2002; Venkatesh 2006). This dichotomizing analytical attention leaves unexamined processes of *making* that are so central to the lives and identities of women "into the sewing." Signature Fashions workers have inserted themselves into a wage labor relationship while still retaining their own ability to design and make clothes. The acuity with which they take "fashion" from the factory to rework as "styles" at home undeniably shapes their subjectivities as workers. With a sense of savvy opportunism, women "into the sewing" express a depth and complexity in their relationship to the things they produce, as well as ambivalence toward them.

Conclusions

Once when Kellisha was showing me how to use the button-tacking machine, the back-area supervisor, Lystra, advised her sternly but not unkindly, "You must learn everything, so if you have to go work somewhere else, you can say you can do everything." Taking skills from the factory helps workers prepare themselves for the intense competition for the few jobs remaining in the formal garment sector. In the process of acquiring these skills from numerous sources, Trinidadian women "into the sewing" become infused with a self-reliant economic selfhood that is ideally fashioned for the requirements of neoliberal capitalism—the spirit of seizing skills wherever one may find them.

Trinidadian garment workers often describe learning to sew as a practice of agency, using a language of self-reliance, freedom, and pleasure: "skills" mean being able to "do something for yourself" as a "way of independence," to "have ideas where you could help yourself," which allows the seamstress to "make the move, do things," and "have real money." These attitudes reflect a valorization of the ability of the individual actor to forge a livelihood under difficult circumstances through self-reliance, bravery, and cunning (Browne 2004). Recent scholarship describes how this treasured Caribbean disposition represents an approach to economic life that is well adapted to managing the complex imperatives of neoliberal globalization (Freeman 2007; Gregory 2007; Mantz 2007; Ulysse 2007).

In the case of Trinidadian women "into the sewing," their relentless pursuit of skill, remaining nimble in the face of economic competition and disappointment, and morally legitimizing illicit acts of "thiefing" prepare them for the flexible demands of contemporary garment work. However, Trinidadian garment workers' attitudes toward skill and work do not simply represent a felicitous convergence of a Caribbean ethos of economic flexibility and the entrepreneurial spirit of neoliberalism. We must consider as well how the willingness of women "into the sewing" to embrace opportunity and change is exploited in contexts of wage employment. Because skills are required for participating in the labor force, garment workers see capturing them as an important individual ambition. Despite the cunning and subterfuge involved in "thiefing" skills behind the boss's back, such acts actually serve management's goals by externalizing the costs of retraining workers—relegating skill acquisition to an informal sector of activity and divesting employers of an obligation to train—at a time when other entitlements like sick leave, vacation leave, and health checks in the factory context have also unraveled.

When they thief a chance, Trinidadian garment workers ratify this managerial vision of the factory as an institution of opportunity rather than one of entitlements. Workers therefore enact what Nikolas Rose (1999) describes as the "responsibilization" of the self: a mode of self-governance grounded in an internalized sense of authorship and culpability over one's own destiny. The mutual acceptance (worker and employer) of skill as not only workers' *responsibility* but also their *pleasure* is deeply embedded in Caribbean ideas of personhood, skill, and the obligation to make one's own luck. Garment workers have fashioned subjectivities that harmonize dominant economic practices with valued Caribbean ways of being-in-the-world. This heightens the uneven stakes of employment in which women "into the sewing" find themselves because relations of power are concealed behind not only a discourse of free choice but also an ethic of pleasure.

Carla Freeman (2005) argues that the neoliberal era has not only demanded the flexibility of labor but also idealized flexibility as a desirable trait. She notes that this "romance of flexibility" is not new in the Caribbean region, where people have long relied upon—and indeed celebrated—occupational multiplicity in livelihoods. What is new, says Freeman, are the ways in which this romance is presented as salve to the uncertainties of neoliberal arrangements in commerce and employment, where jobs may be short-term and workers have to continually retrain. Workers' narrative celebration of thiefing a chance rejoices in a form of individualism that obscures the exploitation of their labor in the factory, an issue explored in more depth in chapter 6, by investigating what happens to these triumphant worker discourses when things go wrong.

Notes

1. Trinidadians of Indian ancestry who have achieved middle-class status followed an economic path different from that of middle-class Afro-Trinidadians. While Afro-Trinidadians pursued formal education and the civil service, Indo-Trinidadians—some of whom had capital assets from land grants following indentureship—used their collateral base to embark on small-scale commercial and manufacturing activities in addition to educational pursuits (Khan 2004:75–76). Thus by the 1970s, Afro-Trinidadians began lagging behind Indo-Trinidadians in ownership and control of private business (Henry 1993:71), although middle- and upper-class Afro-Trinidadians held control of government positions that once belonged to the white elite.

2. The People's National Movement (PNM) ushered the nation through its independence in 1962 and a project of economic modernization. A cornerstone of the PNM's economic policy was "industrialization by invitation," an innovation

of St. Lucian economist W. Arthur Lewis (Lewis 1950; Yelvington 1995:60). Industrialization by invitation entailed the establishment of domestic industry—both import-substitutive and export-oriented—by creating incentives for foreign capital investment. Although the ready supply of Trinidadian labor would be a main draw for investors, the state also supported the expansion of manufacturing with public-sector jobs on infrastructural projects (Henry 1993:66). With the influx of oil money in the 1970s, Trinidad and Tobago took an even stronger turn toward a state-controlled economy, which included the nationalization of key industries (Munasinghe 2001:103).

3. Lynn Bolles (1996) points to the gendered dimensions of occupational multiplicity and how understanding Caribbean women's attempts to "make do" requires attention to the interconnections between the domestic and public spheres.

4. Although I already knew many details of her working life at the time of the interview, Josephine obligingly recounted her story for the tape recorder. For the sake of clarity, I have edited my various interjections out of the conversation. All factories mentioned in Josephine's narrative, as throughout the book, are pseudonyms.

5. Garment workers usually travel to and from the factory dressed in a "professional" style, with neatly pressed skirts and blouses, flat or heeled leather shoes, lipstick, and a leather (or imitation leather) handbag. Once inside the factory, they hang up their blouses and take off their shoes, putting on old T-shirts and plastic slippers for the workday. While Carla Freeman has described Barbadian data-processing workers using professional dress to distinguish themselves from factory workers (who nonetheless earn similar wages), my observation of garment factory workers in Trinidad indicates that they, too, enjoy dressing as professional women (cf. Freeman 2000).

6. Once Signature's clothing appears in stores, some garments are copied by less-expensive retail chains and subsequently sold under cheaper brand names. According to Helene, one competitor, whose manufacturing operations are contracted from China, has become adept at producing quick copies of Signature apparel. Although Helene once threatened legal action against this company, she now just laments the practice, saying, "Every time I see that skirt [that they copied], I get so annoyed, I want to make something even better the next time."

7. While Britain and the United States have long been the source of "fashion" expertise in the Caribbean (Buckridge 2004), the "lag" between fashion trends there and those in the Caribbean has been shortened in recent years by cable television (Wilk 1994), the Internet, international travel, and the "barrels" of garments sent to Trinidad by relatives who have migrated overseas (cf. Freeman 2000:223; Halstead 2002:277). Daniel Miller (1992:175) describes Trinidadian seamstresses in the 1980s

stopping work for an hour each day to watch *The Young and the Restless* on television, so they could memorize the "looks" clients would later demand.

8. Charlotte Street is one of the main retail areas in Port of Spain, catering to the working-class budget.

9. As Deborah Thomas (2004) describes among consumers in Jamaica, black American styles are not imagined as "out there" and latterly adopted into the island context. Rather, consumers see themselves and their countrymen as critical parts of the production of a black vernacular culture, which they see reflected back to them in both American and Jamaican television, music, and film.

6

"Use a Next Hand"

Risk, Injury, and the Body at Work

> I came out of that factory [for good] when I couldn't afford the medicine no more.
> – *Mary, independent seamstress, Port of Spain*

Glenda's eyesight was troubling her. As we stood at the side table to cut and turn collars together, she told me she was having trouble "seeing the work," particularly when it involved looking at dark thread on dark-colored cloth. The prescription glasses Glenda had worn for several years had broken recently, and she replaced them with a pair of reading glasses bought off the rack at a shopping mall. She tried on different pairs and compared their effectiveness by reading the small Bible she carried in her handbag. The glasses she selected were not a good fit, and she would often go without them because they gave her headaches.

As we worked, I asked Glenda how she was managing to cut the edges of the collars, given that she couldn't see them very well. Glenda showed me how she had marked two thick black lines on the table and measured the collar in her hand against them.

"I can do it by average," she said. "I put the two black lines and I can measure it like that. You know how many *years* I doing this? No, I don't have to see."

At fifty-two years old, Glenda was particularly worried about her eyes because her mother had been blinded by glaucoma. Like every health trouble discussed at Signature Fashions, Glenda's eyesight had become something of a public project among her co-workers. When she complained about her difficulty seeing, other workers insisted on various remedies: washing the eye with cow's milk or lemon juice, taking "bush" remedies made from bilberry or *ditay payee* plants, or drinking the water rice had boiled in. Glenda often told her unsolicited advisers, "That will blind me *itself!*" She preferred to stick with her own treatments: bilberry when she could afford it (at TT$16 an ounce) and eating a small bag of carrots she carried in the front of her apron. One day Glenda came in with a vial of sixty bright-yellow vitamin tablets for improving vision that she showed around the factory. She was proud of the purchase because she had seen the bottle sold for TT$120 on Charlotte Street and got it from an optician for "only" TT$85.

Glenda interpreted her failing vision within the biographical trajectory of her life. Whenever we talked about her eyesight, our conversation quickly turned to her secret plan to leave wage employment for good and spend time at home caring for her mother, who is in her eighties. Glenda's mother, who is blind, spent the days in their apartment on her own, and Glenda often spoke about how much better it would be if she could stay home with her. As a Pentecostal Christian, Glenda saw her failing eyesight as both a sign and an opportunity. She repeatedly asked God to "make a way" for her to leave Signature Fashions, whose production of immodest clothing Glenda struggled to reconcile with her notion of a suitable Christian livelihood. The possibility of leaving the factory hinged on whether her brother, a pastor living in South Carolina, would agree to send her US$25 a week to care for their mother at home. Glenda is good at "economizing," as she calls it: finding bargains on food and clothing, sewing for herself and her mother, and growing vegetables in their yard. Although Glenda no longer pursued extra income by sewing for clients, she believed that with her mother's small pension and US$25 a week, she could make ends meet until she began receiving her own state pension. Glenda's husband had been living in New York for the previous seven years, but he did not send maintenance money for her or their nineteen-year-old son and could not be counted on to make a financial contribution.

This chapter explores how the shop floor is experienced by and through workers' bodies, including how they navigate injury and ill health. In previous chapters, we have seen Signature Fashions workers as confident agents, thiefing a chance when the opportunity arises. Even when they work on coordinated activities of covert production, they experience themselves as individuated and independent subjects. In this chapter, I ask whether the material fact of bodily vulnerability—made evident in episodes of injury or illness—poses a challenge to the romantic image of workers' dynamism, flexibility, and autonomy encapsulated in narratives of thiefing a chance. To what extent might incidents of bodily breakdown serve as counterpoint to neoliberal subjectivities that rely on an active subject who is healthy and whole? How do workers reconcile their desire for autonomy from their employers with their need for safety and care in the workplace? Under what conditions might the struggle for occupational health inspire workers to make common cause with one another?

While the body is understood to be a symbolic construct, "full of social meaning" (Sobo 1993:52), anthropologists now recognize the importance of also examining its lived materiality as the site and source of experience (Csordas 1994). At Signature Fashions, the body is a constant presence in two ways: as the material base of experience (the body-as-lived) and as the symbolic grounds for workers' struggles for dignity and self-determination. Even as we focus on the materialities of the shop floor, we must remember that the phenomenological experience of work cannot be abstracted from the "body politic"—the regulation, discipline, and control of bodies that are differentially raced, classed, and gendered (Scheper-Hughes and Lock 1987). Illness and injury are as much social phenomena as physical ones.

Everyday Projects of Health on the Shop Floor

Israel Drori (2000:117), writing about an Israeli garment factory, tells us, "Health is always on the seamstresses' minds." Garment work, as physical labor, relies on the body as a primary instrument. When workers internalize and perform specific bodily postures, physical movements, and spatial and temporal disciplines, their day-to-day activities are generative of somatic experiences, including episodes of pain, fatigue, and injury. Drori explains that for the Israeli workers in his study, concern that garment work would impair their reproductive capacities served as a moral commentary about their abilities to fulfill the roles of wife and mother as well as industrial worker. How workers identify and navigate workplace risks, then, cannot be separated from cultural ideologies and social relations.

Workers at Signature Fashions worry about the industry's health risks, ranging from chronic conditions believed to arise from the sedentary nature of sewing, deteriorating vision from prolonged concentration in low light, the dangers of steam and heat in the pressing section, the aches and pains of musculoskeletal strain, and the risk of inhaling the dust that visibly hangs in the air. In assessing these risks and safeguarding themselves, workers at Signature Fashions approach well-being as a project to be managed. Health ideals do not exist as free-floating concepts but instead are made manifest through everyday practices, such as using West Indian home remedies, over-the-counter painkillers, or herbal vitamins bought from a neighbor to strengthen the body or to combat pain, fatigue, or vision problems. Like the production of garments, health is something to be worked on. Just as workers accept the need to bring their own tools to the factory (small instruments like scissors, tweezers, and nippers) and to make their own protective smocks and kerchiefs out of fabric scraps, they manage physical dangers through their own endeavors of self-care.

The everyday health practices of Signature Fashions workers respond not only to their phenomenological experiences of work but also to wider discourses of health that derive from biomedical knowledge and West Indian "folk" or "bush" medicine of various kinds. Health maintenance in the West Indies has been described by scholars as an eclectic and highly individualized project, whereby individuals draw from both biomedicine and traditional practices to promote health and treat illness and injury (du Toit 2001; Long 1974; Mahabir 1991; Quinlan 2004:63–70). In Trinidad, as elsewhere in the region, personal health practices are generally structured by three principles of well-being: the need for equilibrium (or "flow") in bodily functions, the condition of the blood as indicative of overall health, and the importance of carefully mixing "hot" and "cold" foods and temperatures (Dressler 1982; Littlewood 1988; Quinlan 2004; Sobo 1993). I argue that in taking steps to safeguard their health at home and on the shop floor, Signature Fashions workers participate in the production of a moral economy that defines how much can be reasonably expected of them and how much is too much. Examining the routine ways workers manage their health at work therefore provides a window onto the texture of labor relations, including the everyday means through which workers consent to or resist their conditions of employment. As later sections will show, these "normal" workplace relations, in which safety is entrusted to workers, are disrupted by the intrusion of the injured body.

The factory is a dusty environment; not only do bolts of cloth gather dust wherever they are stacked and stored, stitching the fabric also emits dust from the fibers. Serging, which slices the cloth as it stitches inner seams, sprays dust toward the worker's face. Jean told me, "You know, sometimes in your nostril you see the color we sewing, especially the sergers." Workers at Signature Fashions worry about inhaling dust, not only because it creates a scratchy sensation in the throat but also because of concerns that dust could become trapped inside and interfere with the natural flow of the body's organic processes. Every couple of months Cissy distributed surgical masks made of semi-permeable plastic and cotton. As workers themselves realized, these masks are actually designed for a single use, and wearing one day after day renders it ineffective. Workers therefore fashioned their own dust masks out of small rectangles of cotton cloth and elastic. They applied menthol crystals, crushed into Vaseline, into the insides of their nostrils to increase air flow while trapping dust particles in the nose. Inhaled dust is also managed by the West Indian home remedy of "washout" or "cleanout": drinking a spoonful of olive oil at home after work (cf. Quinlan 2004:109).

Workers feared the deteriorating effects of sewing on their eyesight. As Josephine told me, "This work could bring you blind." Signature Fashions workers experiencing vision problems would pay for eye exams at a commercial optometrist, where many bought glasses for themselves. There was a sense of inevitability that Kavita exhibited in saying, "People in sewing always need glasses." Dolores, a forty-eight-year-old stitcher at Signature Fashions, recalled: "After working a couple of years, your eyes do start to go weak, and like, to make a straight stitch, it might be kind of difficult for me, so that's why I had to go and get my glasses. Because it start to get wavy, and I get frightened. They said the eyes start to get dull, and it start to look that way." Eyeglasses represented a significant expense that most workers could not afford on their own. A factory worker requiring glasses without additional income to rely on (through her own work in the informal sector, from close kin, or through membership in a rotating savings group) might rely on a boyfriend to make the purchase for her. The purchasing of a pair of glasses in the context of a romantic relationship would be taken as an indication that the relationship was serious and that the boyfriend properly attended to his obligations of care. When Kellisha needed glasses, her married boyfriend, Derek, helped her select (and paid for) a pair; even though she felt that wearing glasses ruined her style and only wore them at work, Kellisha let everyone know that Derek had bought them for her.

Workers often complained about the everyday aches and pains that arise from both long periods of sitting and repetitive use of certain muscles. As Donna said, "Sometimes I get so stiff I can't even turn. Sometimes it is so *bad*, and it is only when I'm on the machine." To counteract the pain of sedentary labor, work must be approached with a relaxed and calm attitude. Aparna told me, "You have to loosen your body, you know?" The physical toll of the workplace can be offset by relaxing, or "liming," at home, outside of work hours (cf. Littlewood 1988:132). Without this ability to rest—the result, for example, of an inharmonious domestic situation or the need to sew for clients after work—stress can "build up" in the body and manifest as malaise, chronic pain, and anxiety. As a stitcher named Erica told me, "Everyone work so much now, that's why there's so many people with [high] blood pressure, heart attack, stroke."

When Signature Fashions moved its manufacturing operations from the center of town to an industrial estate on the highway, the wooden chairs in the stitching section were replaced with cushioned, height-adjustable ones. Workers appreciated and acknowledged this token of care, which made them feel, as Jean put it, "[Helene and Robert] really does try to make us happy." In the new factory, workers arrived at 7:30 in the morning and had only thirty minutes for lunch in exchange for being able to go home at 3:30 in the afternoon when overtime was not required. Providing a shorter lunch hour and no afternoon break contravenes national labor law (Moonilal 2001:43), but most Signature workers preferred it because it meant the workday finished earlier.[1] At the same time, Signature workers worried that longer periods of sedentary labor might cause "stagnation" and invite painful congestion of the blood in various parts of the body, reflecting the enduring West Indian principle that health requires the maintenance of blood viscosity and temperature (cf. Quinlan 2004:79–83). Concerns over blood clots, varicose veins, and "fat leg" were countered with biweekly purges and the ingestion of bitter aloes to prevent the blood from becoming too thick. As Jean described it, "We don't have that break time again. So that is why when you see I eating [lunch], I standing up. That's circulation, from sitting there long hours."

Workers do not encounter the factory solely as a hazardous environment; it also represents a place for engaging in proper forms of sociality and attempting to achieve a sense of happiness and well-being. Two principles are central to this endeavor: flow and coolness. "Flow" is a principle of equilibrium. Because the body is a complex system, it remains equalized as long as there is proper internal movement of blood, digestion, and waste. To achieve internal flow, workers often "take a cooling"—drink the water specific herbs or vegetables have steeped in—which is followed by a "purge," taking herbal or commercial laxatives (Littlewood 1988:132). One stitcher sold herbal "colon cleansers" to her co-workers for specifically this purpose, and discussions about the effectiveness of different methods of cooling and purging were commonplace.

The bodily ideal of flow is also achieved through garment workers' attempts to gain control over the pace and progress of their various tasks each day—mastering them rather than feeling at their mercy. Certain tasks, like hemming dresses, are seen as amenable to "flow" because they are quick and easy to accomplish, allowing smooth operation. Tasks that are fiddly, like attaching collars to shirts, are undesirable because they require painstaking concentration, with little possibility of achieving flow. Threats to flow occur when supervisors cajole, scold, or yell at workers and "boss we [around]." A stitcher named Dolores described flow as both a psychological and a somatic state: "You know, sometimes you come, and you come to work with a sort of a down spirit—I would say 'down spirit'—and you come, and you have something nice doing on the machine. You could run that; you ehnt thinking about money or otherwise. You just keep running it." "Running it" allows a worker to engage herself in the immediacy of her work, allowing the mind to wander freely.

Workers often discussed ways to "clean" and "build up" their blood using vitamins and "bush" remedies to contend with the physical demands of factory work. During the pre-Carnival season, when I spent evenings working in a mas camp, some workers were concerned that my body could not "take the jamming"—the additional strain of holding down a second, physically taxing job. I was advised to "put on size" (put on weight) and to take vitamins and bush remedies, as Amanda said, "to build up your blood because you're not sleeping at night."

The Trinidadian body is, in its ideal, cool (ibid.). Too much heat builds up "pressure." Pressure also comes from external forces, such as the occasional presence of Helene, the "boss lady," on the shop floor. As Prabha said to me, anticipating a difficult week of work, "You see it will get real hot in the factory this week. *Real* pressure. Because Cissy want to get the T-shirts done." Coolness is sought not only through action on the physical body but also through performing an external demeanor of calm composure, as demonstrated by Shirley one afternoon when she got up from her machine to go to the bathroom in the back of the factory. She walked slowly to the lavatory and slowly back to her seat. Cissy (the production manager), watching Shirley's movements, called out for her to move more quickly: "Pull your foot, Shirley!" Shirley refused to hasten her pace and continued walking with slow, deliberate steps.

Lata whispered to Dolores, "Take it from me, she don't care. She don't care who boof [scold] she; she don't care."

Dolores said, "That good. You can't take people on."

Lata continued, saying, "When someone tell me something, I ready to fight. But not Shirl. She keep cool-cool. She don't care at all."

"Tha's the way to be," said Dolores, "You keep your cool."

When Signature Fashions workers talk about a healthy working environment, they are quick to evoke the importance of maintaining equilibrium through harmonious social relationships. As Aparna said approvingly of her work in the front area of the factory, "I find myself cool here." Positive social relations not only mimic the state of a healthy body, they allow health to flourish because deficient social relationships may cause illness.[2]

Feeling and acting "cool" is achieved by not internalizing social unrest by gossiping or becoming entangled in other people's concerns. This is best captured through the colloquial phrase "doh [don't] take it on" (Miller 1994b:87). Social strife or criticism should not be taken into the body. Daniel Miller argues that *picong* (teasing) exemplifies this principle. When a person is teased, it is a test of her ability to shrug off criticism and maintain a cool demeanor: "the recipient knows that they are being judged by their ability not to take it on" (ibid.:88; cf. Yelvington 1996:316). Tina was a frequent target of teasing among the back workers, not simply because she was the sole Indo-Trinidadian in the back area but because of her sensitive temperament. Tina's propensity to "take things on" made teasing her a vicious sort of fun, and her tormentors—mostly Carmela, Kellisha, and Audra—persisted until she protested outright. "Taking it on"—internalizing social conflict—disrupts a person's inner equilibrium, leaving her open to the social discord that surrounds her. Although the workplace can be a stressful environment, some workers noted that the factory could also be a place to escape from the dramas and discord of home life. Dolores said that when you come to work you can "throw it off"—cast aside domestic strife and take a break from worrying about home.

While Trinidad's garment industry has always been plagued by poor working conditions (Trinidad and Tobago 1979), many workers at Signature Fashions note a marked decline in factory conditions since the 1980s, which they attribute to the withdrawal of state and trade-union interest in their industry. Workers employed in large factories (100–300 employees) in the 1970s and 1980s remember on-site health care for workers—including eye checks and reproductive health services—even in non-unionized workplaces. Josephine described the decline of conditions in factories like Signature Fashions:

> JOSEPHINE: We should have a kit, a medical kit. We don't have none . . . Longtime and with the government and all used to make sure we have all these kind of things. Why now all yuh stop? [Government inspectors should] pass around the factory and make sure people have the most simple things for people could use.
>
> REBECCA: The government used to inspect?
>
> JOSEPHINE: And now they don't! And all this is . . . they don't look in. They not doing their job. They could do better. They say it's we, ask them, is we the poor people put them there! Is the poor people voted them in.

Neoliberal reforms have not only devastated the local garment industry by thrusting Trinidadian producers into competition with foreign manufacturers; policies of privatization and cuts in public spending have also reduced social welfare provisions by the Trinidadian state (Riddell 2003; Moonilal 2001; Mycoo 2006). However, as Jessica Smith Rolston (2010:332) reminds us, "Neoliberal social processes exist alongside and in tension with others that contradict their logic." In addition to these structural reforms, the 1990s also saw the adoption into national law of maternity leave benefits and a minimum wage (USDS 2001:7). In Trinidad, there remains commitment to various forms of state paternalism, producing a neoliberalism tempered by state-funded ventures, including employment relief programs, basic health services, old-age pensions, youth training programs, and subsidized public housing.[3] For employees, although the minimum wage and statutory maternity leave are enshrined in national law, provisions for medical benefits, paid sick leave, overtime pay, paid public holidays, annual vacation leave, incentive allowance, protective clothing and protective gear, and funeral leave are either noncompulsory or largely unenforced (Moonilal 2001:38–39). Workers at Signature Fashions do not have private medical insurance, sick leave, vacation leave, or a company pension plan.

Although the 1979 Industrial Relations Act enshrines the right of workers to organize their workplace, there is little trade unionism in the garment sector today. Garment workers' belief that trade unions are no longer interested in their welfare is confirmed by trade unionists' own description of the situation. As one labor organizer said to me, the garment industry is not a priority because trade unions have been "on the defensive for very many years," struggling for resources and political clout, while the garment industry is not only small but dwindling.[4] Despite the fact that some Signature Fashions workers secretly belonged to trade unions in case they ever needed to raise a claim in Industrial Court, they had little appetite for collective action. During the oil boom of the 1970s and early 1980s, many garment workers participated in industrial actions that ultimately led to a worsening—not improvement—of their working conditions, leaving workers disheartened by the notion of collective solidarity. As Donna told me, "At a next place I worked, we had a strike and t'ing. We start a union. But they closed down the factory because they didn't want a union running it." Given the ineffectuality and seeming pointlessness of their labor activism, workers choose to remember instead the drama and mayhem of the strikes in which they took part, "marching with placard" and watching "some workers and them beat the supervisor." These memories evoke a Carnivalesque atmosphere that references Trinidad's yearly tradition of public catharsis. Trade unionism is thus understood not to be a sustained movement that could materially benefit workers but instead as a collection of momentary incidents of "confusion" and "bacchanal"—Trinidadian terms that convey useless, if pleasurable, frenzy (Miller 1994a:49, 300; Birth 2008:15).

Given narratives of desertion and decline in the garment industry like the one voiced by Josephine, the passage by Parliament of the Occupational Safety and Health Act (OSHA) in February 2004 caused little stir at Signature

Fashions. Like many trade unionists, journalists, and social commentators, workers believed OSHA was designed specifically for the oil, natural gas, and construction industries, which had experienced a number of high-profile occupational injuries and deaths in previous years. While OSHA's main provisions included the creation of an oversight body with more power than the existing Factories Inspectorate, tighter occupational health guidelines, and broader latitude for workers to challenge the acceptability of their working conditions, many were skeptical of its vigorous application in the garment industry (cf. Danny-Maharaj 2004; Richards 2005).

Garment workers perceive their working bodies to be of little concern to the government agencies tasked with protecting them. Signature Fashions workers believed their employers provided less than they should to protect and maintain the health of the workforce. They attributed this in part to the small size and declining economic importance of their industry and in part to Robert and Helene's improvised and unencumbered approach to factory management. Workers were particularly annoyed that they were only paid for days they worked in the factory (not for sick days or vacation days), as if they were independent contractors rather than full-time employees. They were grateful to Robert and Helene for the cushioned chairs in the new factory, which seemed to demonstrate esteem for the workers' professionalism. Yet the appearance of these chairs highlights the casualization and depoliticization of the employer-employee relationship. Workers did not interpret the chairs within a legalistic framework whereby working conditions constitute a basic labor right. Instead, workers accepted the chairs as a favor from Robert and Helene, for which they were genuinely grateful.

In seeking a felicitous convergence of autonomy, flow, and cool social relationships in the factory, Signature Fashions workers construct a fragile moral economy: collectively defining the tolerable limits of the working body, what a fair distribution of work looks like, and how employers should address workers. Signature Fashions workers do not believe work should never harm. Certain kinds of impairments are considered inevitable, as captured by Kavita's statement, "People in sewing always need glasses." Workers calculate the manageability of these risks when considering whether a job is worthwhile. As the epigraph to this chapter indicates, for some garment workers the burden of self-care is too great, and they leave factory employment when they "couldn't afford the medicine no more."

Just as Signature Fashions workers carry their own tools to the factory, train themselves for new sewing tasks, and pilfer garments, fabrics, and pattern designs, they manage their own health as a self-directed project. In this respect, their experience resonates with that of the Indian factory workers described by Jamie Cross (2010b:233), whose employers have "situated risk at the level of the individual worker and devolved responsibility for health and well-being to them." Where workers are entrusted with this burden of safety and self-care, a claim of injury may be interpreted as a sign of breakdown in the moral order and a challenge to the seemingly consensual labor relations within which neoliberal subjectivities are formed.

"It Hurtin' Meh Hand": Rhonda's Story

During one week in April, I noticed Rhonda operating three machines by herself: a buttonhole stitcher, a button tacker, and a binding-cutting machine. Over two or three days, my attention was drawn to watching her work. Rhonda darted between the machines all day, cutting binding whenever a front worker needed it, tacking buttons when Lystra reprimanded her for not tacking enough buttons, and working the buttonhole maker as well on the growing mound of shirts piled next to the machine.

As I observed Rhonda's perpetual movement, I considered it an apt rendering of Signature's particular form of industrial flexibility. Rhonda's work required her to respond to a constantly changing set of production demands, yet she was not expected to plan, anticipate, or organize her own work. In contrast to the "flat organizational structure [and] decentralized decision making" (Ferguson and Gupta 2002:998) often said to be the hallmarks of post-Fordism, Signature Fashions required Rhonda to be responsive but uninformed. She was obliged to work in a permanent state of readiness, responding to the changing demands of management beneath a spray of criticism that embodied the whip-crack of the "slave-driver situation." More than once I heard Cissy shout, "You not finished with that yet?" Helene was a rare presence on the shop floor that week, only adding to the pressure to be seen as working proficiently.

The button tacker (see figure 6.1) is a small sewing machine that attaches buttons to garments. It rests in the back area because affixing buttons is the final sewing operation, and its location in a low-status part of the shop floor contributes to the perception that button tacking is unskilled labor. It is the first machine I operated when I began doing participant observation in the factory. The machine's action is powerful; the first time I operated it, I nearly jumped out of my chair from the vibrations of the needle pummeling the cloth.

In the weeks leading up to this incident, the button tacker had been increasingly "giving trouble." Its needle, which quickly darts in and out of the buttonholes in a rapid-fire movement—*ratatatatatatatatat*—was constantly falling into misalignment, getting caught on the edge of a button and breaking off. Like many of the machines at Signature Fashions, the button tacker was bought secondhand from another factory that had closed down. Despite the efforts of Cissy, Robert, and the local mechanic who gave the machines a weekly tune-up, the button tacker continued to break needles. Workers described this machine as "givin' trouble" and, when they were more annoyed with it, as being "mash up" because it simply "cyan [can't] work at all."

In March, Lystra berated the back workers who used the machine for breaking too many needles. She decided it was the machine's intense vibrations that caused the needle to skip so wildly out of place and therefore instituted a new rule: a worker should hold the sides of the machine while stitching buttons, wrapping her forearms around its base to cushion the vibrations while it was tacking. When the machine continued to break needles despite being held this way, Lystra decided that only one worker should operate it: Rhonda. Even though Rhonda was already the sole worker on the buttonhole stitcher and binding-cutting machine, Lystra probably selected her to operate the button tacker because she is seen as a relaxed, able, and trusted employee. Rhonda had worked at Signature Fashions for four of her eighteen years in the industry.

Rhonda worked the button tacker for a couple of days until her arms began to ache. Rhonda had seldom experienced physical discomfort from sewing before, but having to use her arms to cover a broken machine proved too much. One afternoon, after working the machine all morning, Rhonda approached Cissy and told her she could no longer work the button tacker. "It hurtin' meh hand," she told Cissy quietly. In Trinidad, the word "hand" is used to refer to the entire arm.

Cissy's response to Rhonda's complaint was immediate. She crossed the shop floor and approached Helene, who was inspecting some finished

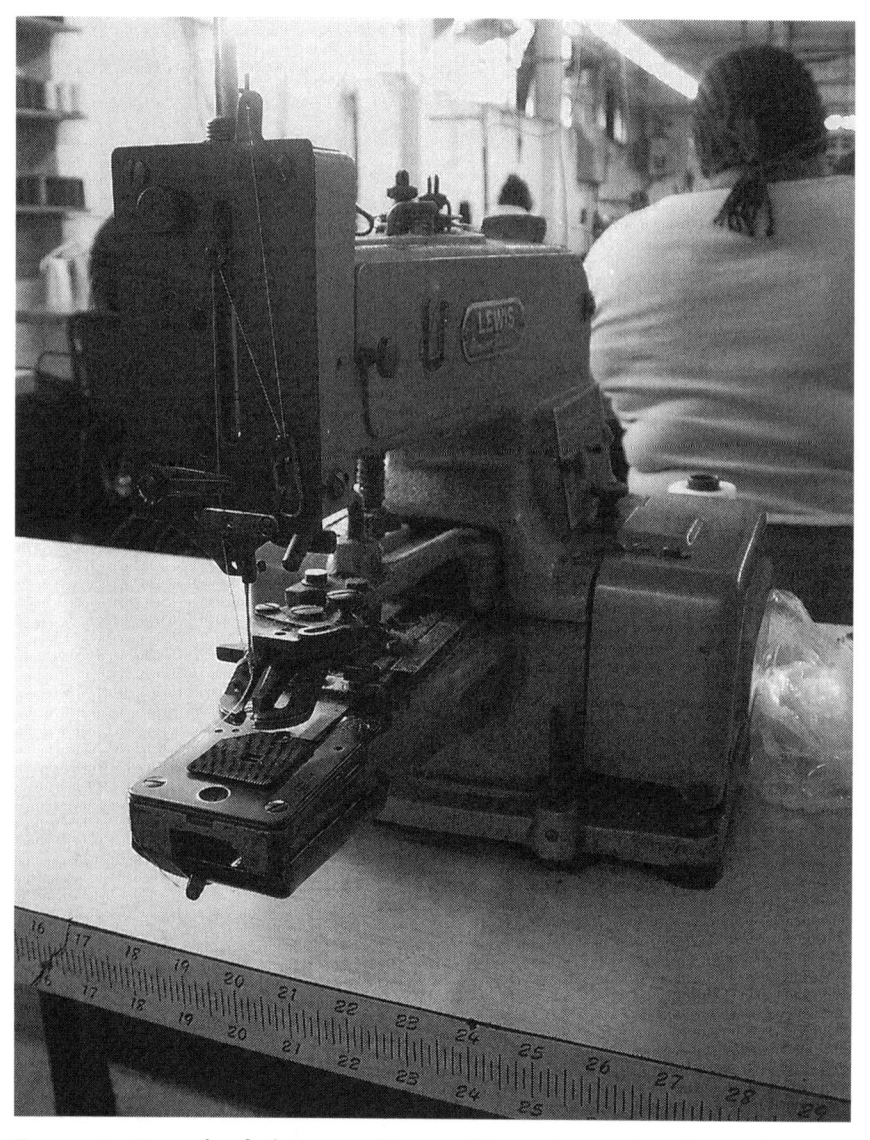

FIGURE 6.1. Example of a button-tacking machine at Universal Uniforms (photo by author)

garments being packaged for sale. Cissy told Helene not that Rhonda was being hurt by the machine but that she had refused to work on it anymore.

"I don't like that at all," announced Helene. "You come here to *work*."

Helene withdrew to her office upstairs, to which Rhonda was soon summoned. The back area grew quiet as the workers watched Rhonda climb the stairs behind Cissy. Around the trimming table where I stood, gossip began circulating.

"That machine ehnt no good," said Carmela with a sniff.

Josephine said, "You could work that machine. Ehnt no problem with that machine."

Lystra came and stood beside me, reminding me that the machine could be made operable if the worker used her whole body: "You see, you does have to hold it at the sides, and she ehnt want to hold the machine. The machine *is* giving trouble, but you have to hold it."

Cissy came back downstairs and asked Josephine to follow her upstairs. Josephine bounded up the stairs behind Cissy, causing Carmela to giggle, "Josey running!" Josephine came back to the shop floor a few minutes later, joining a group of us at the trimming table. As the workers jostled to hear what had happened, Josephine turned to Amanda.

"You tack buttons?" asked Josephine.

Amanda said yes, of course she did.

Josephine continued, "That machine damage your hand?"

Amanda said other than when a needle went in her finger, no.

"Oh ho," said Josephine, nodding as if Amanda had confirmed something for her. Josephine explained that Rhonda was upstairs saying she didn't want to work the button tacker anymore because "it hurt she hand." At this, the workers in the trimming area erupted into fierce debate about the appropriateness and veracity of Rhonda's complaint, which I quickly jotted down:

"That's not right, you do the work they give you."

"If it hurt *my* hand, I use a next hand. That's what you do."

"But that machine *is* giving trouble."

"You come to work, you should do the work."

"That machine ehnt no good."

Josephine explained that Rhonda was complaining about having to cradle the base of the machine while tacking buttons. I had worked the machine only the week before and similarly felt painful vibrations traveling up my arms as I tried to steady it. I was at first surprised by Josephine's lack of support for Rhonda's claim that the machine was hurting her; I then realized that Josephine would probably be called to work the machine if Rhonda did not.

158 THIEFING A CHANCE

I had also never heard Josephine complain about work of any kind, which may be why she was chosen to testify about the machine's condition. As conversations continued to circulate, someone said Rhonda had been overheard talking on her cell phone during lunch and telling her godson, "I fed up."

Sitting upstairs with Helene and Cissy, Rhonda received a scolding and a choice: go back to work on the machine, or go home for good. Cissy declared that Rhonda had a bad attitude because she aspired to work on one of the straight-stitch sewing machines in the front of the factory rather than on her assigned machines "to the back." Rhonda remained in Helene's office for at least ten minutes, after which time she quietly returned to the shop floor, tugging her dust mask across her face. Rhonda's reappearance was greeted with silence from the other workers. Returning to the machine she had complained about and silently taking up her work signaled her capitulation to management's insistence that she operate a broken machine. As she began to tack more buttons, it seemed to me that she was fighting back tears. With the earpieces of her personal radio tucked into her ears, she looked like she wanted to be left alone.

Later, when Rhonda got out of her chair to mark up some shirts for buttons, Helene saw her and called me over. "Tell her you supposed to be marking those shirts." Feeling like a traitor, I walked over to Rhonda and said, "Helene says I am supposed to mark the shirts." As she turned away, I lamely said, "You okay?" Rhonda turned her back to me and sat down without a word.

Discussions over what had happened to Rhonda continued over the next couple of hours and from time to time over the next few days. Workers' opinions on the situation were spatially marked. Those most remote from the scene—like Veena, Veronica, and Prabha, who worked on straight-stitch sewing machines at the opposite end of the shop floor—pressed me for details about what had happened and commiserated over the story as they understood it: that Rhonda had been made to operate a broken machine. Veena regretted the unfairness of the situation: "Rebecca, you see how things does be here?" Rhonda was perceived as being correct for refusing to do work that "t'ing her up" and "damage she hand."

The back workers closer to Rhonda, many of whom had witnessed the actual events that day, expressed a startling hostility toward Rhonda's handling of the situation. All agreed that the machine "does give trouble," but some later described her response that day as far more aggressive and active than I had observed. Rhonda, it was said, should have kept her cool and was wrong to get upset and go "marching" up to the office to complain. No one disputed that the machine was "giving trouble" and that the factory owners frequently bought "some mash-up old thing" instead of newer, costlier machines. What was at issue was whether the machine had "damage she hand."

As Sarah Jain (2006:82) has argued, injuries are not axiomatic but instead require validation within specific institutional frameworks and hierarchies of knowledge. Because a claim of injury may be accepted or rejected, injury-making is a profoundly social process whereby experiences of harm seek acknowledgment and, often, recompense. At Signature Fashions, injuries that draw blood are immediately recognized, as when Ram sliced his hand on the cutting machine or when Nalini broke a needle into her finger. For these acute injuries, the worker immediately leaves the factory (sometimes, but not always, accompanied by Cissy) and walks a short distance across the highway to the free government clinic in El Socorro. National Insurance, deducted weekly from employees' wages, compensates workers for days lost to work-related injury. Small cuts and bruises are dealt with in the factory by supervisors applying iodine solution and wrapping a spare piece of cotton fabric around the wound. While some workers complained about the factory's lack of first-aid necessities, others were more sanguine; said Antoinette, "I does use masking tape and a piece of cloth. I does make my own [bandage]." Unlike the acute injuries that are swiftly addressed, the pain Rhonda complained about is subjective and unverifiable and therefore easy to dismiss (cf. DelVecchio Good et al. 1992).

The shop-floor debates circulating in the wake of Rhonda's confrontation with management shared many characteristics with those that occurred after Lata was caught thiefing a chance (chapter 4). Just as workers did not immediately condemn Lata for snitching to Cissy about Kimberly's shirt, they also did not rush to support Rhonda in her injury claim. Both situations exemplify the thiefing-a-chance subjectivities workers at Signature Fashions have come to embody: independence, autonomy, and a strategizing self. Even though workers rely on one another to complete tasks, to control the pace and sequence of their work, and to covertly make garments for themselves, they embrace a vision of themselves as individuated subjects by framing these activities as personal choices rather than collective enterprises. The intrusion of Rhonda's injury on the shop floor draws attention to the material fact of bodily vulnerability and therefore might have posed a challenge to the triumphant neoliberal rhetoric of thiefing a chance. As Emily Martin (1994) has observed of workers in late-capitalist America, "flexible" subjectivities are threatened by the injured or diseased body, which must be excluded if it cannot be made to fit the discourse. In complaining about the button tacker, Rhonda portrayed herself as vulnerable and needing care, a self-image that violates the individualistic and enterprising ethos of thiefing a chance. As one back worker said of Rhonda's complaint, "If it hurt my hand, I use a next hand. That's what you do."

When I asked Rhonda to recount the incident for my tape recorder some weeks later, she was eager to tell her side of the story. In narrating her experience, she emphasized her reputation as a good worker, which she felt had been tarnished by Cissy's accusations. Rhonda began her story with an assessment of the machine. She said, "Well, the button-tack machine is a machine that does give trouble at times. And sometimes when you see the needle break, as I'm sure you realize, plenty of the workers in the back there don't like to go on the button-tack machine."

Rhonda's recollection of the incident moved quickly from the material fact of the broken machine and her physically having to "cover" it to her indignation over how she had been treated by management: "So when the needle break, sometimes it could hit you in your face, it could hit you in your chest. All those things. And then my fingers, the way how I was holding on both sides of the machine, my fingers and them started hurting—don't [you] mind Helene and them was telling me they don't really see anything wrong in that. I does tell them, since I working at Signature *no* machine is too hard for me to work."[5] With her body rebelling against the task assigned to her, Rhonda perceived the machine not as an object separate from the politics of authority at Signature Fashions but instead as their material form. Rhonda had been pushed hard those days, shifting among three machines, propelled by the incessant reprimands of her supervisors. The discipline required of her was not simply the work rhythms of the industrial factory but also the spatial discipline of commanding three machines simultaneously without the independence to decide how and when to work on each one. Being asked to cover a defective machine with her own body pushed Rhonda past her limit.

Management, in disavowing her claim to injury, invalidated Rhonda's authority to speak from the location of her embodied experience. Although Rhonda asserted a material grievance ("it hurtin' meh hand"), management undermined the principal basis of her allegation by recasting the problem as one of "attitude" rather than injury. Portraying Rhonda as an employee who stubbornly refused to do the work she was assigned, Cissy accused her of wanting to perform the higher-status (and often more highly paid) work in the front of the factory rather than her less-valued back work. Given that the Signature Fashions factory had evolved into a racially marked domain in which the "front" of the factory was mostly occupied by Indo-Trinidadian women, it would indeed have been rare for someone like Rhonda, an Afro-Trinidadian from the East-West Corridor, to advance to the front of the shop floor. The implicit injuries to class and race contained in Cissy's and Helene's words are countered in Rhonda's re-telling of the incident:

> It had times sometimes when we'd be doing buttons, we used to have to tack it with our hands, especially when they doing jackets and things. It has buttons they does buy sometimes. And I will sit down and I will tack out the *majority* of them with my hand. Because the workers and them and all to the back used to tell me, "Rhonda, you does want to play like you is Speedy Gonzales, you does want to do everything," and I say it is not a matter of that. When I come to work, I like to work. I don't like to take my time to do nothing. I just do what I have to do and get it over and done with. I don't like to sit down and linger, that is not *me*.

Rhonda expressed pleasure in her speed and efficiency, rehabilitating an image of self as fast, flexible, and responsive. Rhonda rejected Cissy's assertion that she despised her status as a back worker, proclaiming allegiance with "workers and them to the back." The back workers' recognition of her speed and skill is given as evidence of a strong work ethic. While Rhonda notes the unfairness of being asked to work on a broken machine, she does not linger over an indictment of the factory owners' negligence but instead emphasizes her distress at being depicted as a bad employee.

Lystra, Rhonda's supervisor, played a crucial role in the conflict. Having been scolded by Cissy because too many needles were breaking in her section, Lystra's response was to devise a new bodily discipline—making workers cover the button tacker with their arms—that later gained legitimacy when Cissy and Helene insisted it was the proper way to operate the machine. The Signature Fashions factory thus relies on collusion between supervisors and workers to keep production going, even at the expense of workers' bodies. While Lystra may have been sympathetic to Rhonda's pain, in her role of supervisor she normalized the manipulation of her body to operate the machine: "The machine *is* giving trouble, but you have to hold it."

A worker's experience of pain, anguish, and other forms of social disordering can be considered a somatization of poor working conditions, whereby a hyper-intensive labor regime becomes "imprinted on the body of the working subject" (Cross 2010b:227). The "painful body" in the workplace, then, can be interpreted as a "resistant body"—a body that attests to its own exploitation (Ngai 2005:22). This kind of embodied distress has been written about most famously by Aihwa Ong (1987a:210), who describes Malaysian factory workers' episodes of shop-floor spirit possession as an indirect form of resistance to the trauma of industrial labor. But for women workers, somatic resistance can only ever partially challenge shop-floor authority because it simultaneously reinforces ideologies of female weakness and dysfunction.

The problem for Rhonda is that by presenting herself as vulnerable and needing care, she constructs an image of self that is out of step with the flexible, self-reliant subjectivities her co-workers readily embrace. But management sees the Signature Fashions workers not as flexible, self-reliant actors but instead as an undisciplined and recalcitrant workforce requiring strict orchestration (see chapter 2). When Rhonda complains that her body is being made to replace the broken parts of an old machine, she is presented with a stark choice to realign her interests with those of her employers or to go home.

"It Ehnt Have Anything to Do with the Pressing": Audra's Story

"Labor power," writes John Davis, "is not a commodity which can be detached from a person and bought and sold like dry goods . . . it is an intimate part of the person" (Davis 1992:57, in Jiménez 2003:14). Because workers are social beings, they concern themselves with everyday battles of position to gain control, respect, and tolerable working conditions. An attack on their dignity and sense of self-worth can be as serious as a bodily injury.

Audra had been working as a presser (ironer) at Signature Fashions for more than five years. Mischievous and garrulous, Audra was often described as "a back worker for true," prone to gossip and the boastful chatter known as *picong*. At forty years old, Audra had already raised three children to adulthood, mostly on her own, in the East Port of Spain neighborhood of Morvant. Her previous jobs include working in catering and food services and working as a presser at a laundromat. Although Audra loves to cook and dreams of one day opening her own snack bar, throughout her professional life her jobs have mostly involved heavy physical labor. Her work at Signature Fashions was no different.

Workers considered pressing—ironing the garments once they have been sewn—the most dangerous and demanding work in the factory. When asked what job should be paid best at Signature Fashions, almost every worker said with little hesitation, "The pressers. Because they have to take that *heat*." Standing on one's feet and ironing garments all day is perceived as treacherous work, particularly because of the hazards of working with steam. A serger named Devi said to me, looking over at the pressing area, "That [steam] could rip out your skin. I couldn't work over there with that steam, not me. I say *nah*." I asked her to elaborate why she would not want to work as a presser:

DEVI: Because you pressing whole day and then you go out and rain could be falling. And you know what *that* mean. And the pressers, they have to go home and do their work there, go in the fridge. You have to do water work at home.

REBECCA: And that could make you sick?

DEVI: Yeah, man.

REBECCA: It would make you sick right away or later on?

DEVI: You could get stroke. It could happen then, or it could happen later. Or arthritis from hot and cold. My mother, she have pain in the evening—hand hurting her, foot hurting her. That arthritis.

The insistence that "heat" makes pressing a dangerous job reflects a common Trinidadian health principle ("you know what *that* mean"). Prolonged exposure to heat "opens" the body and renders it vulnerable when quickly followed by a cool element like rainwater or opening a refrigerator door and feeling a blast of cold air (Littlewood 1988:132; Dressler 1982:98).

The heat of pressing makes the work arduous. As Imelda, one of the pressers at Signature Fashions told me: "You know the heat, sometimes it does draw all your strength. You just feel so tired. Sometimes when I does go home in the maxi, I feel so tired that I fall asleep on myself. It so *tiring*. The heat, it does make you weary." Working with heat not only enervates the pressers; doing the job also curtails their ability to perform domestic chores after work that require the use of cold or wet substances, such as cooking, cleaning, and washing clothes. Even leaving work and walking in the evening "dew" can chill a body overheated by steam. Although some workers dismiss the danger of following heat with cold as a superstition, most pressers take steps to manage the risk. One strategy is to try to relax when reaching home and attempt to "cool you-self out" before bathing or cooking. Imelda would "go and sweat out the heat" on her walk home and then, "When I does reach home I *relax* myself a little and then *warm* water and bathe."

Unlike other pressers, Audra rarely worried about the hot-and-cold contrasts in her work. She did not avoid the cool evening air and said she would rather hurry home in a little rainfall than stand under the factory's front awning and delay her departure until the showers had passed. Her indifference to the supposed dangers of working as a presser was notable, given a very public conflict that had taken place between Audra and Helene the year before.

One afternoon, Audra was working in the pressing area, next to a younger employee named Dora, when Libby, the cleaner, started mopping the floor where they were working. Dora, according to Audra, "is very fussy. So the cleaner's cleaning, and she's wetting the area where we were pressing. I don't fuss over them things. But Dora said, 'Don't wet here, we're pressing.'" Dora's comment to Libby led to some back-and-forth bickering between them. The commotion was overheard by Helene, who had been standing in the cutting room. Helene came into the pressing area and approached Audra directly. Audra recounts:

> I wasn't saying anything, I wasn't involved in it. But Helene came straight at me. What she always does. If something is not done properly, she always comes straight at *me*. She came straight at me, and . . . she started quarrelling with me.
>
> I said, "I didn't say anything!"

So she say to me, "So you mean if you get wet, it's not go do you anything? What's your problem? If you're pressing, and she's mopping here and you're pressing, ehnt nothing go happen to you."

And so I said, "I didn't say *anything*."

Audra has long believed that Helene dislikes her, and she saw Helene's intervention in the quarrel between Dora and Libby as an attempt to hassle her. Audra told me that Helene often blamed her for "making trouble" and had once accused her of stealing, asking to see the contents of her bag before she left work. She said, "Some people just don't like [some] people. I figure that Helene and me just didn't really get along."

Helene demanded that Audra admit that getting wet while pressing did not constitute a health hazard. Because it was Dora, not Audra, who had complained about it, Audra refused to take a position on the matter and only repeated, "I didn't say anything about that." Lystra tried to intervene on Audra's behalf, declaring, "Helene, Audra didn't say anything." Says Audra:

> AUDRA: [Helene] didn't want to hear that. She carried on. And she pick up this bottle of water. She say, "So let's see if you get wet—if you're pressing and you get wet—if you'll die tomorrow!"
>
> REBECCA: She said that?
>
> AUDRA: Yes. She take a bottle of water and say, "Can I wet you? Can I wet you?" Well, I usually wash my hands when I'm pressing, so I know I'm not going to die if I get wet . . . I said, "Well, you could wet my hands, yes." She wet my hands. "What about your foot? I could wet your foot?" I said, "No, I don't want my foot wet."

Despite Audra's protestations, Helene sprayed the water bottle onto Audra's leg, "wetting it up" as she stood there. Audra finished her story: "I [had] said, 'Helene, don't wet my foot.' And she went and wet my foot anyhow. I didn't say anything. I just went home and didn't go back." The incident took place on a Friday; Audra collected her pay packet and left work at the end of the day, intending never to return to Signature Fashions. Over the weekend she was able to secure a new job as a presser at a nearby factory, where she worked for two days. She found the working conditions in the other factory intolerable, so when Cissy called her the following week to say that Helene would apologize if she came back to work, Audra agreed.

This story resonates because it depicts "the body" center stage in the struggle for authority and dignity on the shop floor. Helene sprayed Audra purportedly to disprove a false notion that mixing the "heat" of the steam with the "cool" of soapy water posed a threat to a worker's health. Audra read Helene's action as a profound assault on her sense of personhood. What began as a dispute about the dangers of mixing hot and cold had ended in a physical display of Helene's power, which for Audra transgressed reasonable authority in both its arbitrariness and its intimate nature. For Audra, her only choice was to quit her job. She maintained a cool demeanor and simply walked out the door after receiving her pay. She said later: "You see, when I get really vex, I try not to say anything . . . I went home and I didn't come back. Nobody knew I wasn't coming back."

Although physical discipline was not uncommon at Signature Fashions, the incident between Audra and Helene diverged considerably from the usual forms of discipline to which workers were accustomed. Cissy was an ever-present figure on the shop floor, but Helene was generally removed from the factory's daily operations. With their rare appearances in the "downstairs" of the factory, Helene and Robert were often invoked by workers as the sympathetic but remote "bosses" of the operation, in comparison to Cissy, the unrelenting figure of direct supervision. Workers bragged when they had work to do "for Helene"—specific projects she brought to them—taking delight in telling Cissy that they could not do *her* work at the time. Once, when Robert witnessed a metal horse fall on Bernice's leg, his solicitous aid was well appreciated, and afterward Bernice kept repeating, "Robert said I supposed to sit down today." The widespread characterization of Robert and Helene as tightfisted was always shadowed by a secondary depiction of the factory owners as potential patrons, if only a worker could somehow activate a relationship of mutual obligation and care. This image of the factory owners as distantly benevolent made both Audra's and Rhonda's confrontations with Helene particularly bitter.

In Audra's re-telling of her story, she emphasized that the conflict had not been about the dangers of mixing hot and cold elements. Audra understood Helene's behavior as a high-handed attempt to disabuse her of an old-fashioned belief; she also believed that Helene specifically had it in for her. Although Audra never directly critiqued Helene's behavior in class or racial terms, such elements are clearly in evidence in the story: the asserted superiority of Helene's biomedical understandings of illness etiology over the folk beliefs she projected onto Audra, Helene's easy appropriation of Audra's body, and Audra's conviction that she, an Afro-Trinidadian back worker, was simply not "liked" by Helene. This is why Audra refused to be drawn into a debate about the health risks of mixing hot and cold—not with Helene during the incident or with me when I interviewed her later with an anthropologist's curiosity about traditional belief systems. For Audra, the confrontation represented the much deeper issue of her physical autonomy:

[Helene] said, "Why you don't want your foot wet?"

I said, "Because I don't *want* my foot wet." It didn't have nothing to do with . . . I don't like my foot wet, it feeling *funny*. So, it ehnt have anything to do with the pressing [hot-and-cold contrasts] and all that. It just feel funny if it get wet.

Helene later claimed she had been joking and had not meant to hurt Audra's feelings. Audra accepted Helene's apology as a condition of returning to work "because it's Helene's factory. So I couldn't come back without that from her." Yet Audra refused to accept Helene's interpretation of the incident as joking gone awry; she knew that for that to have been the case, Audra and Helene would have to have been on far more equal footing than they were.

Aihwa Ong (1991:286) has described the disciplining of the industrial workforce as "an intricate, long-drawn-out process involving a mixture of repression, habituation, co-option, and cooperation within the workplace and throughout society." Within factory structures of hierarchy and authority, workers usually consent to their working conditions. While Foucault's notion of "governmentality" captures the ways workers participate in the governance of themselves by enacting the various bodily disciplines required of them, Gramsci reminds us that seemingly consensual relations can be haunted by the threat of coercion (Foucault 1991; Gramsci 1971). When an argument on the shop floor between Donna and Cissy once culminated in Cissy's announcement to the workers "who don't want to work can *leave*," Jean said to me later, "Everyone there needs the money. No one was going to go." Workers are keen to hold on to their jobs at Signature Fashions, which pays the minimum wage and provides steady work in an air-conditioned setting. Workers consent to some aspects of their exploitation, believing what is otherwise available may be worse.[6]

Rhonda's and Audra's stories are curiously claustrophobic, referring only to the tightly woven relationships between workers and managers in a small factory; neither account evokes external agencies, laws, or even a broader discourse of labor rights. Although occupational injury in some instances can form the critical base for an emergent worker consciousness (Susser 1988:195), both Rhonda's and Audra's accounts exemplify instead the individual and individualizing strategies of Signature Fashions workers. The construction of a worker collectivity that could struggle together seems absent, even from the workers' imagination. Their memories of failed labor activism in the 1980s evoked feelings of disappointment and convinced them of the futility of collective solidarity. Trade unions are perceived to be rife with political in-fighting and leaders trying to "get for themselves" rather than a sustained movement that could actually help them. The use of trade unions now is strategic: some workers joined in secret as a type of insurance in case they should someday need to raise a claim in the Industrial Court, which can only be done through a recognized trade union (Moonilal 2001). These two stories demonstrate some of the different strategies workers enact. While management's judgment of the situation holds sway, workers are left to pursue their own tactics of acceptance, withdrawal, playful ridicule, or pursing their own projects (thiefing a chance).

Rhonda's and Audra's stories demonstrate how power relations on the shop floor are mediated by technology. While some scholars argue that working bodies within a Fordist labor regime become an extension of factory tools, "the final attachment to the industrial machine" (Belmonte 1979, in Scheper-Hughes and Lock 1987:23), workers at Signature Fashions constantly struggle with and against their machines. Labor discipline is most fully achieved through workers' willingness to take on these machines as individual struggles (Ong 1987b). Because workers have to match their bodies to requirements, the manufacturing process individuates workers through their responses to these material conditions. Lateral conflict between themselves and their machines can therefore obscure and even preclude direct struggles with management.

The factory owners' procurement of cheap, secondhand machines is a continual source of discussion. Their reputed desire to "get a good bargain" on "old, old machines" is constant fodder for joking among workers. These jokes form a critique of workplace conditions and what workers are asked to endure. Yet behind the jokes about their employers' stinginess lies resentment for the fact that the old machines and lack of benefits sometimes make workers' already difficult position intolerable.

Conclusions

A year after returning to England, I received a letter from Glenda. She told me she had stopped working at Signature Fashions and was staying at home with her mother instead: "I prayed God make a way for me, and I took it." She was receiving US$99 a month from her brother in the United States and an additional US$200 from her husband. Her son had found a job. She wrote, "The workers [at Signature] always wanted to know how I made out, but I never told them. It's one thing that I'm glad for Rebecca, is I never had to go back and ask back for my work because things didn't work out, I didn't want to go back either." She had begun treatment for glaucoma at a hospital clinic. She wrote, "This is the best my eyes has ever seen & felt to the past 2 to 2½ years . . . am eating oranges and carrot for the eyes, orange has vitamin E for the eyes."

Glenda also reported some changes in the factory:

> Several workers left Signature, besides myself. Peggy in the cutting room left, she got a job at Mount Hope hospital. Shirl on the machine, she stay home with the kids. Kimberly on the machine got another job. Jean got another job, they wanted to put her to iron, Helene gave her the offer, but she said no. The two pressers (ironers), Audra & Dora got other jobs, they moved Amanda from tagging too slow & talking too much. Robert (the boss) on the job, is on the floor and he have them straight as a pin, no sitting down for the trimmers, and he moved them more up to the front, where Cissy could see them.

While reading the letter, I remembered Glenda's advice whenever I was frustrated at work. One time after Brenda approached me and said, "Oh, so you didn't cut the straps?" I became upset because no one had told me to cut them. Glenda said to me, "Don't take that on. Count the days, count the days until you go."

I said with a laugh, "Is that what you do?"

"Yes," she said, "I do."

For Glenda, retiring from Signature Fashions was only partially catalyzed by her deteriorating eyesight; she had cultivated a desire to leave the factory for some time, and her failing vision gave her the leverage to acquire financial support from her brother. Her strategy of withdrawal resonates with many workers at Signature Fashions. Workers frequently responded to workplace difficulties with the phrase "I leaving just now": an individualized tactic of endurance, then escape once another opportunity (or "chance") could be seized. Glenda portrays her successful departure from Signature Fashions as an act of rebellion, imbued with the furtive pleasure of running away. I was not surprised to learn that several workers have left Signature Fashions since the completion of my fieldwork; the trope of escape was constantly evoked in the factory and represented one of the most popular strategies of personal resistance.

Glenda's letter also describes changes to the arrangement and supervision of the shop floor. The spatial logics of "front" and "back" divided workers at Signature Fashions into a racialized landscape of production. Glenda's description of the trimming section being moved to the front of the shop floor implies a disruption to this spatial ordering of the factory and so, potentially, its most trenchant racial features. Yet Helene's reported attempt to move Jean out of her stitching job and into a pressing one suggests that the logics of front-and-back organization—in which classed and raced subjects are perceived as appropriate for different types of factory work—still prevailed.

I have argued throughout this book that it is Signature Fashions workers—through their labors, patience, and creative willingness to withstand contingency—who impute flexibility into what is often an unwieldy, inflexible production system. Workers try to make the most of what the factory can offer them: new skills and access to new ideas, opportunities to thief a chance, a day-to-day work regimen that is usually perceived to be tolerable and comparatively well-paid, and the local status that comes from working for one of the "best" brands in the country. Within the material context of the factory, workers experience themselves as individuated subjects, capable of making and taking opportunities. Placing "the body" at the center of analysis asks to what extent bodily vulnerability disrupts the triumphant narratives of autonomy encapsulated in thiefing a chance. As Emily Martin (1994) tells us, the dynamic, flexible, and individualistic subjectivities that characterize the late capitalist era rely on bodies that are healthy and active. However, while incidents of distress, pain, and illness might have served to counter the triumphalism of thiefing a chance, they instead reveal how depoliticized and individuated the worker-employer relationship is. Although worker flexibility is essential, styles of management at Signature Fashions can be punitive and intrusive; the employee's dynamism is not recognized, and neither is the company's dire need for it.

Turning to chapter 7, we do well to keep in mind Sherry Ortner's assertion that "vulnerable bodily beings are also bearers of reflective consciousness, who can always imagine or fantasize escapes and alternatives" (Ortner 1996:14). The question becomes what spaces are available for garment workers to challenge or critique the economic conditions of their lives, given that their strategizing tactics of cunning self-reliance so often foreclose collective solidarity. Everyday discussions about "crime" (particularly kidnapping) on the shop floor are shown to be a means through which workers (and managers) narrate their experience of the neoliberal order. The language and conceptual categories with which they construct "talk of crime" (Caldeira 2000) reveal not only their perceptions about violence and insecurity but also how an attempt to critique a global economic order can become entangled in local politics of race and class.

Notes

1. This is one example of how illegal employment arrangements may actually correspond to workers' own preferences.

2. This is evident in *obeah* (sorcery) practices. Illness can be caused by animosity projected onto the person by an enemy aided by an obeah practitioner. While many Trinidadians dismiss obeah as superstitious witchcraft, most of the Trinidadians I knew, when faced with a persistent and seemingly incurable ailment, would at some point wonder if it was caused by the ill will of others: "if somebody want to do me something" (cf. Khan 2003:772).

3. Michelle Mycoo (2006:136) notes that despite Trinidad's prior commitment to a "philosophy of state paternalism," the reduction of state spending imposed by structural adjustment has necessitated severe cutbacks in education, housing, and health, which disproportionately affect the poor.

4. Trinidadian garment workers, it should be noted, played a key role in labor activism throughout the twentieth century (Kiely 1996; Reddock 1994). The 1930s labor revolts included a great deal of activity within the "women's sections" of trade unions, such as a prolonged strike of the Renown Garment Factory in 1939

over wages and working conditions (Concerned Women for Progress 1982:2; Reddock 1993:254–55). During the oil boom (1971–83), membership in trade unions peaked in Trinidad and Tobago as unions sought to press their advantage in a context of swift economic growth and labor shortages (Kiely 1996:156; Yelvington 1995:73). However, organized labor activities in garment factories could lead to firings, reprisals, and factory closures—frequently followed by reopenings under a new name (Trinidad and Tobago 1979). During the recession that followed the oil boom, "trade unions and their leaders were widely blamed for low worker productivity and high wages that combined to cripple industry" (Yelvington 1995:73). The post-boom period saw an overall decline in trade unionism not only in the garment industry but across all sectors (Kiely 1996:152). The National Trade Union Centre reported a net decline of trade-union membership of 40 percent between 1980 and 1998 (Moonilal 2001:15).

5. In the Chinese silk-weaving factory described by Lisa Rofel (1999), the "efficiency" and "productivity" of individual workers was publicly recorded and posted for all to see. In contrast, workers' "performance" in the Signature Fashions factory was mystified. Without a piece rate to measure their work against, workers had little sense of how much was required of them or how their performance rated against that of their co-workers. Cissy claimed to keep all of this information in a ledger. With no record of work performance available to public scrutiny, Cissy maintained absolute authority in naming who was working well and who was not. The decision to grant salary increases to some workers but not others relied on Cissy's records of employee performance.

6. As Kevin Yelvington and Trinidadian commentators have noted, dismissing a worker is not without costs for the employer. Trinidad's formula for severance pay "required the company to pay two weeks' pay for every year completed for workers with one to five years' service and three weeks' pay for every year completed for those workers with more than five years' service" (Yelvington 1995:113; ILO 2004). Thus an employer like Signature Fashions has a financial incentive to retain workers like Rhonda and Audra, who have worked at the company for more than four years. However, garment workers often complained of not receiving the amount due to them, and the cost of challenging severance pay was prohibitive (requiring the worker to first join a trade union, then open a claim in the Industrial Court). This demonstrates how the interests of workers (to keep their job) and employers (to avoid costly severance pay) sometimes converge, although workers perceive employers to have the upper hand.

7

"Kidnapping Go Build Back We Economy"

Criminal Tropes in Neoliberal Capitalism

VELMA: When it comes to *crime*, the Negro on the corner with the gold tooth is going to get stopped, but nobody stops the big man—the man bringing in the things. Who could bring in the guns, the little man or the big man? No, it's coming in the containers, in the containers with the cloth and all that.

REBECCA: Is it specifically fabric and clothes containers that smuggle in drugs and guns?

VELMA: Look who's bringing it in! How they could get so much money from cloth alone?

— *Velma, independent seamstress, Port of Spain*

Trinidad real nice. The onliest thing is the crime.
— *Kavita, Signature Fashions worker*

Fifteen days into my fieldwork, I sat watching the six o'clock news with two fellow residents of the Port of Spain women's hostel where I was living. The three of us sat on wooden chairs with plastic cushions, huddled around a television set in the front room of the hostel. My two companions, Arlene and Thea, were Afro-Trinidadian women from southern Trinidad attending nursing school in Port of Spain. The newsreader announced the recent kidnapping of fifty-six-year-old businessman Vernon Roopnarine, who had been seen by witnesses being bundled into a car outside his home in west-central Trinidad. Shortly after, Roopnarine's captors called his family and demanded a TT$500,000 ransom for his safe return.[1]

On the television, Roopnarine's brother wept openly as he pleaded for Vernon's release. I felt sympathetic tears springing to my own eyes—surprising myself—and turned to Arlene and Thea. "That's sad, eh?" I said.

"I don't find it so sad," said Thea.

Over the next half-hour, Arlene and Thea explained the situation as they understood it—"because you're not from here, you wouldn't know"—beginning with their assessment of Roopnarine's case. They told me that over the previous year, kidnapping-for-ransom had emerged as a new crime in Trinidad, the latest "fashion" among "bandits" looking for easy money. Arlene and Thea said they had little sympathy for Roopnarine's family because it had become commonplace for victims' families to cry on television, pleading their inability to meet the kidnappers' demands, even when it seemed evident that they could afford to pay ransom. Arlene suggested that the Roopnarine family was acting similarly to an "East Indian" family she knew in southern Trinidad whose eldest daughter had been kidnapped. She described the opulence and expanse of the family's home: "from this wall here, quite down to the main road" (a distance of forty yards). She said, "They say, 'We can't afford to pay . . .' They *lying*." Concerned that she had stoked my anxiety, Arlene added, "But don't worry, they ehnt go take some foreign person, you *perfectly* safe."

I could not have known it at the time, but my discussion with Arlene and Thea was to become emblematic of the many conversations I would have pertaining to class, race, politics, and crime both outside and inside the Signature Fashions factory. During my fifteen months of fieldwork, Trinidad's crime rate reportedly soared and was a constant source of daily discussion, political hand-wringing, and letters to the editor in national newspapers. Kidnapping became particular fodder for conversation because it produced such dramatic spectacle—the tearful family on the six o'clock news, for example—and provided an opportunity to engage themes of race and class that Trinidadians frequently discuss. Who deserved sympathy and who deserved blame were not universally agreed; individuals variously positioned in the social and economic matrices of society generated diverse and irreconcilable interpretations of events.

When I began working at Signature Fashions, I quickly discovered that crime was a topic of daily discussion on the shop floor. Conversations about crime were a means through which workers and managers could articulate their interpretations of recent changes in Trinidadian society and revealed the conceptual categories with which they diagnosed who might be to blame. During a dramatic rise of ransom abductions in 2003 and 2004, the garment industry found itself uniquely entangled in a national kidnapping crisis, for two reasons. First, Indo-Trinidadian owners of family enterprises like garment manufacturing were often represented in the public imaginary as prime targets for abduction by poor black criminals. Garment factories, with their legion of Indo-Trinidadian owners and managers and many workers from impoverished Afro-Trinidadian neighborhoods, became conceptualized as sites of a potentially risky mixture between antagonistic categories of people. Second, the widespread accusation that fabric importers were smuggling drugs and guns into Trinidad ("How they could get so much money from cloth alone?") interpreted the wealth of industry leaders as ill-gotten and their abduction as morally justifiable.

Recent anthropological literature explores how growing inequalities in Latin America and the Caribbean have been experienced and expressed in reference to crime (Auyero 2000; Caldeira 2000; Godoy 2006; Goldstein 2003; Taylor 2009). As neoliberal economic programs widen the gap between rich and poor and etch these inequalities into the landscape of the "dual city" (Mollenkopf and Castells 1991), the elite see their access to public spaces shrinking because of the fear of crime, which they experience as a deterioration of class privilege. The rise of gated communities in Trinidad reflects this "new form of territorial organization," whereby private security measures taken by upper-income and middle-income classes signal mistrust over the state's ability to safeguard its citizens (Mycoo 2006:132, 141).

Donna Goldstein (2003:175), writing about the Brazilian context, argues that Rio's wealthy citizens feel a keen sense of vulnerability that is expressed through recursive "talk of crime" (Caldeira 2000). Through such talk, they narrate their relationship to what they perceive to be an increasingly violent and dangerous society and craft justifications for brutal forms of residential segregation and personal security. Talk of crime is also ubiquitous among the poor but is more often tied to the direct experience of violence. For the poor, talk of crime may focus equally on criminals and the police, whom they position on a continuum of violence and victimization rather than in opposition to each other (Caldeira 2000:186; Goldstein 2003:206–7; Gray 2004:296–305). The poor may even celebrate the heroism, freedom, and pure justice represented by the outlaw who "rights wrongs" as a means of telescoping their own discontent over economic injustice (cf. Hobsbawm 1969).

Yet the existing literature on crime perception has led to a troubling bifurcation, whereby rich and poor are depicted as socially, economically, and residentially segregated. This neglects the fact that diverse social groups necessarily interact at the point of production. Factories like Signature Fashions represent an important site for shaping perceptions of crime because it is where people actually contend with social mixture (see chapter 3). On the shop floor, ideologies of social incompatibility confront the inherent interdependence of economic classes. An analytical emphasis on rich and poor has also left under-theorized the experiences and perceptions of a middle strata of owners and managers of small garment factories who feel vulnerable to crime yet do not possess the wealth to construct a "fortified enclave" (Caldeira 1996) for personal protection.

This chapter examines circulating discourses of crime at Signature Fashions and in a second factory, Universal Uniforms. By comparing the narratives of factory owners, who are manifestly anxious about kidnapping, and those of workers, who use talk of kidnapping to critique the relationship among race, class, business, and the neoliberal state, this chapter looks out to contemporary Trinidadian society from the situated place of the shop floor while at the same time looking *into* the factory from the external vantage of current events. In discussing the kidnapping crisis, workers, managers, and factory owners expressed anxiety about emerging inequalities that have slipped from the moorings of established economic and social hierarchies.

KIDNAPPING, CRIME, AND SECURITY

During my fieldwork, Trinidad's rising crime rate was a frequent source of day-to-day discussion, media commentary, debates on the floor of Parliament, and sermons from the pulpit (e.g., Beharry 2004; Johnson 2003; Pires 2004; Sooknanan 2004). With 260 murders during 2004, local reports described Trinidad as the world's fifth-most-"murderous" country per capita (*Trinidad Guardian* 2004, 2005). Although statistics are incomplete, kidnapping-for-ransom appeared to grow steeply over the same period, with as many as 163 abductions reported to the police and dozens more rumored to have been settled privately (Mahabir 2005). Some commentators have fixed blame for violent crime on local actors by citing youth unemployment, despair, and drug use as criminal motivations (Guardian South Bureau 2004:5). The intensification of a transnational trade in drugs and firearms—with Trinidad serving as a thoroughfare between South American producers and North American markets—contributed not only to the proliferation of guns in Trinidad but also to the rise of gang violence as competing groups vie for market control (Charan and Heeralal 2004; UNODC and World Bank 2007).[2]

Many analysts locate the beginning of Trinidad's kidnapping "epidemic" in the 2002 abduction of Anthony Sabga, the son of a prominent Syrian-Trinidadian family whose fortunes had been made through textile importing and real estate development. Sabga's family paid a reported TT$5 million ransom for his safe return (Sheppard 2005). Yet the most curious thing about media commentary and everyday talk about kidnapping in Trinidad is the persistent assertion that it is Trinidadians of Indian descent, rather than wealthy whites or Afro-Trinidadians, who are kidnapped for ransom. Indo-Trinidadians supposedly hold a near-monopoly as victims of abduction. After compiling kidnapping statistics from the three national newspapers in 2004, the anthropologist Kumar Mahabir (2005) created this profile: "The average kidnapping victim appears to be a middle aged Indian businessman. He resides in South Trinidad, the East-West Corridor, or Port of Spain and is likely to be snatched in or close to his home. If the hefty ransom of about half a million dollars is paid, he is likely to return safely to his family." The classed and raced character of kidnapping in Trinidad was perceived with mounting horror by garment factory owners, most of whom are Indo-Trinidadian.[3] As I made my way around various factories as part of a survey of the garment industry, their fear of violent crime and obsession with security were palpable. Factory owners talked about how "horrible" and "unlivable" the country had become, a place that is "not good for business" in the words of one and "not good for we families" in the words of another. Homes and factories were secured with high fences, "burglar-proofing" (bars on windows), and sometimes alarm systems, private security guards, and CCTV. Factory owners described their vulnerability as a function of both their class visibility as business owners and the belief that a police force largely composed of Afro-Trinidadians treated kidnapping as the small problem of a marginal community rather than a national crisis.

The anxiety of garment factory owners was vividly expressed by Bernard and Zarin, proprietors of Universal Uniforms, a factory just outside Port of Spain. A married couple in their late thirties, they claimed to restrict their movements to the home and workplace for fear of armed robbery and abduction. Bernard and Zarin hoped to emigrate before their two small children were old enough to begin secondary school. They often asked me, a foreign visitor, to validate their assessment that, as Zarin put it, "Crime here is so bad, you wouldn't find it so in America there or England." For Bernard, their vulnerability derived from the social heterogeneity of the factory and the perilous intimacies garment manufacturing necessitates between diverse categories of people:

> Remember, you hire people from urban areas and every area. And you open them up to your business in terms of that they know you *have* a business. You don't know what kind of children [they have] and culture they come from. But once they here, you know it is not accepted at that point, but you don't know if they go home and tell somebody, *"I working for people so much years . . ."* or whatever. But crime has an inside connection. So you don't know where it comes from. Maybe it is an employee, maybe you go to the bank too often or something. But you're being watched.

Factory owners like Bernard saw crime as spiraling upward, perpetrated by "worthless" individuals drawn to the easy money kidnapping and robbery provided. Like many Trinidadians, garment factory owners pointed to the densely populated, economically depressed neighborhoods clustered in the hills of East Port of Spain (especially Laventille and Morvant) as the place where criminal activity fomented. The Community-Based Environmental Protection and Enhancement Programme (CEPEP), which organizes unemployed workers to maintain public areas, was cited by many factory owners as having instilled a "something for nothing" mentality among poor Afro-Trinidadians by requiring little labor for a day's wages. The charge that CEPEP contracts were distributed through criminal gangs in Laventille with links to the People's National Movement (PNM) added to a perception that political patronage "organizes" crime and a sense that the state is unwilling rather than unable to combat lawlessness.

Fear of the workforce is not new to the Caribbean region, where the planter elite once dreaded above all else "the simple, brooding physical proximity of their slaves" (Walvin 2001:153). Today, managers imagine workers as the vectors through which violent crime will infiltrate the shop floor. When Bernard says "it" is "not accepted" in the factory, he emphasizes that delinquent or disruptive behavior would not be tolerated in the workplace. Yet he asserts that a disgruntled worker (saying *"I working for people so much years,"* with a voice of mock discontent) might urge someone from her "urban area" to harm Bernard. Thus, he notes, "crime has an inside connection." He suggests a threat from his workers' "children," whom I took to be the grown sons of the women he employs. For Bernard, the factory has become a place of risky mixture, where close and exploitative relationships threaten to ignite violence. Universal Uniforms was a notorious sweatshop, where workers were paid below the minimum wage, hired when government contracts were secured, and then fired when the work dried up. Bernard and Zarin were a constant presence in the cramped, dark factory located above a fabric shop on a busy main road. Bernard worked as the production manager, distributing sewing, dispersing payment, and settling shop-floor disputes. Workers from Laventille were aware of the menace their neighborhood evoked. On Fridays, each of the workers stood in line at Bernard's desk to sign his ledger and receive their pay. When Rose believed she had been underpaid for her week's work, she peeled back the paper stapled to the bills she received and announced, "Two hundred and seventy dollars? Somebody round here go get *kidnapped*." At minimum wage, Rose should have been paid close to TT$320 for the week.

Returning to Signature Fashions, we have to recognize that although factory owners share a fear of crime, there is no homogeneous group of owner-managers that speaks with unanimity about kidnapping. Although Bernard and Zarin's feelings are common, factory owners are differentiated along axes of race, class, and access to social, cultural, and political capital. Helene and Robert share a less intimate relationship with their workforce and exhibited less worry about crime. Operating from offices above the shop floor, Helene and Robert were not involved in the day-to-day business of hiring, payment, and supervision. They also occupy a more rarefied sphere of society: Helene is a popular, well-known businesswoman, fashion designer, and friend of local celebrities. Despite sharing an Indo-Trinidadian heritage, Helene and Robert clearly possess more social capital than Bernard and Zarin, who felt besieged by a pervasive sense of menace.

Helene and Robert echoed Bernard's assertion that crime has an "inside connection," but they experienced it as a source of relief rather than anxiety. As Helene said, "[Kidnapping is] based on *money*. They do their checks, you know, and they know who has money . . . I knew I didn't have any money stashed away in some bank, where someone could know about it to say, 'Well okay, Helene has two million stashed away in the bank. Let's grab her.'" Robert claimed that individuals who are kidnapped have often been mixed up in illegal activities, like drug dealing, themselves and are taken as payment for deals gone awry. I asked him why so many Indo-Trinidadians have been kidnapped; he replied, "Most of the people that are involved in actually touching the drugs are East Indian in Trinidad. That is a fact. Well-known fact. Most of the actual drug lords are East Indian. I'm not kidding. You ask a kid who the pusher is, they know."

Factory owners who were troubled by kidnapping experienced two sources of vulnerability: their perceived neglect, as Indo-Trinidadians, by state institutions like the police and their public visibility as owners of small businesses. Although an unofficially "East Indian" political party, the United National Congress (UNC), ruled from 1995 to 2001, in 2001 the PNM returned to what many of its Afro-Trinidadian supporters saw as its rightful place in power. Given the low representation of Indo-Trinidadians in the police force, many Indo-Trinidadians believed its inability to handle the kidnapping crisis was indicative of the malicious neglect with which they would be treated now that the PNM once again commanded the state apparatus.

Garment factory owners also felt vulnerable because of their public visibility and approachability. Although the growth of gated communities shows an increasing separation of entire neighborhoods into privatized, fortified enclaves (Mycoo 2006), the pursuit of security is exemplified in Trinidad by the fortification of the individual home or business. High fences ring upscale homes in wealthy neighborhoods northwest of Port of Spain, and Trinidadian elites—particularly the white minority—retreat into cars and privatized spaces rather than endure the rough-and-tumble of the public streets, parks, and shops, preferring the air-conditioned, exclusive, and controlled arenas of shopping malls in the northern and western suburbs of Port of Spain. Yet as Kevin Yelvington (1995:66) reminds us, "The high visibility of the retail sector belies its generally low income, thus giving the false impression of East Indian economic strength" (see Dookeran 1985:72–73). Many garment factory owners had neither the wealth nor liberty to carry out many "strategies of protection" (Caldeira 1996:307), and they lived in respectable but open neighborhoods and worked in factories exposed to main roadways. Helene and Robert's social prestige and security techniques insulated them from the worst anxiety. At Signature Fashions it was Cissy, the production manager, who seemed to carry a weight of constant dread, often asking me with disbelief, "You *see* how things going here in Trinidad?"

"Is *Them* Making Laventille Look So": Back Worker Views of Crime

While kidnapping represents for factory owners a dramatic example of Trinidad's degeneration—compelling them to constrict their movements for the sake of personal security—for many garment workers, particularly in the back area, the transformation of their home neighborhoods into violent, besieged places has been the greater preoccupation. With the intensification of the hard-drugs trade in and through Trinidad, gang clashes in Laventille, and the easy availability of guns (Charan and Heeralal 2004; Economist Intelligence Unit 2003; UNODC and World Bank 2007), workers from East Port of Spain were made anxious by the dangers of stray bullets, street violence, and police corruption. A frequent topic of factory conversation was police brutality in Laventille and Morvant, which reached a fever pitch after the police shooting of an unarmed woman, Galene Bonadie, in Morvant. Bonadie, a forty-one-year-old mother on her way to work, reportedly stumbled upon four police officers beating a man they had pulled from his automobile. In the verbal altercation that followed, Bonadie was shot in the head and then dragged into the police van and driven away (Heeralal 2004; Lord 2004). Audra claimed her eldest son had heard the gunshots. She said, "[When] I take a drop from the taxi, I go home *straight*. I'm not on the road." Where police, like bandits, seem to victimize with impunity, the threat of street violence made lingering outside a risk.

Many workers from East Port of Spain described neighbors growing more detached and suspicious of one another over a period of ten or fifteen years as crime rates escalated. Nancy, for example, said that "before," if you had to leave your home on an errand, you could call out to any neighbor and ask them to "throw an eye" on your children from time to time, to make sure they were alright. She said she could no longer do this: "They might do your chirren something while you not there." Crime was certainly seen as originating *in* the community, as a result of "evil," "worthless" individuals with deficient upbringing who steal from their neighbors, deal drugs, or engage in reprisal killings. Glenda suggested, "It come from the parents." Some workers noted a need for stronger emphasis on Christian values (to "change people's heart"), while Evangelical Christians—such as Jean, Glenda, and Josephine—also described rising crime as an intrinsic characteristic of the "last days" of this world. Said Josephine, "If you read your Bible, it will tell you, you will see for yourself. It will have lots of war and crime, more will come again. No government could stop that . . . only one man could stop it, is God."

Although Trinidad's GDP grew in 2003—mostly as a result of the expansion of the capital- and technology-intensive energy sector—unemployment remained persistently high during the same period, and non-energy exports declined (IMF 2004). The rising prices of food, gasoline, and transportation have increased the real cost of living in the face of depressed and stagnant wages, while deep cuts in social expenditures meant the experience of poverty worsened (Mycoo 2006:136–37). In the midst of such daily anguish, garment workers rarely summoned sympathy for victims of kidnapping-for-ransom. A common way of delegitimizing the kidnapping "epidemic" was to deny the very *existence* of kidnapping in Trinidad. PNM supporters might suggest that episodes of "people get snatched" were nothing more than an elaborate ruse staged by the UNC to destabilize a predominantly Afro-Trinidadian government. When UNC leader Basdeo Panday suggested that his supporters should challenge institutional discrimination against Indo-Trinidadians using "civil disobedience," some of his critics took this as an admission that kidnappings were a farce devised to make the government look bad on law-and-order issues. The well-reported cases of two Indo-Trinidadian teenagers staging their own abductions to extort money from their parents bolstered the sense that many kidnappings were bogus (Seetahal 2005).

Yet even while dismissing the kidnapping crisis or describing it as God's plan, back workers might also insist that abductions were morally justified. If "worthless" individuals from poor communities were the proximate cause of crime, its prime authors and beneficiaries are "big-money people"—wealthy Trinidadians who have a master hand in running drugs and guns through the country and whose social positioning renders them beyond scrutiny. For this reason, many workers at the Signature Fashions factory enjoyed Cro Cro's calypso hit "Face Reality" during the 2004 Carnival season:

> Remember the master say
> If you do wrong you have to pay
> So dey tief out de treasury
> And dey living hoity-toity
> Dey dress with jacket and tie
> Dey tief and living a lie
> Dey better pay back
> All de wrong ting dey do,
> Or the bandit coming for you.
> So all dem Carlos, dem jefe sefe, dem who tief
> And dem who doh pray
> Ah begging mi bandit friend
> *Kidnap dem!*
> All who have coke in water tank
> Drug money in foreign bank
> Doh mind how de plea and beg
> *Kidnap dem!*
> All who money ho-to-to
> All who know dey rip off Tidco
> All dem who brother is hen
> *Kidnap dem!*
> Dey have we money in London and Miami
> Kidnapping go build back de economy.
> Ah wrong deserves punishment
> Tha's why dey 'fraid to walk de pavement
> Launder all Dole Chadee money
> . . .
> All dem big, big, big store owners
> Who does bring coke in cloth containers
> to fry brain ah we children
> *Kidnap dem!*
> Dey children happy in London
> We kids turning pusher-man,

> Laventille children ketchen de ne-nen
> *Kidnap dem!*
> Dey have we money in London and Miami
> Kidnapping go build back we economy . . .
>
> *(Cro Cro 2004)*

With its catchy refrain *"Kidnap dem!"* Cro Cro's song led to immediate controversy. Calypso music has always been a popular form of satire and political commentary in Trinidad (Birth 2008; Regis 1999; Rohlehr 1990). From the end of Christmas until the beginning of Lent, calypsonians perform their latest songs in tents staged throughout the country. Cro Cro's tent, *Calypso Revue*, located in downtown Port of Spain, is uncompromisingly political, tending to be either supportive of or indulgent toward the PNM. As any local listener would know, "Face Reality" accuses the UNC of corruption during its years in power (1995–2001) with its quotation "So dey tief out de treasury," its evocation of "[their] money in London and Miami," and the connection it draws between kidnapping victims and supporters of the UNC party.[4]

Cro Cro's song was enjoyed by many Signature Fashions workers, particularly those in the back area. Audra and Jean took to quietly singing "Kidnap dem!" along with their personal radios. When Lata complained, "Stop singing that *blasted* song," Jean shot back, "It's just a song, and it's *true*." What appealed to Jean and the back workers—other than the catchy sound of the song itself—was how it conveyed a critique of both the wealthy, corrupt Trinidadians believed to be running guns and drugs into the country ("All dem big, big, big store owners / Who does bring coke in cloth containers") and the UNC party, which supposedly "tief[ed] out de treasury" while in power, then hid the money in private bank accounts in "London and Miami." Thus Cro Cro's call to repatriate the money: "Kidnapping go build back we economy."

The song was for these workers a convincing recitation of the causes of the devastating transformation of their home communities, as exemplified in an interview with Josephine from the back area:

> JOSEPHINE: And why Laventille so bad and have so much of gun? They shooting everybody with their gun. Poor people with the gun. Laventille people not getting a gun just *so*. They not bringing it in just *so*. It is the bigger men and them bringing in the guns, that's why we have so much of crime.

REBECCA: So what did you think about [the] Cro Cro controversy? Remember—

JOSEPHINE: I don't have nothing wrong with Cro Cro. I find nothing wrong with Cro Cro. I *love* his song.

REBECCA: You love his song?

JOSEPHINE: I love his song—

REBECCA: So you felt, what, that was a perspective that needed to be said?

JOSEPHINE: Rebecca, you need to be listening to the song. Whatever message he sending out. He didn't say for nobody to hold nobody, but listen to what he trying to tell the people and them. Listen, all yuh they say here, they say, what he say? "Kidnap dem!" Everybody get vex. He say, "Kidnap dem." Is *them* who making Laventille look so! What those hungry-tail boys working to get for? Where they looking to get guns? *[Long pause.]* Where they getting the guns from?

REBECCA: Somebody with a lot of money is bringing that?

JOSEPHINE: Oh ho! Alright. So when they say "Laventille"—I live Laventille all my *life*, I used to walk one o'clock, six o'clock, five o'clock in the morning. I used to walk any hour. Have a quarrel with my boyfriend, and he get vex and turn back, I used to take my cool walk, continue taking my cool walk up the road.

REBECCA: And now you wouldn't do it?

JOSEPHINE: No, I can't do because it have guns. Where they getting the guns from? Nobody want to admit where they getting the guns from. All they want to put is a big headline: "LAVENTILLE."

Josephine's words trace a complex logic of blame for the current conditions in East Port of Spain. She emphasizes that while "guns" are plaguing her neighborhood, no one *in* the neighborhood is "bringing it in just so." The guns have been distributed by those with money, power, and connections: "the bigger men." Signature Fashions workers who enjoyed Cro Cro's song favor an alternate reading of the kidnapping-crime nexus from the one most frequently portrayed in the media, by politicians, and by factory owners. Workers who support the song urge us to consider not the "small man" who may be visible but instead the "big man" who profits somewhere offstage. A common perception among back workers was that such crimes were committed by two particular groups of "big-money people": first, Syrian-Trinidadian families, who established themselves in textile importing and garment manufacturing in the 1950s and later moved into real estate development. The other "big-money people," as Robert describes it, are the "East Indian" business owners who are seen to have a hand in crime. As Glenda told me, "Don't shed a tear for those kidnapped people. They brought it on their-selves."

Josephine's account depicts the gendered dimensions of living with street violence: her "cool walk" interrupted by the threat of stray bullets suggests a constriction of women's physical mobility and social power. Her gendered/classed/raced grievances, however, are importantly framed as a critique of the state. Josephine's discussion of crime, kidnapping, and the decline of Laventille was immediately preceded in the interview by her indictment of the government for no longer inspecting garment factories to make sure workers were fairly treated (see chapter 6). Josephine had worked in the industry for twenty years and saw conditions decline over that period as both the state and trade unions withdrew their concern for the welfare of garment workers because of the sector's small size and weakening economic position. As Josephine grasps for an explanation of what has happened and a target for whom to blame, she interprets as a single phenomenon the collapse of the garment sector in the post-liberalization era, the reduction in state and trade-union interest in her welfare, and the violent disintegration of her neighborhood. Eric Hobsbawm's cross-cultural study of social banditry suggests that the romanticization of the outlaw is keenest when a traditional moral economy is in disarray. The bandits most celebrated in poems, ballads, and legends not only victimize the elite through attack and robbery but also set the moral world to right by enforcing a traditional obligation to share. Social bandits, like those depicted in Cro Cro's song, are "reformers not revolutionaries" because they commit themselves to the restoration of a prior, imagined order rather than the forging of a new one (Hobsbawm 1969:21).

"You See How We Is Treated?": The Predicament of Indo-Trinidadian Workers

Enjoyment of, and opposition to, Cro Cro's song fell along clear lines in the factory. Those who enjoyed the song were Afro-Trinidadians, while those who decried it were Indo-Trinidadian. (Still, many workers refused to take any position on the song.) Clearly, some of the back workers took to singing the song as a quiet taunt to front workers, emphasizing their opposition to what they perceived to be a shared ethnic interest between Indo-Trinidadian workers and the Indo-Trinidadian victims of kidnapping. Front workers found themselves accused of being apologists for corrupt political classes and for having inappropriate ethnic loyalties.

The fact that most of the kidnapping victims reported on the nightly news were "East Indian" was both indisputable and worrying for Indo-Trinidadian workers in the factory. As Tina said, "It is all the words that describe to be frightening, it is all of that. All the big words you use to be frighten, it is like that." They felt wounded by their co-workers' dismissal of the kidnapping problem as solely the concern of the Indo-Trinidadian community. Many believed police corruption allowed kidnapping to flourish; as Kavita exclaimed: "It have certain police have a hand in it!" These workers saw racism at the heart of kidnapping, on a spectrum from plain indifference to outright violence toward Indo-Trinidadians—a position made more convincing by the fact that the police force, like the government in power, was predominantly composed of Afro-Trinidadians. Said Gita, "Take a Negro, they go catch you *one time* [i.e., right away]; come snatch a Indian and you go on your way."

Tina, the sole Indo-Trinidadian working in the back area of the factory, was particularly concerned about crime. Because she possessed a sensitive temperament, some of her co-workers found teasing her a cruel sort of fun. For example, one afternoon Tina had planned to go to Port of Spain with Dolores, an Afro-Trinidadian stitcher who lived near Tina in Chaguanas. When Dolores was unable to go at the last minute, Tina decided to go straight home from work instead of into town. The next day, Carmela teased Tina mercilessly, announcing to all of us working in the back area, "Tina afraid to go town by she-self!"

Tina protested, "Me and Dolores were go go to town together."

"So?" said Carmela. "You could still go to town by you-self."

"I didn't want to go to town by myself," said Tina.

"Because she frighten," announced Carmela. Carmela accentuated her words with the broken pair of scissors she used to trim pockets, punctuating the air with each word. She was clearly revving up for a bout of picong, struggling to make sense of these changes, they have tried and often failed to identify and articulate connections between them. Citizens who never experienced the state as an abstract, impersonal entity remain convinced that it always operates through biased actors with ethnic and party-political allegiances. Workers who have always been impoverished know that capital moves in remote and mysterious ways.

The back workers at Signature Fashions who praised kidnapping as retribution against a corrupt elite present their communities as besieged by the actions of greedy businesspeople and politicians. They emphasize Trinidad's rising rates of violent crime, the increasingly fortified urban landscape, income disparities between rich and poor, and the complicity of the state in each of these concerns. The phrase "kidnapping go build back we economy" may appear prima facie to critique transnational capitalism by presenting a means of repatriating Trinidadian wealth from bank accounts in "London and Miami." But it is the growing economic and political might of Indo-Trinidadians that the Afro-Trinidadian working class perceives to be the most troubling disruption to the normal order of society. We must recognize in Cro Cro's song long-standing racist stereotypes of Indo-Trinidadians as clannish, acquisitive, and disloyal to the nation, redeployed in an analysis of social inequality. An economic critique from the shop floor, then, is mired in historical resentments and jealousies stoked by a continuing ethnic politics that has "consistently posed African and Indian economic advancement in mutually exclusive terms" (Puri 1999:239).

When back workers celebrate banditry by singing "*Kidnap dem!*" on the shop floor, the song works as a taunt directed toward Indo-Trinidadian co-workers. The narratives of Indo-Trinidadian workers reveal the difficulties of and ambivalence toward their position in the factory and in society as a whole, where mainstream political parties are envisioned foremost through ethnic rather than class-based politics. Indo-Trinidadian front workers find themselves addressed by their co-workers as apologists for middle- and upper-class Indo-Trinidadians (imagined to be both rich and corrupt). As they themselves struggle to make sense of "crime" in Trinidad, with all its raced and classed dimensions, they are left feeling vulnerable and beleaguered. Forced to choose between class and race loyalties, they struggle to find a "place" from which to speak, where their emotions (particularly fear of crime and sympathy for victims) are given legitimacy.

As the nightly news recounted nearly a murder each day in 2003 and 2004, Trinidadians of all economic backgrounds responded by fortifying their homes, curtailing after-dark activities, and becoming suspicious of strangers and neighbors alike. At Signature Fashions, workers and managers use the topic of kidnapping as a means of talking about race, class, and politics in contemporary Trinidad. Imbricated within a highly racialized organization of production, these conversations reveal its very contours. Just as Kevin Yelvington found in a Trinidadian factory in the 1980s, raced, classed, and gendered relations are constructed, consented to, and experienced on the shop floor. Kidnapping talk offers a window onto the emotional texture of these relations because diverse and irreconcilable views are not merely of opinion but also of affect. "Interests" and "allegiances" are not a matter of means-ends rationality; they are crafted through registers of sympathy, fear, ridicule, blame, and vengeance. In this respect, kidnapping stories do not merely reflect prior subjectivities but instead show themselves to be constitutive of them.

Notes

1. TT$500,000 was roughly equivalent to US$83,000.

2. Although statistics for the region are incomplete, the Economist Intelligence Unit estimates that 50 percent of the cocaine that enters the North American and European markets arrives from South America by way of the Caribbean islands (EIU 2003:7). The narcotics trade has facilitated the availability and use of firearms by organized gangs that require them for protection, smuggle them along with drugs, trade them for drugs, and use them to maintain discipline and execute informers (UNODC and World Bank 2007:133). Therefore, while it is widely recognized that the narcotics trade has led to an expansion of organized crime in Trinidad and throughout the region (*The Economist* 2008), the proliferation of guns has meant that spikes in violence can occur equally when the drug market expands or when it contracts, as rival organizations struggle over shipment routes in the first instance and narcotics in the second (UNODC and the World Bank 2007:15).

3. My assertion that most garment factory owners in Trinidad are Indo-Trinidadian derives from my survey of the industry, which included field visits and a compilation of the names of business owners in the *Trinidad and Tobago Export Directory 2002* (TIDCO 2002) and *Trinidad and Tobago Export Directory 2003* (TIDCO 2003b). The white and Syrian-Trinidadian families who initiated garment

manufacturing in the early twentieth century have, for the most part, achieved upward mobility and capital expansion, now investing in property development and the importation rather than manufacturing of fabric and garments.

4. In 2004, a government inquiry into UNC corruption revealed that its leader, Basdeo Panday, owned property and savings accounts in London. Panday was arrested on corruption charges in 2005, although his conviction was later overturned (Loutoo 2007).

5. Worker narratives reveal the profoundly local nature of their understandings of political and economic transformations, even when these conditions have been shaped by the kinds of neoliberal policies variously embraced the world over. Karla Slocum (2006:192) makes a similar observation in her analysis of how the changing global governance of the banana industry has affected farmers in St. Lucia: "growers' efforts at analyzing and making sense of the shifting banana industry drew significantly on local and national resources, categories, meanings, and relations, illustrating that growers 'thought locally.'" Todd Sanders (2008:111) rightly draws attention to anthropologists' discomfort with such "local" critiques of global capitalism when informants arrive at interpretations whose politics are dissonant with those of our own, wryly commenting, "Wouldn't it be nice, after all, if anthropology's Others recognized and criticized, always and forever, their own conditions of subordination and exploitation in a highly immoral capitalist/modern/neoliberal/global economy?"

8
Conclusion

> The world has been made with blunt power
> but also with sleights of hand.
> – *Cynthia Enloe, Bananas, Beaches and Bases*

Neoliberal restructuring has changed the face of the global garment sector. Fewer and fewer countries now dominate production for the world market, while other parts of the globe—where wages are comparatively high and workers' rights relatively secure—have been increasingly priced out of competition, even for domestic consumption. The 2005 expiration of the Multi-Fibre Agreement, an international quota system that dispersed garment manufacturing around the world, has accelerated this process of industrial clustering in places where cheap labor, industrial specialization, and economies of scale represent "ideal" market conditions (Gereffi and Frederick 2010; Lu 2013; Rivoli 2005; Frederick and Staritz 2012; Özden and Sharma 2006).

These developments have inspired a number of scholarly accounts that examine the growth of export-oriented garment and textile production in places where business is booming (Caraway 2007; De Neve 2005; Hewamanne 2010; Kabeer and Mahmud 2004; Kim 2013; Lynch 2007). Anthropological studies have explored what new trade arrangements mean for the organization of labor, the politics of production, and working conditions in various local contexts. The growth of this scholarship reflects what Jennifer Bair and Marion Werner (2011:989) have called academia's "inclusionary bias" toward examining places where production is expanding. The story told far less often is that of dissolution, disappointment, and decline in parts of the world where the logics of market capitalism cannot support a thriving garment sector. This book represents an attempt to grapple with the conditions on the ground in one such place.

During my fieldwork in Trinidad, I was often told that I should be examining the oil industry, the natural gas sector, or tourism during the country's annual Carnival. Such assertions exemplify the notion that our concerns should rest with industries considered economically significant. Yet in an attempt to illuminate the everyday struggles of "real people doing real things" (Ortner 1996:2), the working lives of women in an industry that is peripheral to both the national economy and the national imagination constitute a fitting object of inquiry. For it is here, at the margins, that we can see the challenges facing those who have been presented most unambiguously with the neoliberal edict to be resourceful, adaptive, and self-reliant.

This book about a factory in Trinidad challenges us to rethink the story of the global garment industry. Because Trinidadian producers of standard clothing like T-shirts, shirts, and trousers cannot compete solely on price in a global market, mass-production factories that relied for profitability on cheap labor alone have slowly closed down. But this has not meant the loss of an entire sector. What has remained in Trinidad is a constellation of enterprises: sweatshops that hire and fire in accordance with contractors' demands, independent seamstresses and tailors operating from their own shops and homes, and designer firms like Signature Fashions that quickly respond to local fashion trends and benefit from the remaining tariffs on non-CARICOM (Caribbean Community) imports. Some of these enterprises cannibalize the old equipment and infrastructure of a former era; some take advantage of the industry's low status and diminished regulatory apparatus to casualize the relationship between workers and employers. With shrinking opportunities for wage employment, women devoted to making a living in this sector survive by cobbling together livelihoods with formal employment and own-account work.

Trinidadian firms that have survived trade liberalization have, as theorists predicted, been those able to achieve some form of flexible production to meet the needs of a quickly changing and competitive market, although less frequently through the "high road" of staff empowerment and continual training than through the "low road" of casualization, labor intensification, intermittent layoffs, invasive forms of surveillance, and an erosion of workers' rights (Collins 2001; De Neve 2005; Dunn 2004; Holmström 1998; Wright 2001).[1] Without the presence of trade unions or the vigorous enforcement of existing state regulations, Signature Fashions would meet its just-in-time manufacturing demands through a creeping informalism. Although Signature Fashions workers describe the manufacturing process as chaotic, "disorganized," and "now for now," these characteristics actually aid production by orchestrating employees to respond to fluctuations in market demand with quickened tempos and overtime work. Paying workers late symbolizes unequal power in the employer-employee relationship and reflects an improvised approach to management that downplays employers' legal obligations to provide ample notice and proper remuneration for overtime work.

But my research shows that workers do not simply contribute to the flexibility of the firm through their vulnerability to exploitation; they also contribute to it through their own agency. A Fordist organization of production that insists on a separation between mental and manual labor is poorly adapted for flexible production. At Signature Fashions, workers face a changing array of expectations from managers who demand an outward face of acquiescence. But by resisting the organization of production and attempting to wrest control of it, Signature workers contribute to industrial flexibility, although in unacknowledged ways. Despite their managers' insistence that each operator should be fixed and atomized, Signature workers engage in "productive sociality" to help one another move up the line, quickly repair each others' mistakes, and learn new skills by operating machines they have not been trained or sanctioned to use. Through thiefing a chance, workers satisfy the contradictory mandates to be both enterprising and quiescent. They skill up for new sewing tasks, learn how to work together, and become invested in the smooth functioning of the factory because only then can they pursue their own side projects on the shop floor.

On my visits to more than a dozen other factories in Trinidad, I discovered that worker theft is a regular source of joking discussion among managers, who marvel at their employees' outrageous ingenuity in sneaking garments out of the factory gate. Indeed, some of the remaining factories that produce commodity garments like T-shirts have instituted group-based piece rates not only so employees will incentivize one another but also to prevent them from copying or taking garments from the assembly line. But in the small-scale, retail-driven production regime at Signature Fashions, thiefing a chance flourishes. Paid hourly instead of by the piece, workers can channel additional efforts into making garments for themselves rather than devoting all their time to beating a quota.

At Signature Fashions, thiefing a chance serves a unique role in resolving the paradox of flexibility created by the manufacturing of a variable product in a Fordist regime. When I asked Robert and Helene about the extent to which their workers used factory materials and machines for their own purposes, they used the same moral frameworks workers did in distinguishing "stealing" from "thiefing." Taking a finished garment from the assembly line, of which Annie had been accused (see chapter 4), is treated as stealing, a serious offense. But Robert and Helene also understood that workers frequently "thiefed" little moments to make the most of the factory resources, making up their own clothes on factory machines or working on "private jobs" for clients during work hours. Although they described these activities as bothersome and potentially disruptive to production (and therefore to be officially discouraged), they are tolerated because, as Robert told me, "that ehnt go wear out the machines," after all.

What Robert and Helene did not recognize was how thiefing practices might actually contribute to flexible production. Echoing Melissa Wright's (2001) characterization of labor relations in a Mexican maquiladora, Robert and Helene do not treat their employees as dynamic and flexible but rather as an undisciplined and recalcitrant labor force that has to be strictly orchestrated. The factory is run with a top-down management style that attempts to atomize workers by allocating each of them to a particular part of the assembly process. The presumed need to control the workers means that thiefing is understood as inconvenient but external to production. Although the managerial vision of orderly obedience in the factory is never achieved, it is an aspiration that precludes recognition of any positive effects of thiefing a chance on the production process.

As Michel Anteby (2008:151–71) has argued, allowing workers to engage in side production can extend managerial control by providing a space in which workers voluntarily meet official production demands so they can quietly make their own crafts and in so doing perform a self-authored occupational identity. Although my conclusions resonate with those of Anteby in that we both identify ways that management relies on workers' subjectivities to govern them more effectively, I emphasize the mismatch between management's stated desire for an orderly workplace and its unresolved need for a more dynamic one.

The illicit activities that workers call "thiefing a chance" are productive because they engender self-reliant, strategizing subjectivities. These subjectivities have also been developed by women "into the sewing" through many years of working in the industry and accumulating skills. These are not simply the technical skills of how to produce garments but also a neoliberal disposition of flexibility that is vital to making a living in a competitive economic environment (Urciuoli 2008). Many workers gained exposure to sewing as children at home or from being sent "by a lady who sews" in their neighborhoods, yet their narratives of skill acquisition show the imperative to "thief" skills as well. Whether at home watching a sister sew or in the factory sneakily using a machine until caught by a manager and then made to work it outright, thiefing a chance is an important practice for women who make a living in the garment industry. Thiefing a chance is also an apt description of life under neoliberalism, whereby garment workers cobble together a livelihood through formal, informal, and illicit means.

Although Trinidadian garment workers' responses to trade liberalization and the withdrawal of state spending on their welfare do to a certain extent include their acceptance of the need to become the "responsibilized citizen-subjects" neoliberalism is said to require (Ferguson 2009:172; Rose 1999), this is importantly localized within Caribbean cultural mores and social histories. Thiefing a chance belongs to the "reputation" strand of the dualistic, mutually reinforcing value system at work within Caribbean societies. While "respectability" reflects Euro-centric colonial standards—such as deference to social hierarchy, religiosity, and moral rectitude—reputation is allied with the "autochthonous" (Mantz 2007:21) ethics of Caribbean social life: spontaneity, self-invention, and an ethos of equality. A growing anthropological literature has challenged the status of respectability as handmaiden to the colonial project by showing that it constitutes an arena of dignified resistance, particularly in the private spaces of home life (Besson 1993; Miller 1994a). In the neoliberal era, the values and activities encompassed by "reputation" now also require reassessment, to probe whether its anti-establishment values still obtain.

Carla Freeman (2005, 2007), writing about Barbados, observes that despite its oppositional and contestatory ethos, cultural practices associated with "reputation" values have been reconfigured to support and extend a neoliberal agenda. In a context of heightened economic insecurity, the confidence, flexibility, and self-reliance realized in "reputation" practices like thiefing a chance have become newly appreciated as the creative means through which Caribbean people contend with the opportunities and challenges of global capitalism. In describing the prevalence of thiefing a chance, my intention is not to suggest that Trinidadian workers exploit their workplaces at a higher rate than workers elsewhere in the world. I argue instead that in Trinidad, as perhaps throughout the Caribbean, these kinds of illicit activities are uniquely valorized, not as "everyday resistance" to the hegemonic interests of employers but instead as the embodiment of an enterprising ethos (Bolles 1996; Browne 2004). This shows how treasured Caribbean ways of being-in-the-world have been refashioned for the competitive demands of the neoliberal era.

If we accept Loïc Wacquant's contention that neoliberal governmentality renders "the trope of individual responsibility" a central, even "motivating" discourse (Wacquant 2012:72), then thiefing a chance is an example of how this trope of individual responsibility is materialized in a particular place and time. Long-standing Trinidadian cultural values, such as risk taking, entrepreneurialism, and self-reliance, have become activated and thereby reaffirmed in the context of factory employment. Individual responsibility, framed here as "thiefing a chance," gains legitimacy and staying power from its roots in Caribbean culture.

I hope this book, in conveying something of the enthusiasm and energy of women workers, challenges the stereotype of garment workers as low-skilled, compliant victims of a capitalist economic order. At the same time, analytical attention to "neoliberal subjectivities"—the ways people navigate new forms of economic insecurity by developing a self-governing self—helps us to critically assess garment workers' celebratory narratives of their own empowerment. There is no doubt that thiefing a chance is an empowering discourse. It resonates with the jubilant ways workers describe themselves as "into the sewing," claiming a far more dynamic, entrepreneurial, and self-authored subjectivity than the phrase *garment worker* conveys to them. Although they are well aware of the structural constraints and social hierarchies that impede their lives both in the factory and outside it, Signature Fashions workers also see themselves as agents in their own right.

However, as Carole Greenhouse (2010:7) has argued, neoliberal conditions pose a unique predicament for theorizing the agency of individual subjects because the languages of empowerment, freedom, self-reliance, choice, and indeed "agency" itself are such defining features of "neoliberalism's ideological charter." In this respect, analyzing agency under neoliberalism shares with the social study of race the danger of reproducing rather than interrogating local interpretive categories (Khan 2004:5; Munasinghe 2001:11). To understand how a rhetoric of "empowerment" can serve capitalist ends that ultimately disadvantage workers requires an ethnographic view that also appreciates the politics of labor. When they repudiate the label "garment worker" for the identity of being "into the sewing," Signature Fashions workers choose to embrace an entrepreneurial ethos at the expense of identifying with the legacy of industrial labor. This, I suggest, reflects a neoliberal denigration of the dignity of labor in favor of individualized forms of autonomy encapsulated in self-employment.

Where does economic life begin and end for a woman who "loves" to sew? If the subjectivities of workers are implicated in the firm's flexibility, so, too, is their sense of pleasure. Just as the livelihoods of garment workers confound a public-private division in regard to where and how work takes place, economic logics and the logics of desire intermingle in their occupational strategies. Women in the Trinidadian garment industry often continue to sew because they "love" to, even when that devotion is tempered by difficulty, pain, or injury. When Rhonda complained that she was injured by a broken machine (chapter 6), what distressed her most was the way her grievance was used to assault her reputation as a good employee. The enjoyment workers derive from learning, sewing, and becoming economic actors is therefore an intimate source of their exploitation in the context of wage employment. Workers subsidize factory production by internalizing the costs of their own retraining because skill is regarded not only to be the worker's property but also an expression of her own project of self-making. Although garment workers depict "thiefing" as daringly taking advantage of the structural conditions in which they find themselves, we must not conflate intentions and effects. In pursuing their own projects of production and self-making, Signature Fashions workers consistently conform to the "flexible" requirements of the neoliberal economic order (Harvey 1990; Martin 1994).

Turning to what an ethnography of the illicit can tell us about how factories work, I argue the need for a new conceptualization of the factory, not as a stable or bounded unit but instead as the productive intersection of a wide range of social and material processes. Signature Fashions workers enter the factory to enact specific types of projects: whether earning a wage, learning new skills, coming "out" for the experience of employment, escaping an inharmonious home life, to thief a chance, or for a combination of reasons. These are not a pure set of intentions but are instead crafted in relation to the opportunities the factory represents. At the same time, owners and managers carry their own goals, plans, expectations, and practices to the shop floor, where they converge with those of the workers and become transformed. The competing interests of workers, managers, and factory owners sometimes find themselves in alignment and at other times in conflict.

Thiefing a chance is a structuring feature of shop-floor life at Signature Fashions, lending a view of the factory as constituted through authorized and unauthorized action, acknowledged and unacknowledged interests, planned and unintended consequences. My book therefore problematizes our conventional understandings of what a factory *is* by emphasizing the productive power of unsanctioned activities and the variability of their effects. It raises questions for further research, about to what extent capitalist institutions rely on chance alignments of this kind and how we can make them theoretically visible.

Conceptualizing the factory as a social and material assemblage, in which different practices and plans can find themselves in productive rhythm, allows us to move beyond a Gramscian analytics that specifies how workers are exploited through modes of coercion and consent, to embrace as well a Foucaultian understanding that discipline's power is diffuse and that all actors become swept up in it. When stitchers are expected to operate a broken machine, for example, they are enlisted into a shared project to keep the factory working by placing their own bodies into the breach. There is no acknowledgment that their bodies replace faulty machine parts. When Rhonda complains that she can no longer operate her machine (chapter 6), it is not simply that coercion in the form of threatened job loss supplants her consent to the terms of employment but rather that her interests and those of her employers are not the same, and for all the times they are aligned, there are instances when they most resolutely are not.

In thinking about how to improve conditions for workers who make garments for the global market, Marion Werner and Jennifer Bair have pointed to the need to move beyond ineffectual technocratic solutions such as codes of conduct to "mobilize against the neoliberal orthodoxies that have failed workers in the North *and* South" (Werner and Bair 2009:7; emphasis mine). To generate a fundamental rethinking of global systems of production and distribution, we first have to understand not only the localized ways in which a doctrine of market supremacy has circulated and become materialized in the form of specific policies and practices (Ferguson 2009:170) but also how it has shaped the everyday lives, habits, and imaginations of workers, consumers, and citizens. Such an endeavor requires the kinds of rich, complex empirical engagements ethnographic study can provide.

This book tells us how neoliberalism is made local in Trinidad through specific practices in an industry shaped by new economic pressures. As women workers navigate the opportunities and challenges represented by this economic order, they activate strategies of coping that are always culturally inflected. A disposition toward "flexibility" and the local valorization of a wide variety of strategies of cunning adaptation are mobilized in this effort. Even as we esteem and honor these strategies, our task is to continue to probe how culture is used and remade within these processes while holding in tension their multiple effects.

Note

1. My survey of Trinidad's garment sector revealed that while most firms have addressed the imperatives for flexible production through a "low road" of informalization, a few firms have instead put their energies into technical innovation and staff empowerment.

Cohen, Robin. 1980. "Resistance and Hidden Forms of Consciousness amongst African Workers." *Review of African Political Economy* 7 (19): 8–22. http://dx.doi.org/10.1080/03056248008703437.

Collins, Jane L. 2001. "Flexible Specialization and the Garment Industry." *Competition and Change* 5 (2): 165–200.

Collins, Jane L. 2003. *Threads: Gender, Labor and Power in the Global Apparel Industry.* Chicago: University of Chicago Press. http://dx.doi.org/10.7208/chicago/9780226113739.001.0001.

Comaroff, John L., and Jean Comaroff. 2006. "Law and Disorder in the Postcolony: An Introduction." In *Law and Disorder in the Postcolony*, ed. Jean Comaroff and John L. Comaroff, 1–56. Chicago: University of Chicago Press. http://dx.doi.org/10.7208/chicago/9780226114101.001.0001.

Comitas, Lambros. 1973 [1964]. "Occupational Multiplicity in Rural Jamaica." In *Work and Family Life: West Indian Perspectives*, ed. Lambros Comitas and David Lowenthal, 157–73. New York: Anchor Books.

Concerned Women for Progress (CWP). 1982. "The Garment Industry in Trinidad and Tobago." *Women in Struggle* 1 (1): 1–5.

Craig, Susan. 1975. "Political Patronage and Community Resistance: Village Councils in Trinidad and Tobago." In *Rural Development in the Caribbean*, ed. P. I. Gomes, 173–93. Kingston: Heinemann.

Cro Cro. 2004. "Face Reality." Lyrics published in the *Trinidad Guardian*. Tuesday, January 27, 33.

Cross, Jamie. 2009. "From Dreams to Discontent: Educated Men and the Politics of Work at a Special Economic Zone in Andhra Pradesh." *Contributions to Indian Sociology* 43 (3): 351–79. http://dx.doi.org/10.1177/006996670904300301.

Cross, Jamie. 2010a. "Neoliberalism as Unexceptional: Economic Zones and the Everyday Precariousness of Working Life in South India." *Critique of Anthropology* 30 (4): 355–73. http://dx.doi.org/10.1177/0308275X10372467.

Cross, Jamie. 2010b. "Occupational Health, Risk, and Science in India's Global Factories." *South Asian History and Culture* 1 (2): 224–38. http://dx.doi.org/10.1080/19472491003592912.

Crowley, Daniel J. 1957. "Plural and Differential Acculturation in Trinidad." *American Anthropologist* 59 (5): 817–24. http://dx.doi.org/10.1525/aa.1957.59.5.02a00060.

Csordas, Thomas J., ed. 1994. "Introduction: The Body as Representation and Being-in-the-World." In *Embodiment and Experience: The Existential Ground of Culture and the Self*, ed. Thomas J. Csordas, 1–24. Cambridge: Cambridge University Press.

Danny-Maharaj, Phoolo. 2004. "UNC: Government Too Slow on Safety Act." *Trinidad and Tobago Express*. Monday, June 7, 21.

Davis, John. 1992. *Exchange*. Minneapolis: University of Minnesota Press.

de Certeau, Michel. 1984. *The Practice of Everyday Life*. Trans. Steven Rendall. Berkeley: University of California Press.

De Neve, Geert. 1999. "Asking for and Giving *Baki*: Neo-bondage, or the Interplay of Bondage and Resistance in the Tamilnadu Power-Loom Industry." In *The Worlds of Indian Industrial Labour*, ed. Jonathan Parry, Jan Breman, and Karin Kapadia, 379–406. London: Sage. http://dx.doi.org/10.1177/006996679903300116.

De Neve, Geert. 2001. "Towards an Ethnography of the Workplace: Hierarchy, Authority and Sociability on the South Indian Textile Shop-Floor." *South Asia Research* 21 (2): 133–60. http://dx.doi.org/10.1177/026272800102100201.

De Neve, Geert. 2005. *The Everyday Politics of Labour: Working Lives in India's Informal Economy*. New Delhi: Social Science Press.

DelVecchio Good, Mary-Jo, Paul E. Brodwin, Byron J. Good, and Arthur Kleinman. 1992. *Pain as Human Experience: An Anthropological Perspective*. Berkeley: University of California Press.

Dilley, Roy. 1999. "Ways of Knowing, Forms of Power." *Cultural Dynamics* 11 (1): 33–55. http://dx.doi.org/10.1177/092137409901100103.

Dookeran, Winston. 1985 [1974]. "East Indians and the Economy of Trinidad and Tobago." In *Calcutta to Caroni: The East Indians of Trinidad*, ed. John Gaffar La Guerre, 69–83. London: Longman Group.

Dressler, William W. 1982. *Hypertension and Culture Change: Acculturation and Disease in the West Indies*. South Salem, NY: Redgrave.

Drori, Israel. 2000. *The Seam Line: Arab Workers and Jewish Managers in the Israeli Textile Industry*. Stanford, CA: Stanford University Press.

Drosdoff, Daniel. 2004. "Women of Steel." *IDB America: Magazine of the Inter-American Development Bank*. August. http://www.iadb.org/idbamerica/index.cfm?thisid=2937. Accessed May 28, 2007 (page no longer available).

du Toit, Brian M. 2001. "Ethnomedical (Folk) Healing in the Caribbean." In *Healing Cultures: Art and Religion as Curative Practices in the Caribbean and Its Diaspora*, ed. Margarite Fernández Olmos and Lizabeth Paravisini-Gebert, 19–28. New York: Palgrave.

Dunn, Elizabeth C. 2004. *Privatizing Poland: Baby Food, Big Business, and the Remaking of Labor*. Ithaca, NY: Cornell University Press.

Dypski, Michael Cornell. 2002. "The Caribbean Basin Initiative: An Examination of Structural Dependency, Good Neighbor Relations, and American Investment." *Journal of Transnational Law and Policy* 12: 95–136.

Economist, The. 2008. "A Caribbean Crime Wave." *The Economist*, March 20. http://www.economist.com/displayStory.cfm?story_id=10903343&fsrc=RSS. Accessed January 31, 2014.

Economist Intelligence Unit (EIU). 2003. *Country Report 2003: Trinidad and Tobago*. London: EIU.

Economist Intelligence Unit (EIU). 2005. *Country Report 2005: Trinidad and Tobago*. London: EIU.

Elson, Diane. 1983. "Nimble Fingers and Other Fables." In *Of Common Cloth: Women in the Global Textile Industry*, ed. Wendy Chapkis and Cynthia Enloe, 5–14. Amsterdam: Transnational.

Elson, Diane, and Ruth Pearson. 1981. "Nimble Fingers and Cheap Workers: An Analysis of Women's Employment in Third World Export Manufacturing." *Feminist Review* 7 (1): 87–107. http://dx.doi.org/10.1057/fr.1981.6.

England, Sarah. 2008. "Reading the Dougla Body: Mixed-Race, Post-Race, and Other Narratives of What It Means to Be Mixed in Trinidad." *Latin American and Caribbean Ethnic Studies* 3 (1): 1–31. http://dx.doi.org/10.1080/17442220701865820.

Enloe, Cynthia. 1989. *Bananas, Beaches, and Bases*. Berkeley: University of California Press.

Enslin, Elizabeth. 1994. "Beyond Writing: Feminist Practice and the Limitations of Ethnography." *Cultural Anthropology* 9 (4): 537–68. http://dx.doi.org/10.1525/can.1994.9.4.02a00040.

Eriksen, Thomas Hylland. 1990. "Liming in Trinidad: The Art of Doing Nothing." *Folk (Kobenhavn)* 32 (1): 24–43.

Ferguson, James. 2009. "The Uses of Neoliberalism." *Antipode* 41 (1): 166–84.

Ferguson, James, and Akhil Gupta. 2002. "Spatializing States: Toward an Ethnography of Neoliberal Governmentality." *American Ethnologist* 29 (4): 981–1002. http://dx.doi.org/10.1525/ae.2002.29.4.981.

Fernandes, Leela. 1997. *Producing Workers: The Politics of Gender, Class, and Culture in the Calcutta Jute Mills*. Philadelphia: University of Pennsylvania Press.

Foucault, Michel. 1979. *Discipline and Punish: The Birth of the Prison*. Trans. Alan Sheridan. New York: Vintage Books.

Foucault, Michel. 1991. "Governmentality." In *The Foucault Effect: Studies in Governmentality*, ed. Graham Burchell, Colin Gordon, and Peter Miller, 87–104. London: Harvester Wheatsheaf.

Frederick, Stacey, and Cornelia Staritz. 2012. "Developments in the Global Apparel Industry after the MFA Phaseout." In *Sewing Success? Employment, Wages, and Poverty following the End of the Multi-Fibre Arrangement*, ed. Gladys Lopez-Acevado and Raymond Robertson, 41–85. Washington, DC: World Bank. http://dx.doi.org/10.1596/9780821387788_CH03.

Freeman, Carla. 1993. "Designing Women: Corporate Discipline and Barbados's Off-Shore Pink-Collar Sector." *Cultural Anthropology* 8 (2): 169–86. http://dx.doi.org/10.1525/can.1993.8.2.02a00030.

Freeman, Carla. 1997. "Reinventing Higglering in a Transnational Arena: Barbadian Women Juggle the Triple Shift." In *Daughters of Caliban: Caribbean Women in the 20th Century*, ed. Consuelo Lopez Springfield, 68–95. Bloomington: Indiana University Press.

Freeman, Carla. 1998. "Femininity and Flexible Labor: Fashioning Class through Gender on the Global Assembly Line." *Critique of Anthropology* 18 (3): 245–62. http://dx.doi.org/10.1177/0308275X9801800302.

Freeman, Carla. 2000. *High Tech and High Heels in the Global Economy: Women, Work, and Pink-Collar Identities in the Caribbean*. Durham, NC: Duke University Press. http://dx.doi.org/10.1215/9780822380290.

Freeman, Carla. 2001. "Is Local:Global as Feminine:Masculine? Rethinking the Gender of Globalization." *Signs* 26 (4): 1007–37. http://dx.doi.org/10.1086/495646.

Freeman, Carla. 2005. "Neoliberalism, Respectability, and the Romance of Flexibility in Barbados." Working Paper no. 40, Emory Center for Myth and Ritual in American Life. Atlanta: Emory University.

Freeman, Carla. 2007. "The 'Reputation' of Neoliberalism." *American Ethnologist* 34 (2): 252–67. http://dx.doi.org/10.1525/ae.2007.34.2.252.

Fuentes, Annette, and Barbara Ehrenreich. 1983. *Women in the Global Factory*. Boston: South End.

Garni, Alisa. 2014. "Transnational Traders: El Salvador's Women Couriers in Historical Perspective." *Sociological Forum* 29 (1): 165–88. http://dx.doi.org/10.1111/socf.12074.

Genovese, Eugene D. 1976. *Roll, Jordan, Roll: The World the Slaves Made*. New York: Vintage.

Gereffi, Gary, and Stacey Frederick. 2010. "The Global Apparel Value Chain, Trade, and the Crisis: Challenges and Opportunities for Developing Countries." In *Global Value Chains in a Postcrisis World: A Development Perspective*, ed. Olivier Cattaneo, Gary Gereffi, and Cornelia Staritz, 157–208. Washington, DC: World Bank.

Godoy, Angelina Snodgrass. 2006. *Popular Injustice: Violence, Community, and Law in Latin America*. Stanford, CA: Stanford University Press.

Goldstein, Donna M. 2003. *Laughter Out of Place: Race, Class, Violence, and Sexuality in a Rio Shantytown*. Berkeley: University of California Press.

Gramsci, Antonio. 1971. *Prison Notebooks: Selections*. Trans. Quintin Hoare and Geoffrey N. Smith. New York: International Publishers.

Gray, Obika. 2004. *Demeaned but Empowered: The Social Power of the Urban Poor in Jamaica*. Kingston: University of the West Indies Press.

Greaves, Ynolde. 1974. "Conditions and Problems Affecting Productivity in the Garment Industry." BA dissertation, University of the West Indies, St. Augustine, Trinidad and Tobago.

Greenhouse, Carol J. 2010. "Introduction." In *Ethnographies of Neoliberalism*, ed. Carol J. Greenhouse, 1–10. Philadelphia: University of Pennsylvania Press. http://dx.doi.org/10.9783/9780812200010.1.

Gregory, Steven. 2007. *The Devil behind the Mirror: Globalization and Politics in the Dominican Republic*. Berkeley: University of California Press.

Griffith, Winston H. 1990. "CARICOM Countries and the Caribbean Basin Initiative." *Latin American Perspectives* 17 (1): 33–54. http://dx.doi.org/10.1177/0094582X9001700103.

Guardian South Bureau. 2004. "PM to Address Nation on New Crime Strategy." *Trinidad Guardian*. Monday, July 12, 5.

Hale, Angela, and Jane Wills, eds. 2005. *Threads of Labour: Garment Industry Supply Chains from the Workers' Perspective*. London: Blackwell. http://dx.doi.org/10.1002/9780470761434.

Halstead, Narmala. 2002. "Branding 'Perfection': Foreign as Self; Self as 'Foreign-Foreign.'" *Journal of Material Culture* 7 (3): 273–93. http://dx.doi.org/10.1177/135918350200700302.

Haraszti, Miklos. 1978. *A Worker in a Worker's State: Piece-Rates in Hungary*. Trans. Michael Wright. New York: Universe Books.

Harrington, Christy. 2000. "Fiji's Women Garment Workers: Negotiating Constraints in Employment and Beyond." *Labor and Management in Development Journal* 1 (5): 2–22.

Harris, Wilson. 1995. *History, Fable, and Myth: In the Caribbean and the Guianas*. Wellesley, MA: Calaloux.

Harrison, Faye V. 1998. ""Women in Jamaica's Urban Informal Economy: Insights from a Kingston Slum." *Nieuwe West-Indische Gids / New West Indian Guide* 62 (3–4): 103–28.

Hart, Keith. 1973. "Informal Income Opportunities and Urban Employment in Ghana." *Journal of Modern African Studies* 11 (1): 61–89. http://dx.doi.org/10.1017/S0022278X00008089.

Hart, Keith. 2010. "Informal Economy." In *The Human Economy: A Citizen's Guide*, ed. Keith Hart, Jean-Louis Laville, and Antonio David Cattani, 142–53. Cambridge: Polity.

Harvey, David. 1990. *The Conditions of Postmodernity: An Enquiry into the Origins of Cultural Change*. Oxford: Blackwell.

Heeralal, Daryl. 2004. "Morvant 'Don's' Ex Shot Dead." *Trinidad and Tobago Saturday Express*. Saturday, April 3, 3.

Henry, Ralph M. 1993. "Notes on the Evolution of Inequality in Trinidad and Tobago." In *Trinidad Ethnicity*, ed. Kevin A. Yelvington, 56–80. London: Macmillan.

Henry, Ralph M., and Gwendoline Williams. 1991. "Structural Adjustment and Gender in Trinidad and Tobago." In *Social and Occupational Stratification in Contemporary Trinidad and Tobago*, ed. Selwyn Ryan. St. Augustine: Institute of Social and Economic Research, University of the West Indies.

Heron, Adom Philogene. 2011. "Taming the Spider Man: From Anticolonial Hero to Neoliberal Icon." Paper presented at the Société Internationale d'Ethnologie et de Folklore (SIEF) Conference, Lisbon, Portugal, April 17–21.

Herzfeld, Michael. 2004. *The Body Impolitic: Artisans and Artifice in the Global Hierarchy of Value*. Chicago: University of Chicago Press.

Hewamanne, Sandya. 2010. *Stitching Identities in a Free Trade Zone: Gender and Politics in Sri Lanka*. Philadelphia: University of Pennsylvania Press.

Higman, Barry W. 1984. *Slave Populations of the British Caribbean 1807–1834*. Baltimore: Johns Hopkins University Press.

Hilaire, Alvin D.L. 2000. "Caribbean Approaches to Economic Stabilization." International Monetary Fund (IMF) Working Paper WP/00/73. Washington, DC: IMF Western Hemisphere Department.

Hobsbawm, Eric J. 1969. *Bandits*. Worcester, MA: Trinity.
Holland, Dorothy, William Lachicotte Jr., Debra Skinner, and Carole Cain. 1998. *Identity and Agency in Cultural Worlds*. Cambridge, MA: Harvard University Press.
Holmström, Mark. 1998. "Introduction: Industrial Districts and Flexible Specialization: The Outlook for Smaller Firms in India." In *Decentralized Production in India: Industrial Districts, Flexible Specialization, and Employment*, ed. Philippe Cadène and Mark Holmström, 7–41. London: Sage.
Hosein, Roger. 2006. *Aspects of the Labour Market in a Small Oil Rich Economy and Some Associated Policy Suggestions*. Port of Spain: ILO Caribbean.
Hsiung, Ping-Chun. 1996. "Between Bosses and Workers: Dilemmas of a Keen Observer and a Vocal Feminist." In *Feminist Dilemmas in Fieldwork*, ed. Diane L. Wolf, 122–37. Boulder: Westview.
International Labour Organization (ILO). 2004. *National Labour Law Profile: Trinidad and Tobago*. Geneva: ILO. http://www.ilo.org/public/english/dialogue/ifpdial/info/national/tt.htm. Accessed July 28, 2007.
International Labour Organization (ILO) Caribbean. 1997. *Women Entrepreneurs in Micro and Small Businesses in Trinidad and Tobago*. Port of Spain: ILO Caribbean.
International Monetary Fund (IMF). 2004. *Article IV Consultation with Trinidad and Tobago: Public Information Notice (PIN) no. 04/136*. Washington, DC: IMF Printing. http://www.imf.org/external/np/sec/pn/2004/pn04136.htm. Accessed July 27, 2007.
Jain, Sarah S. Lochlann. 2006. *Injury: The Politics of Product Design and Safety Law in the United States*. Princeton, NJ: Princeton University Press.
Jayasinghe, Daphne. 2001. "'More and More Technology, Women Have to Go Home': Changing Skill Demands in Manufacturing and Caribbean Women's Access to Training." *Gender and Development* 9 (1): 70–81. http://dx.doi.org/10.1080/13552070127730.
Jiménez, Alberto Corsín. 2003. "Working out Personhood: Notes on 'Labour' and Its Anthropology." *Anthropology Today* 19 (5): 14–17. http://dx.doi.org/10.1111/1467-8322.00217.
Johnson, Tony. 2003. "T&T 2nd in Kidnap World." *Trinidad and Tobago Sunday Express*. Sunday, October 19. http://www.trinidadandtobagonews.com/forum/webbbs_config.pl/noframes/read/1233. Accessed January 19, 2007.
Kabeer, Naila, and Simeen Mahmud. 2004. "Globalization, Gender and Poverty: Bangladeshi Women Workers in Export and Local Markets." *Journal of International Development* 16 (1): 93–109. http://dx.doi.org/10.1002/jid.1065.
Karides, Marina. 2010. "Theorizing the Rise of Microenterprise Development in Caribbean Context." *Journal of World-Systems Research* 16 (2): 192–216.
Khan, Aisha. 1998. "Constructing Identities in Trinidad." *American Ethnologist* 25 (3): 499–500. http://dx.doi.org/10.1525/ae.1998.25.3.499.
Khan, Aisha. 2003. "Isms and Schisms: Interpreting Religion in the Americas." *Anthropological Quarterly* 76 (4): 761–74. http://dx.doi.org/10.1353/anq.2003.0056.

Khan, Aisha. 2004. *Callaloo Nation: Metaphors of Race and Religious Identity among South Asians in Trinidad*. Durham, NC: Duke University Press. http://dx.doi.org/10.1215/9780822386094.

Kiely, Ray. 1996. *The Politics of Labour and Development in Trinidad*. Kingston: University of the West Indies Press.

Kim, Jaesok. 2013. *Chinese Labor in a Korean Factory: Class, Ethnicity, and Productivity on the Shop Floor in Globalizing China*. Stanford, CA: Stanford University Press. http://dx.doi.org/10.11126/stanford/9780804784542.001.0001.

Kincaid, Jamaica. 1983. *At the Bottom of the River: Stories*. New York: Farrar, Straus and Giroux.

Ladoo, Harold Sonny. 1972. *No Pain Like This Body*. London: Heinemann.

Lamphere, Louise. 1987. *From Working Daughters to Working Mothers: Immigrant Women in a New England Industrial Community*. Ithaca, NY: Cornell University Press.

Lee, Ann. 1997. "The Steelband Movement and Community Politics in Laventille." In *Behind the Bridge: Poverty, Politics and Patronage in Laventille, Trinidad*, ed. Selwyn Ryan, Roy McCree, and Godfrey St Bernard, 69–89. St. Augustine: Institute of Social and Economic Research, University of the West Indies.

Lessinger, Johanna. 2002. "Work and Love: The Limits of Autonomy for Female Garment Workers in India." *Anthropology of Work Review* 23 (1–2): 13–18. http://dx.doi.org/10.1525/awr.2002.23.1-2.13.

Levine, Lawrence W. 1977. *Black Culture and Black Consciousness: Afro-American Folk Thought from Slavery to Freedom*. Oxford: Oxford University Press.

Lewis, W. Arthur. 1950. "The Industrialisation of the British West Indies." *Caribbean Economic Review* 2 (1): 1–61.

Lieber, Michael. 1981. *Street Scenes: Afro-American Culture in Urban Trinidad*. Cambridge, MA: Schenkman.

Littlewood, Roland. 1988. "From Vice to Madness: The Semantics of Naturalistic and Personalistic Understandings in Trinidad Local Medicine." *Social Science and Medicine* 27 (2): 129–48. http://dx.doi.org/10.1016/0277-9536(88)90322-X.

Long, Joseph K. 1974. "Jamaican Medicine: Choice between Folk Healing and Modern Medicine." PhD dissertation, University of North Carolina, Chapel Hill.

Lord, Richard. 2004. "Mark Slams Police on Bonadie Killing." *Trinidad and Tobago Express*. Wednesday, April 7, 3.

Loutoo, Jada. 2007. "Appeal Court Quashes Panday's Conviction." *Trinidad Guardian*. Wednesday, March 21. http://guardian.co.tt/archives/2007-03-21/news8.html. Accessed August 3, 2007.

Lovelace, Earl. 1998 [1979]. *The Dragon Can't Dance*. London: Faber and Faber.

Lu, Sheng. 2013. "Impacts of Quota Elimination on World Textile Trade: A Reality Check from 2000 to 2010." *Journal of the Textile Institute* 104 (3): 239–50. http://dx.doi.org/10.1080/00405000.2012.717753.

Luvaas, Brent. 2010. "Designer Vandalism: Indonesian Indie Fashion and the Cultural Practice of Cut 'n' Paste." *Visual Anthropology Review* 26 (1): 1–16. http://dx.doi.org/10.1111/j.1548-7458.2010.01043.x.

Lynch, Caitrin. 2007. *Juki Girls, Good Girls: Gender and Cultural Politics in Sri Lanka's Global Garment Industry*. Ithaca, NY: Cornell University Press.

Mahabir, Kumar. 1991. *Medicinal and Edible Plants Used by East Indians of Trinidad and Tobago*. San Juan, Trinidad and Tobago: Chakra.

Mahabir, Kumar. 2005. "Kidnappings in Trinidad: A Statistical Analysis." Paper presented at public lecture hosted by the Global Organization of People of Indian Origin (GOPIO), Divali Nagar, Trinidad, Sunday, April 3.

Maher, Vanessa. 1987. "Sewing the Seams of Society: Dressmakers and Seamstresses in Turin between the Wars." In *Gender and Kinship: Essays toward a Unified Analysis*, ed. Jane Fishburne Collier and Sylvia Junko Yanagisako, 132–59. Stanford, CA: Stanford University Press.

Manning, Patrick. 2005. "Prime Minister's Statement on Reform of the Non-Energy Tax Regime." *Trinidad Guardian*. Wednesday, September 28. http://www.guardian.co.tt/archives/2006-04-19/b9.html. Accessed July 26, 2007.

Mantz, Jeffrey W. 2007. "How a Huckster Becomes a Custodian of Market Morality: Traditions of Flexibility in Exchange in Dominica." *Identities: Global Studies in Culture and Power* 14 (1): 14–38. http://dx.doi.org/10.1080/10702890601102506.

Marchand, Trevor H.J. 2003. "A Possible Explanation for the Lack of Explanation; or, Why the Master Builder Can't Explain What He Knows: Introducing Informational Atomism against a 'Definitional' Definition of Concepts." In *Negotiating Local Knowledge: Power and Identity in Development*, ed. Johan Pottier, Alan Bicker, and Paul Silitoe, 30–50. London: Pluto.

Marchand, Trevor H.J. 2008. "Muscles, Morals and Mind: Craft Apprenticeship and the Formation of Person." *British Journal of Educational Studies* 56 (3): 245–71. http://dx.doi.org/10.1111/j.1467-8527.2008.00407.x.

Mars, Gerald. 1982. *Cheats at Work: An Anthropology of Workplace Crime*. London: Unwin.

Martin, Emily. 1994. *Flexible Bodies: The Role of Immunity in American Culture from the Days of Polio to the Age of AIDS*. Boston: Beacon.

Masi de Casanova, Erynn. 2011. *Making up the Difference: Women, Beauty, and Direct Selling in Ecuador*. Austin: University of Texas Press.

Massiah, Joycelin. 1986. "Work in the Lives of Caribbean Women." *Social and Economic Studies* 35 (2): 177–239.

Meighoo, Kirk. 2004. "Strength and Transformation." *Trinidad and Tobago Sunday Express*. Sunday, October 31, 13.

Mendes, John. 1986. *Cote Ce Cote La: Trinidad and Tobago Dictionary*. Arima, Trinidad and Tobago: Self-published.

Merleau-Ponty, Maurice. 1962. *The Phenomenology of Perception*. Trans. Colin Smith. London: Routledge.

Miller, Daniel. 1992. "The Young and the Restless in Trinidad: A Case of the Local and the Global in Mass Consumption." In *Consuming Technologies: Media and Information in Domestic Spaces*, ed. Roger Silverstone and Eric Hirsch, 163–82. London: Routledge. http://dx.doi.org/10.4324/9780203401491_chapter_10.

Miller, Daniel. 1994a. *Modernity, an Ethnographic Approach: Dualism and Mass Consumption in Trinidad*. Oxford: Berg.

Miller, Daniel. 1994b. "Style and Ontology." In *Consumption and Identity*, ed. Jonathan Friedman, 71–96. Chur, Switzerland: Harwood Academic.

Miller, Daniel. 1997. *Capitalism: An Ethnographic Approach*. Oxford: Berg.

Mills, Mary Beth. 1997. "Contesting the Margins of Modernity: Women, Migration and Consumption in Thailand." *American Ethnologist* 24 (1): 37–61. http://dx.doi.org/10.1525/ae.1997.24.1.37.

Mills, Mary Beth. 1999. *Thai Women in the Global Labor Force: Consuming Desires, Contested Selves*. New Brunswick, NJ: Rutgers University Press.

Mintz, Sidney W. 1976. *The Birth of African-American Culture: An Anthropological Perspective*. Boston: Beacon Press.

Mintz, Sidney W. 1996. "Enduring Substances, Trying Theories: The Caribbean Region as Oikoumenê." *Journal of the Royal Anthropological Institute* 2 (2): 289–311. http://dx.doi.org/10.2307/3034097.

Mintz, Sidney W. 1998. 'The Localization of Anthropological Practice: From Area Studies to Transnationalism.' *Critique of Anthropology* 18 (2): 117–33.

Mohammed, Patricia. 1989. "Women's Responses in the 70s and 80s in Trinidad: A Country Report." *Caribbean Quarterly* 35 (1–2): 36–45.

Molé, Noelle J. 2010. "Precarious Subjects: Anticipating Neoliberalism in Northern Italy's Workplace." *American Anthropologist* 112 (1): 38–53. http://dx.doi.org/10.1111/j.1548-1433.2009.01195.x.

Mollenkopf, John Hull, and Manuel Castells, eds. 1991. *The Dual City: Restructuring New York*. New York: Russell Sage.

Mollona, Massimiliano. 2005. "Factory, Family and Neighbourhood: The Political Economy of Informal Labour in Sheffield." *Journal of the Royal Anthropological Institute* 11 (3): 527–48. http://dx.doi.org/10.1111/j.1467-9655.2005.00249.x.

Mollona, Massimiliano. 2009. *Made in Sheffield: An Ethnography of Industrial Work and Practice*. New York: Berghahn.

Momm, Willi. 1999. "Restructuring Caribbean Labour Markets in the Context of Globalization and Trade Liberalization." In *Labour Issues in the Context of Economic Integration and Free Trade: A Caribbean Perspective*, ed. Willi Momm, 49–54. Port of Spain: ILO Caribbean.

Monsegue, Horace. 1989. "Garment Industry 'Alive and Well': High Praise for IDC Graduates." *Trinidad Guardian*. Sunday, July 25, 14.

Moonilal, Roodal. 2001. "Workers' Protection: The Case of Trinidad and Tobago." Working Paper no. 7, International Labour Organization (ILO) Caribbean Working Papers Series. Port of Spain: ILO Caribbean Office.

Mose Brown, Tamara. 2011. *Raising Brooklyn: Nannies, Childcare and Caribbeans Creating Community.* New York: New York University Press.

Mose Brown, Tamara, and Erynn Masi de Casanova. 2014. "Representing the Language of the 'Other': African American Vernacular English in Ethnography." *Ethnography* 15 (2): 208–31.

Munasinghe, Viranjini. 2001. *Callaloo or Tossed Salad? East Indians and the Cultural Politics of Identity in Trinidad.* Ithaca, NY: Cornell University Press.

Munasinghe, Viranjini. 2002. "Nationalism in Hybrid Spaces: The Production of Impurity out of Purity." *American Ethnologist* 29 (3): 663–92. http://dx.doi.org/10.1525/ae.2002.29.3.663.

Munasinghe, Viranjini. 2006. "Theorizing World Culture through the New World: East Indians and Creolization." *American Ethnologist* 33 (4): 549–62. http://dx.doi.org/10.1525/ae.2006.33.4.549.

Mycoo, Michelle. 2006. "The Retreat of the Upper and Middle Classes to Gated Communities in the Poststructural Adjustment Era: The Case of Trinidad." *Environment and Planning A* 38 (1): 131–48. http://dx.doi.org/10.1068/a37323.

Naipaul, V. S. 1967. *A Flag on the Island.* New York: Macmillan.

Naipaul, V. S. 1981 [1962]. *The Middle Passage.* New York: Vintage.

Naipaul, V. S. 2001 [1961]. *A House for Mr. Biswas.* New York: Vintage.

Ngai, Pun. 2005. *Made in China: Women Factory Workers in a Global Workplace.* Durham, NC: Duke University Press.

Nordas, Hildegunn Kyvik. 2004. *Global Textile and Clothing Industry Post the Agreement on Textiles and Clothing.* Geneva: World Trade Organization.

O'Connor, Peter. 2007. "We Cringe in Shame!" *Trinidad and Tobago's Newsday.* Sunday, March 11. http://www.newsday.co.tt/commentary/0,53646.html. Accessed June 5, 2007.

O'Malley, Michael. 1992. "Time, Work and Task Orientation: A Critique of American Historiography." *Time and Society* 1 (3): 341–58. http://dx.doi.org/10.1177/0961463X92001003002.

Olmstead, Frederick Law. 1856. *A Journey in the Seaboard Slave States, with Remarks on Their Economy.* New York: Dix and Edwards.

Ong, Aihwa. 1987a. *Spirits of Resistance and Capitalist Discipline: Factory Women in Malaysia.* Albany: State University of New York Press.

Ong, Aihwa. 1987b. "Review Essay: Disassembling Gender in the Electronics Age." *Feminist Studies* 13 (3): 609–26. http://dx.doi.org/10.2307/3177883.

Ong, Aihwa. 1991. "The Gender and Labor Politics of Postmodernity." *Annual Review of Anthropology* 20 (1): 279–309. http://dx.doi.org/10.1146/annurev.an.20.100191.001431.

Ong, Aihwa. 2006. *Neoliberalism as Exception: Mutations in Citizenship and Sovereignty.* Durham, NC: Duke University Press. http://dx.doi.org/10.1215/9780822387879.

Ortiz, Sutti. 2002. "Laboring in the Factories and in the Fields." *Annual Review of Anthropology* 31 (1): 395–417. http://dx.doi.org/10.1146/annurev.anthro.31.031902.161108.

Ortner, Sherry B. 1996. *Making Gender: The Politics and Erotics of Culture*. Boston: Beacon.

Ortner, Sherry B. 2005. "Subjectivity and Cultural Critique." *Anthropological Theory* 5 (1): 31–52. http://dx.doi.org/10.1177/1463499605050867.

Osirim, Mary Johnson. 1997. "We Toil All the Livelong Day: Women in the English-Speaking Caribbean." In *Daughters of Caliban: Caribbean Women in the Twentieth Century*, ed. Consuelo Lopez Springfield, 41–67. Bloomington: Indiana University Press.

Özden, Çaglar, and Gunjan Sharma. 2006. "Price Effects of Preferential Market Access: Caribbean Basin Initiative and the Apparel Sector." *World Bank Economic Review* 20 (2): 241–59. http://dx.doi.org/10.1093/wber/lhj008.

Peña, Devon G. 1997. *The Terror of the Machine: Technology, Work, Gender, and Ecology on the US-Mexican Border*. Austin: University of Texas Press.

Piore, Michael J., and Charles F. Sabel. 1984. *The Second Industrial Divide: Possibilities for Prosperity*. New York: Basic Books.

Pires, B. C. 2004. "Yes to State of Emergency." *Trinidad and Tobago Sunday Express*. Sunday, October 31, 6.

Pollard, H. J. 1985. "The Erosion of Agriculture in an Oil Economy: The Case of Export Crop Production in Trinidad." *World Development* 13 (7): 819–35. http://dx.doi.org/10.1016/0305-750X(85)90110-X.

Pollard, Velma. 2005. "Woman and Family in the African Diaspora: Mother and the Sewing Machine in Caribbean Literature." *Changing English* 12 (1): 53–60. http://dx.doi.org/10.1080/1358684052000340452.

Portes, Alejandro, and John Walton. 1981. *Labor, Class, and the International System*. New York: Academic.

Premdas, Ralph. 1993. "Ethnic Conflict in Trinidad and Tobago: Domination and Reconciliation." In *Trinidad Ethnicity*, ed. Kevin A. Yelvington, 136–60. Knoxville: University of Tennessee Press.

Prentice, Rebecca. 2008. "Knowledge, Skill, and the Inculcation of the Anthropologist: Reflections on Learning to Sew in the Field." *Anthropology of Work Review* 29 (3): 54–61. http://dx.doi.org/10.1111/j.1548-1417.2008.00020.x.

Prentice, Rebecca, and Gavin Hamilton Whitelaw. 2008. "Introduction to Special Issue, Embodying Labor: Work as Fieldwork." *Anthropology of Work Review* 29 (3): 53–54. http://dx.doi.org/10.1111/j.1548-1417.2008.00019.x.

Puri, Shalini. 1999. "Race, Rape, and Representation: Indo-Caribbean Women and Cultural Nationalism." In *Matikor: The Politics of Identity for Indo-Caribbean Women*, ed. Rosanne Kanhai, 238–82. St. Augustine: University of the West Indies School of Continuing Studies.

Quinlan, Marsha B. 2004. *From the Bush: The Front Line of Health Care in a Caribbean Village*. Belmont, CA: Wadsworth.

Rahman, Mustafizur, Asif Anwar, Fida-e- Tashfia, and Zebulun Kreiter. 2008. "Global Trade in T&C after the MFA Phase-Out: Emerging Trends and Challenges for Low-Income Developing Countries." Occasional Paper 70A, Centre for Policy Dialogue. Dhaka: Centre for Policy Dialogue.

Ramprasad, Frank. 1997. *The New World Trade Order: Uruguay Round Agreements and Implications for CARICOM States*. Kingston: Ian Randle.

Ramsaran, Ramesh F. 1992. *The Challenge of Structural Adjustment in the Commonwealth Caribbean*. New York: Praeger.

Reddock, Rhoda E. 1984. "Women and Garment Production in Trinidad and Tobago 1900–1960." Working Paper no. 2, Sub-Series on Women's History and Development. The Hague: Institute of Social Studies.

Reddock, Rhoda E. 1993. "Transformation in the Needle Trades: Women in Garment and Textile Production in Early Twentieth Century Trinidad and Tobago." In *Women and Change in the Caribbean*, ed. Janet H. Momsen, 249–62. Bloomington: Indiana University Press.

Reddock, Rhoda E. 1994. *Women, Labour, and Politics in Trinidad and Tobago: A History*. London: Zed Books.

Reddock, Rhoda E. 1998. "Women's Organizations and Movements in the Commonwealth Caribbean: The Response to Global Economic Crisis in the 1980s." *Feminist Review* 59 (1): 57–73. http://dx.doi.org/10.1080/014177898339451.

Regis, Louis. 1999. *The Political Calypso: True Opposition in Trinidad and Tobago, 1962–1987*. Gainesville: University Press of Florida.

Richards, Peter. 2005. "Labour-Trinidad: Outdated Law Costs Lives, Unions Charge." *Inter-Press Service News Agency*. Saturday, August 26. http://ipsnews.net/news.asp?idnews=30040. Accessed February 12, 2007.

Riddell, Barry. 2003. "The Face of Neo-liberalism in the Third World: Landscapes of Coping in Trinidad and Tobago." *Canadian Journal of Development Studies* 24 (4): 592–615. http://dx.doi.org/10.1080/02255189.2003.9668947.

Rivoli, Pietra. 2005. *The Travels of a T-Shirt in the Global Economy: An Economist Examines the Markets, Power, and Politics of World Trade*. Hoboken, NJ: Wiley and Sons.

Roberts, John W. 1978. "Slave Proverbs: A Perspective." *Callaloo* 4 (4): 129–40. http://dx.doi.org/10.2307/2930902.

Roberts, John W. 1989. *From Trickster to Badman: The Black Folk Hero in Slavery and Freedom*. Philadelphia: University of Pennsylvania Press. http://dx.doi.org/10.9783/9780812203110.

Robotham, Don. 1998. "Transnationalism in the Caribbean: Formal and Informal." *American Ethnologist* 25 (2): 307–21. http://dx.doi.org/10.1525/ae.1998.25.2.307.

Robotham, Don. 2003. "Review of *Callaloo or Tossed Salad: East Indians and the Cultural Politics of Identity in Trinidad*, by Viranjini Munasinghe." *Transforming Anthropology* 11 (2): 68–70. http://dx.doi.org/10.1525/tran.2003.11.2.68.

Rodman, Hyman. 1971. *Lower-Class Families: The Culture of Poverty in Negro Trinidad*. New York: Oxford University Press.

Rofel, Lisa. 1992. "Rethinking Modernity: Space and Factory Discipline in China." *Cultural Anthropology* 7 (1): 93–114. http://dx.doi.org/10.1525/can.1992.7.1.02a00070.

Rofel, Lisa. 1999. *Other Modernities: Gendered Yearnings in China after Socialism*. Berkeley: University of California Press.

Rohlehr, Gordon. 1990. *Calypso and Society in Pre-Independence Trinidad*. Port of Spain: Self-published.

Rolston, Jessica Smith. 2010. "Risky Business: Neoliberalism and Workplace Safety in Wyoming Coal Mines." *Human Organization* 69 (4): 331–42.

Rose, Nikolas. 1999. *Powers of Freedom: Reframing Political Thought*. Cambridge, UK: Cambridge University Press. http://dx.doi.org/10.1017/CBO9780511488856.

Rothstein, Frances Abrahamer. 2005. "Flexibility for Whom? Small-Scale Garment Manufacturing in Rural Mexico." In *Petty Capitalists and Globalization: Flexibility, Entrepreneurship, and Economic Development*, ed. Alan Smart and Josephine Smart, 67–82. Albany: State University of New York Press.

Ryan, Selwyn. 1997. "Party Politics and Laventille." In *Behind the Bridge: Poverty, Politics and Patronage in Laventille, Trinidad*, ed. Selwyn Ryan, Roy McCree, and Godfrey St Bernard, 153–82. St. Augustine: Institute of Social and Economic Research, University of the West Indies.

Ryan, Selwyn. 2003. *Deadlock: Ethnicity and Electoral Competition in Trinidad and Tobago, 1995–2002*. St. Augustine: Sir Arthur Lewis Institute of Social and Economic Studies, University of the West Indies.

Ryan, Selwyn, Roy McCree, and Godfrey St Bernard, eds. 1997. *Behind the Bridge: Poverty, Politics and Patronage in Laventille, Trinidad*. St. Augustine: Institute of Social and Economic Research, University of the West Indies.

Sabel, Charles F. 1994. "Flexible Specialization and the Re-emergence of Regional Economies." In *Post-Fordism: A Reader*, ed. Ash Amin, 101–56. Cambridge: Blackwell. http://dx.doi.org/10.1002/9780470712726.ch4.

Salzinger, Leslie. 1997. "From High Heels to Swathed Bodies: Gendered Meanings under Production in Mexico's Export-Processing Industry." *Feminist Studies* 23 (3): 549–74. http://dx.doi.org/10.2307/3178386.

Salzinger, Leslie. 2003. *Genders in Production: Making Workers in Mexico's Global Factories*. Berkeley: University of California Press.

Sanders, Todd. 2008. "Buses in Bongoland: Seductive Analytics and the Occult." *Anthropological Theory* 8 (2): 107–32. http://dx.doi.org/10.1177/1463499960809 0787.

Scarry, Elaine. 1985. *The Body in Pain: The Making and Unmaking of the World*. Oxford: Oxford University Press.

Scheper-Hughes, Nancy, and Margaret M. Lock. 1987. "The Mindful Body: A Prolegomenon to Future Work in Medical Anthropology." *Medical Anthropology Quarterly* 1 (1): 6–41. http://dx.doi.org/10.1525/maq.1987.1.1.02a00020.

Scott, James C. 1985. *Weapons of the Weak: Everyday Forms of Peasant Resistance*. New Haven, CT: Yale University Press.

Scott, James C. 1990. *Domination and the Arts of Resistance: Hidden Transcripts*. New Haven, CT: Yale University Press.

Scott, James C. 2005. "Afterword to 'Moral Economies, State Spaces, and Categorical Violence.'" *American Anthropologist* 107 (3): 395–402. http://dx.doi.org/10.1525/aa.2005.107.3.395.

Seetahal, Dana. 2005. "A Dose of Reality?" *Trinidad Guardian*. Sunday, September 25. http://www.guardian.co.tt/archives/2005-09-25/dana.html. Accessed August 3, 2007.

Segal, Daniel A. 1994. "Living Ancestors: Nationalism and the Past in Postcolonial Trinidad and Tobago." In *Remapping Memory: The Politics of Time and Space*, ed. Jonathan Boyarin, 221–39. Minneapolis: University of Minnesota Press.

Senior, Olive. 1991. *Working Miracles: Women's Lives in the English-Speaking Caribbean*. Cave Hill, Barbados: Institute of Social and Economic Research.

Sergeant, Kelvin, and Penelope Forde. 1992. "The State Sector and Divestment in Trinidad and Tobago: Some Preliminary Findings." *Social and Economic Studies* 41 (4): 173–204.

Shah, Alpa. 2006. "The Labour of Love: Seasonal Migration from Jharkhand to the Brick Kilns of Other States in India." *Contributions to Indian Sociology* 40 (1): 91–118. http://dx.doi.org/10.1177/006996670504000104.

Sheppard, Suzanne. 2005. "Kidnapping Becoming a Growing Global Business." *Trinidad and Tobago Newsday*. Sunday, April 10. www.newsday.co.tt/news/print,0,26903.html. Accessed January 12, 2015.

Simpson, Edward. 2006. "Apprenticeship in Western India." *Journal of the Royal Anthropological Institute* 12 (1): 151–71. http://dx.doi.org/10.1111/j.1467-9655.2006.00285.x.

Singh, Sherry Ann. 2004. "Handicapped by Imports." *Trinidad Guardian*. Tuesday, March 25. http://www.guardian.co.tt/archives/2004-03-27/bussguardian3.html. Accessed May 24, 2007.

Slocum, Karla. 2006. *Free Trade and Freedom: Neoliberalism, Place, and Nation in the Caribbean*. Ann Arbor: University of Michigan Press.

Smith, Gavin. 1999. *Confronting the Present: Towards a Politically Engaged Anthropology*. Oxford: Berg.

Smith, Michael. 2003. "Police in Trinidad Find Body of Kidnapped Business Owner." Associated Press Worldstream, Tuesday, September 9. http://www.highbeam.com/doc/1P1-79530317.html. Accessed August 16, 2011.

Sobo, Elisa J. 1993. *One Blood: The Jamaican Body*. Albany: State University of New York Press.

Sooknanan, Devika. 2004. "Letter to the Editor: Crime a Disease in Trinidad." *Trinidad and Tobago's Newsday*. Saturday, January 31. http://www.newsday.co.tt/letters/0,14761.html. Accessed August 3, 2007.

Stacey, Judith. 1988. "Can There Be a Feminist Ethnography?" *Women's Studies International Forum* 11 (1): 21–27. http://dx.doi.org/10.1016/0277-5395(88)90004-0.

Stoller, Paul. 2002. *Money Has No Smell: The Africanization of New York City*. Chicago: University of Chicago Press. http://dx.doi.org/10.7208/chicago/9780226775265.001.0001.

Index

advertising, 25–26, 28
Afro-Trinidadians: categorization of, 19, 84n1; and East Port of Spain, 55–56; economic advancement of, 29, 140n1; and nationalism, 55; and party politics, 56, 84–85n3, 180, 188–89; at Signature Fashions, 52, 53–54, 63, 65–67, 69; and social hierarchy, 115; stereotyping of, 67–68. *See also* back workers
agency: concept of, 201; economic, 11–12; and flexible production, 45, 197; and learning to sew, 103–104, 139
All Trinidad Sugar and General Workers' Trade Union, 59
Anderson, Elijah, 57
Anteby, Michel, 88, 95–96, 109n5, 198–99
assembly line, 5, 34–35, 43–44; global, 49, 72

bacchanal, 57, 152
back area, 33–34, 45–48, 170. *See also* back workers
back workers: concept of, 51–53, 60–62; ethnic composition of, 52, 63–64; solidarity among, 62–63, 161; views of crime, 181–86, 191. *See also* organization of production
Bair, Jennifer, 195–96, 203
Beckles, Hilary, 115
Belmont, 18, 55, 57–58, 70
Birth, Kevin, 50n5, 85n5, 188
Bolles, Lynn, 141n3
Bourdieu, Pierre, 127

Braverman, Harry, 122–23
Browne, Katherine, 9–10, 14, 99–100, 118, 128. *See also* creole economics
Burawoy, Michael, 36–37, 107
button tacker, 154–55, 156(photo), 157, 160, 161–62

calypso, 55, 130, 183–84, 189
capitalism: early, 10–11; global, 7, 11; incidental nature of, 6, 202; mercantile, 52; neoliberal, 22–23n2, 27, 122, 139
capitalists, 6, 20–21, 31, 48, 107
Caribbean Community (CARICOM), 7–8, 22n1, 29, 117, 196
carnival, 18, 55, 128, 152, 196; clothing for, 38, 125, 130
Caroni, 58–59, 71
Chaguanas, 57, 60(photo); as home to Indo-Trinidadian workers, 52, 53, 54, 58–60
Charlotte Street, 70, 137, 142n8, 144
China, 3, 8, 32; subcontracting from, 27, 30, 141n6
clothing: brand-name, 9, 20, 26, 27; imported, 8, 129; symbolic importance of, 92–93, 129, 131, 134; worn by workers, 70, 82, 96, 141n5. *See also* garment industry
Cohen, Robin, 99
Collins, Jane, 40, 45
Comaroff, Jean and John, 190
Comitas, Lambros, 118

225

Community-Based Environmental Protection and Enhancement Programme (CEPEP), 56, 65, 178
creole economics, 9–10, 99
crime, 59–60, 173–75, 190–91; fear of, 58, 178–79; in Laventille, 56–57, 178, 181–82, 184–85; origins of, 177, 180, 182; and security, 175, 180. *See also* drugs; guns; kidnapping
Cro Cro, 183–86, 189, 191
Cross, Jamie, 22–23n2, 154, 162

de Certeau, Michel, 88
De Neve, Geert, 40, 108
desire: as a force of production, 5–6, 36–37, 48–49; to learn how to sew, 114, 127
discipline: and the body, 127; and industrial labor, 167, 168; and power, 202; at Signature Fashions 40–43, 65–67; and subjectivity, 11. *See also* "slave-driver situation"
Drori, Israel, 145
drugs, 22, 173, 177, 180, 181, 192n2

East Port of Spain, 52, 54, 55–58, 181, 185. *See also* Laventille
emancipation, 7, 55, 116
empowerment: concept of, 200–201
Enloe, Cynthia, 49, 195
entrepreneurialism: and Caribbean culture, 11, 200; and factory owners, 29–30; and neoliberalism, 10, 101, 201; petty, 113; and seamstresses, 132; and thiefing a chance, 108
Eriksen, Thomas, 99, 128
ethnography, 11–12, 16–17, 19–20, 202. *See also* fieldwork

factory, 5, 14; as a social and material assemblage, 6, 21, 202; as a source of knowledge, 113, 122–23, 133–34. *See also* Signature Fashions
fashion, 26, 28–29, 30, 38; concept of, 132–34, 135–37; workers' knowledge of, 113, 138
Fernandes, Leela, 53
fieldwork, 3–5, 15–20, 28
flexibility: and Caribbean culture, 101, 139, 200; in garment manufacturing, 27, 36–37, 44–45; and neoliberalism, 12, 140, 199. *See also* paradox of flexibility
flexible production, 114, 196–98; role of illicit work practices in, 6, 27, 44–45, 49, 107. *See also* "now for now"; paradox of flexibility; thiefing a chance
flexible specialization, 5, 35
flow: concept of, 90, 146, 149
Fordism, 4, 5, 34–35, 122, 168; as inflexible, 45, 197, 198
formal economy, 108, 113–14, 117, 126. *See also* informal economy
Foucault, Michel, 11, 45, 167, 202
Freeman, Carla, 1, 10, 51, 72, 82, 101, 140, 141n5, 199–200
free trade. *See* trade liberalization
front workers: concept of, 51–53, 60–62; ethnic composition of, 52, 63–64

garment industry, 7–9, 73, 151, 196–97, 203; and kidnapping, 175; state policies toward 75, 116–17; and trade unions, 152. *See also* trade liberalization
garment workers, 19, 72–73, 119–20; and labor activism, 152, 171–72n4; and neoliberalism, 12; resistance to label of, 71–72; stereotypes of, 11–12, 200. *See also* "into the sewing"; garment industry; Signature Fashions workers
Garni, Alisa, 73
gender, 17, 82; norms, 80–81, 135–36; production of, 12, 52–53, 69
governmentality, 45, 167, 200
Gramsci, Antonio, 14, 107, 167, 202
Gregory, Steven, 15, 124
guns, 22, 177, 181, 184–85, 192n2

Hart, Keith, 126
Harvey, David, 27
health concerns: blood-related, 148, 149; dust-related, 147; heat-related, 163–64; musculoskeletal, 148, 155–57; and temperature mixing, 146, 163, 164–67; vision-related, 143–44, 147–48. *See also* injury; occupational health
herbal remedies, 113, 144, 146, 149
Herzfeld, Michael, 127
Hobsbawm, Eric, 186
Holmström, Mark, 25
hucksters, 11, 116

identity: concept of, 52–53; and consumption, 82, 128, 133; and work, 62, 132, 198, 201
illicit work practices, 4–5, 12–14, 100, 199, 202; and flexible production, 6, 44–45, 107, 198;

valorization of, 99, 200. *See also* thiefing a chance
indentured laborers, 7, 19, 54, 58, 67, 140n1
individualism, 98, 101, 102, 107–108, 140
Indo-Trinidadians: categorization of, 19, 84n1; and Chaguanas, 58, 59–60; economic advancement of, 29–30, 80–81, 116, 140n1; and kidnapping, 175, 177, 187, 188; and nationalism, 55; and party politics, 180, 189; at Signature Fashions, 52, 53–54, 63; stereotyping of, 67–68, 189, 191
Industrial Court, 152, 168, 172n6
Industrial Relations Act, 152
informal economy, 9, 99, 113–15, 126, and skill acquisition, 139. *See also* illicit work practices; occupational multiplicity
injury, 9, 161, 168; concept of, 154, 159; unsuccessful claim of, 155–59, 201
interest: concept of, 6, 107, 202
International Monetary Fund (IMF), 2, 7, 26
"into the sewing": concept of, 71–72, 73, 200–201; and occupational multiplicity, 112, 117, 126; and skill, 123, 199. *See also* love

Jain, Sarah, 159

Khan, Aisha, 84n1
kidnapping: epidemic of, 174, 176–77, 182, 189; fear of, 178–80, 187–88
Kim, Jaesok, 40
Kincaid, Jamaica, 118–19

labor activism, 152. *See also* trade unions
Ladoo, Harold Sonny, 58
Laventille, 55–58, 57(photo), 59; association with crime, 60, 178, 181
Lieber, Michael, 17
liming, 16, 18, 148
love: of sewing, 21, 126–27, 132, 201; and skill, 108, 114, 126–27; and romantic partnership, 75
Lovelace, Earl, 128
Luvaas, Brent, 30

Maher, Vanessa, 121, 131, 134
Mantz, Jeffrey, 11, 199
Martin, Emily, 160, 170
Massiah, Joycelyn, 114
Miller, Daniel, 7, 17, 84n1, 92–93, 119, 129, 132–33, 138, 150, 190

Mills, Mary Beth, 49
Mintz, Sidney, 10
Multi-Fibre Agreement (MFA), 26, 117, 195
Munasinghe, Viranjini, 19, 54, 55, 58, 67, 129
Mycoo, Michelle, 171n3, 175

Naipaul, V.S., 58, 68
neoliberalism: and Caribbean culture, 10–11, 101, 139–40, 199–200; concept of, 15; and crime, 190–91; exceptional nature of, 22–23n2; and flexibility, 27, 199, 201; resistance to, 203; spaces for commentary within, 190–91. *See also* neoliberal subjectivities; trade liberalization
neoliberal subjectivities, 114, 154, 189–90, 200; and Caribbean culture, 10, 107, 140. *See also* subjectivity
Ngai, Pun, 162
"now for now," 42, 43, 46, 50n5, 197

occupational health, 9, 146–47, 151, 153, 154; and injuries 155–59. *See also* health concerns
occupational multiplicity, 117–18, 126, 140
Occupational Safety and Health Act, 152–53
oil boom, 7, 30–31, 56, 58, 152; and trade unions, 171–72n4
Olmstead, Frederick, 100
Ong, Aihwa, 162, 167
organization of production, 34–35, 154, 197; and race, 51–53, 64, 69, 83–84. *See also* flexible production
Ortner, Sherry, 14, 83, 171, 196

Panday, Basdeo, 54, 59, 182, 193n4
paradox of flexibility, 4–6, 35, 43, 198
People's National Movement (PNM), 55–56, 84–85n3, 85n5, 178, 184, 189; and Afro-Trinidadians, 54, 180, 182; industrialization policy of, 140–41n2
picong (teasing), 150, 163, 187
piece-rate payment, 13, 35, 50n6, 74–75, 172n5. *See also* wages
plantation: as master symbol, 68; as prototypical factory, 10
plantation economy, 7; and racialization, 12, 52, 67–68
Port of Spain, 17, 19, 26, 115, 177, 180. *See also* East Port of Spain
post-Fordism, 27, 114, 117, 154. *See also* Fordism

228 INDEX

pressing, 34, 45–46, 61; health concerns associated with, 146, 163–64
productive sociality, 44–45, 88, 197
progressive bundle system, 33, 40
Puri, Shalini, 67, 189, 191

race, 67; and class, 12, 138; and occupational identity, 68–69; and organization of production, 51–53, 83–84, 170. *See also* Afro-Trinidadians; Indo-Trinidadians; kidnapping
recession, 7, 26, 31, 73, 113, 172n4
reputation, 99, 199–200
resistance: and the body, 162; escape as a form of, 170; everyday, 13–14, 100, 200; to racialization, 70; respectability as, 199; and thiefing a chance, 2, 101
respectability, 10, 98–99, 115, 118, 199
Roberts, John, 100–101
Robotham, Don, 11, 85n3
Rofel, Lisa, 63, 172n5
Rolston, Jessica Smith, 153
Roopnarine, Vernon, 173–74, 190
Rose, Nikolas, 139–40

Salzinger, Leslie, 52–53
Sanders, Todd, 193n5
Scarry, Elaine, 22
Scott, James, 13–14, 90, 100. *See also* resistance
seamstresses, 127–28, 129–30; as garment workers, 119–20, 131–32; history of, 115, 116; and occupational multiplicity, 117–18; as sewing instructors, 119–20. *See also* garment industry; "into the sewing"
Segal, Daniel, 67–68
sentiment: as a force of production, 5–6, 48–49. *See also* desire
sewing, 116, 119, 120. *See also* garment industry; seamstresses
sewing machines, 129–30, 168–69; broken, 155, 202. *See also* button tacker; trimming machine
side production. *See* thiefing a chance
Signature Fashions, 3–4, 26; business strategy, 27; customers 26, 135–37; factory, 27–28, 32, 36; fieldwork entry into, 15, 28, 31–32; owners, 28–32; products, 30; as a pseudonym, 20. *See also* organization of production; Signature Fashions workers

Signature Fashions workers, 72–73; diversity among, 82–83; and occupational multiplicity, 117–18; racial categorization of, 53–54; residential patterns of, 54, 55, 58. *See also* back workers; front workers
skill, 119, 120; and deskilling 109n5, 122–23; and racial categorization, 68–69; and Signature Fashions workers, 39, 61. *See also* "into the sewing"; sewing
skill acquisition, 138–40, 199; as self-making, 126–27, 201; and thiefing a chance, 5, 102–106, 120–22. *See also* thiefing a chance; training
"slave-driver situation," 42–43, 46, 65, 154
slavery, 7; cultural responses to, 9–10, 99; and seamstresses, 115; and taking, 100–101; and Trinidadian racial categories, 67–68. *See also* plantation economy
Slocum, Karla, 193n5
Smith, Gavin, 111, 117
Sobo, Elisa, 129, 145
solidarity, 16, 60, 62, 152, 168, 171
sou sou, 77
spatial relations: racializing effects of, 63, 69, 83–84
Stacey, Judith, 19–20
stitchers, 116; and seamstresses, 119–20; at Signature Fashions, 39, 60–61. *See also* front workers
stitching section, 32, 33, 39–45
structural adjustment, 7, 113, 151–52, 171n3
style, 82, 128–29, 132–33, 138. *See also* fashion
subjectivity: Caribbean forms of, 11, 107, 140; concept of, 14–15; and neoliberalism, 107, 114, 170–71; and thiefing a chance, 10, 159–60, 199; and workers, 49, 108, 132, 138, 198–99, 201. *See also* neoliberal subjectivities
supervisors, 33–34, 40, 45; and thiefing a chance, 92
supervisory pyramid: as spatial trope, 34–35, 36
surplus value, 13, 100, 101
Syrian-Trinidadians, 29–30, 115, 116, 186, 192–93n3

tailors, 116, 117, 121(photo), 127–28, 129
taking, 100–101; and thiefing a chance, 14, 106
tariffs, 7–8, 26, 29, 116
Taylorism, 40, 45

thiefing a chance: apolitical nature of, 14, 100–101; author's complicity in, 88–90, 106–107; and Caribbean culture, 9–10, 101, 199–200; concept of, 2, 4, 20, 21, 87–88, 90; and flexible production, 5, 107, 197; justifications for, 97; moralities of, 93–97, 99, 197–98; and neoliberalism, 9, 20, 21, 199; and skill acquisition, 5, 102–106, 114, 120–22, 139–40, 199; subjectivity, 90, 107, 159–60, 199. *See also* flexible production; individualism

Thomas, Deborah, 87, 101, 142n9, 118

Tobago, 7

trade liberalization, 7–8; and the garment industry, 3, 9, 26, 113, 117, 195

trade unions, 36, 75, 152, 168, 171–72n4

training, 5, 77, 102, 119, 125–26. *See also* skill acquisition

transportation: cost of, 17–18, 71

trimming machine, 46–48

trimming section, 33–34, 170. *See also* back area

Trinidad, viii(map), 6–7; economy of, 182; party politics in, 54; population of, 54, 84n1, 115; residential patterns in, 53

Ulysse, Gina, 11

United National Congress (UNC), 54, 59, 180, 182, 189; allegations of corruption against, 184, 193n4

Universal Uniforms, 77–78, 117, 178–79

Wacquant, Loïc, 200

wages: hourly, 50n6; at Signature Fashions, 35, 36, 40. *See also* piece-rate payment

"we own factory," 90, 96, 107

Werner, Marion, 195–96, 203

white Trinidadians, 29–30, 116, 180, 192–93n3

Williams, Eric, 55

Wilson, Peter, 10, 98–99

Wolf, Eric, 52

World Bank, 7, 77

Wright, Melissa, 125, 198

Yanagisako, Sylvia, 6, 31, 48

Yelvington, Kevin, 12, 15, 30, 52, 53, 69, 83, 118, 171–72n4, 180, 188, 192

Youth Training and Employment Partnership Programme, 77

playful mockery at Tina's expense. As Tina protested that she simply did not want to go to town by herself after planning the trip with Dolores, Carmela kept up her teasing: "What she frighten of? She frighten they go rape she. Or kidnap she."

Kellisha added, sarcastically, "They go kidnap she."

Carmela said, "She frighten getting kidnap. You got money?"

Kellisha said, "She ehnt got money." Kellisha considered for a moment and said, "What they go kidnap she for, nuts?" Laughter broke out all around. Tina's husband sells bags of peanuts on the highway outside Chaguanas, and Tina also sells nuts in the factory. "They go kidnap she for nuts! They go kidnap she for the *peanut cart!*"

For Carmela and Kellisha, Tina's anxiety over crime is a form of presumption. Threats to her of kidnapping, rape, or theft are treated with equal mockery because of Tina's poverty and social marginality. Although Tina protested this characterization by insisting that fear of crime did not prevent her from visiting Port of Spain, Carmela and Kellisha knew of Tina's worries and would have found it hard to believe that fear had played no role in her choice to go home.

Kevin Birth reminds us that Trinidadians, like all people, speak from "positioned" identities, which he defines as "statuses that people recognize they occupy and to which they assume others react" (Birth 2008:22; cf. Holland et al. 1998). Indo-Trinidadian workers like Tina found themselves struggling to establish a position from which to speak and a means of presenting their own fears as legitimate. These feelings are underpinned by what Kevin Yelvington (1995:139) describes as "the rivalry between blacks and East Indians over scarce resources and the mutual fear that a member of the other group will be in a position of authority and thus extract historical revenge." Workers like Kavita ("police have a hand in it") and Tina see the kidnapping crisis as evidence of malicious neglect of the safety of Indo-Trinidadians by a state apparatus perceived to protect Afro-Trinidadian interests at the expense of Indo-Trinidadians. With the prevailing feeling that the kidnapping crisis meant Indo-Trinidadians were vulnerable not only to violent crime but also to official indifference, being criticized for fear only compounded their sense of victimization.

At Signature Fashions, Afro-Trinidadians found themselves reflecting on the state of affairs in a different way from their Indo-Trinidadian co-workers.

Because electoral politics so often generated material benefit in the form of local employment and targeted public works projects, Afro-Trinidadians experienced the UNC's years in power as a loss of access to the state's benevolence. During my fieldwork, the country had just emerged from six years of government by a self-confidently (but unofficially) "Indian" political party, whose rule was dogged by allegations of corruption and allocation of state expenditure directed toward "Indian" communities (Ryan 2003). However, Shalini Puri (1999) draws our attention to the historical ways Indo-Trinidadians have been repeatedly caricatured as acquisitive, treacherous, conniving, and disloyal. Writing about a 1958 calypso by Lord Superior (whose refrain *"Tax them!"* resonates with Cro Cro's message more than forty years later), Puri argues that "the recurrent theme of Indian wealth is framed here as a fear of Indian economic dislocation of Afro-Trinidadians" (ibid.:241). In a context in which the first inheritors of the post-colonial state apparatus were the colored middle classes—who drew on the histories and symbols of the urban black poor to create a national identity that reflected their experiences (Munasinghe 2002; Ryan 1997)—Afro-Trinidadians were perhaps still coming to terms with the emergence of Indo-Trinidadians as a political force in addition to an economic one. Jean, a stitcher from East Port of Spain, told me: "When the [UNC] talk about civil disobedience, all these things is *one*. High prices [in stores], so when you say, 'See [what's wrong with] this government,' and you seeing prices going up and crime and all this kind of thing, kidnappings when you see most of them is a hoax, you wouldn't want to vote for PNM again." Here, Jean presents herself as a victim of the Indo-Trinidadian middle classes, who own the factories she works in and the stores she shops in. The notion that this same constituency, in the form of the UNC party, also has the intention of destabilizing a PNM government becomes yet another outrage. For workers who encountered street violence, negotiated the stigma of living in East Port of Spain, and regretted the state neglect of their welfare in the garment factories, their resentment toward the political and economic ascendancy of Indo-Trinidadians is a mirror of their own marginalization.[5]

Although Signature Fashions workers frequently present themselves as triumphant agents who can thief a chance, they also continually reflect upon relations of power from their vantage point as working-class people. Neoliberal subjectivities do not exclude alternate ways of thinking about the self and the collective, and garment workers criticize those seen as possessing power at their expense. Yet Afro-Trinidadian workers' depiction of themselves as dominated by the Indo-Trinidadian middle class rests on racist representations of Indo-Trinidadian greed and a common view of ethnic politics as a zero-sum game in which each party advances at the expense of the other. As Daniel Miller (1994a:22) reminds us, "What has remained [in Trinidad] is a legacy of deep inequalities, within which virtually all contemporary groups feel aggrieved."

Conclusions

Vernon Roopnarine's body was recovered from a roadside four days after he was kidnapped. He had been beaten and strangled to death (Smith 2003). As with all incidents of kidnapping in Trinidad, there was a proliferation of interpretations regarding why Roopnarine was killed. A widely accepted view was that ransom negotiations between his family and captors had soured, but other possibilities were also imagined. I evoke Roopnarine to remind us that the kidnapping drama does not always conform to script; the image of his murdered body is a reminder of the gruesome materiality underpinning debates inside and outside the factory. The perpetrators, as in many kidnapping ordeals, were not apprehended and so remain shadow figures upon whom multiple fears are projected.

What kinds of spaces of commentary open up under neoliberal capitalism? In recent years, anthropologists working in diverse locations have detected a widespread phenomenon described by John Comaroff and Jean Comaroff (2006) as "disorder in the postcolony": a growing sense of lawlessness, anxiety, and violent disruption that has gripped much of the developing world. Fueled by transnational underground economies, unleashed by the shrinking of the welfare state, and gaining expression in violent crime and extra-judicial lynchings, disorder in the post-colony seems to expose the fragility of the neoliberal state and its inability to contain violence and maintain order. Yet as the case of Trinidad shows, neoliberalism is not a monolithic process; its mantra of "deregulation, privatization, and free trade" is enacted in partial, incomplete, and intensely local ways. The changes Signature Fashions workers perceive as significant—rising crime rates, the emergence of Indo-Trinidadian political power, and the decline of the garment manufacturing sector—appear to them to be related. In

References

Anderson, Elijah. 2001. *Code of the Street: Decency, Violence, and the Moral Life of the Inner City*. New York: Norton.

Andrews, William L., and Henry Louis Gates Jr., eds. 1999. *The Civitas Anthology of African American Slave Narratives*. Washington, DC: Civitas Counterpoint.

Anteby, Michel. 2008. *Moral Gray Zones: Side Productions, Identity, and Regulation in an Aeronautic Plant*. Princeton, NJ: Princeton University Press.

Anthony, Michael. 1997. *Historical Dictionary of Trinidad and Tobago*. Lanham, MD: Scarecrow.

Appadurai, Arjun. 1986. "Introduction: Commodities and the Politics of Value." In *The Social Life of Things: Commodities in Cultural Perspective*, ed. Arjun Appadurai, 3–63. Cambridge: Cambridge University Press. http://dx.doi.org/10.1017/CBO9780511819582.003.

Argenti, Nicolas. 2002. "People of the Chisel: Apprenticeship, Youth, and Elites in Oku (Cameroon)." *American Ethnologist* 29 (3): 497–533. http://dx.doi.org/10.1525/ae.2002.29.3.497.

Auyero, Javier. 2000. "The Hyper-Shantytown: Neo-liberal Violence(s) in the Argentine Slum." *Ethnography* 1 (1): 93–116. http://dx.doi.org/10.1177/14661380022230651.

Bair, Jennifer, and Marion Werner. 2011. "Commodity Chains and the Uneven Geographies of Global Capitalism: A Disarticulations Perspective." *Environment and Planning A* 43 (5): 988–97. http://dx.doi.org/10.1068/a43505.

Baldeosingh, Kevin. 2004. "In de Gayelle." *Trinidad and Tobago's Newsday*. Friday, April 16, 24.

Barrow, Christine. 1986. "Finding the Support: A Study of Strategies for Survival." *Social and Economic Studies* 35 (2): 131–76.

Beckles, Hilary McD. 1999. *Centering Woman: Gender Discourses in Caribbean Slave Society*. Kingston: Ian Randle.

Behar, Ruth, and Deborah Gordon, eds. 1995. *Women Writing Culture*. Berkeley: University of California Press.

Belmonte, Thomas. 1979. *The Broken Fountain*. New York: Columbia University Press.

Beharry, Prior. 2004. "Moonilal: T&T Now 'Colombianised.'" *Trinidad and Tobago Express*. Tuesday, May 18, 14.

Besson, Jean. 1993. "Reputation and Respectability Reconsidered: A New Perspective on Afro-Caribbean Peasant Women." In *Women and Change in the Caribbean*, ed. Janet Momsen, 15–37. London: James Curry.

Birth, Kevin K. 1999. *"Any Time Is Trinidad Time": Social Meanings and Temporal Consciousness*. Gainesville: University Press of Florida.

Birth, Kevin K. 2008. *Bacchanalian Sentiments: Musical Experience and Political Counterpoints in Trinidad*. Durham, NC: Duke University Press.

Bolles, A. Lynn. 1996. *Sister Jamaica: A Study of Women, Work, and Households in Kingston*. Lanham, MD: University Press of America.

Bolt, Maxim. 2012. "Waged Entrepreneurs, Policed Informality: Work, the Regulation of Space and the Economy of the Zimbabwean–South African Border." *Africa* 82 (1): 111–30. http://dx.doi.org/10.1017/S0001972011000751.

Bourdieu, Pierre. 1977. *Outline of a Theory of Practice*. Trans. Richard Nice. London: Cambridge University Press. http://dx.doi.org/10.1017/CBO9780511812507.

Bourdieu, Pierre. 1998. "The Essence of Neo-Liberalism: Utopia of Endless Exploitation." Trans. Jeremy J. Shapiro. *Le Monde Diplomatique*. December. http://mondediplo.com/1998/12/08bourdieu. Accessed May 5, 2007.

Bourgois, Philippe. 1988. "Conjugated Oppression: Class and Ethnicity among Guyami and Kuma Banana Workers." *American Ethnologist* 15 (2): 328–48. http://dx.doi.org/10.1525/ae.1988.15.2.02a00080.

Braverman, Harry. 1974. *Labor and Monopoly Capitalism: The Degradation of Work in the Twentieth Century*. New York: Monthly Review.

Brenner, Neil, and Nik Theodore. 2002. "Cities and the Geographies of 'Actually Existing Neoliberalism.'" *Antipode* 34 (3): 349–79. http://dx.doi.org/10.1111/1467-8330.00246.

Brereton, Bridget. 1981. *A History of Modern Trinidad 1783–1962*. Oxford: Heinemann.

Brereton, Bridget. 1993. "Social Organisation and Class: Racial and Cultural Conflict in Nineteenth Century Trinidad." In *Trinidad Ethnicity*, ed. Kevin A. Yelvington, 33–55. London: Macmillan.

Brewster, David. 2004. "Cut Supply of Drugs in West . . . Crime Wave Will Be Solved, Says Fr Henry." *Trinidad and Tobago Express*. http://www.trinidadexpress.com/index.pl/article_archive?id=29548984. Accessed January 19, 2007.

Brown, Karen McCarthy. 1987. "'Plenty Confidence in Myself': The Initiation of a White Woman Scholar into Haitian Vodou." *Journal of Feminist Studies in Religion* 3 (1): 67–76.

Browne, Katherine E. 2004. *Creole Economics: Caribbean Cunning under the French Flag*. Austin: University of Texas Press.

Browne, Katherine E., and B. Lynne Milgram, eds. 2009. *Economics and Morality: Anthropological Approaches*. Lanham, MD: AltaMira.

Buckridge, Steeve O. 2004. *Language of Dress: Resistance and Accommodation in Jamaica, 1760–1890*. Mona: University of the West Indies Press.

Burawoy, Michael. 1979. *Manufacturing Consent: Changes in the Labor Process under Monopoly Capitalism*. Chicago: University of Chicago Press.

Burawoy, Michael. 1985. *The Politics of Production: Factory Regimes under Capitalism and Socialism*. New York: Verso.

Bynoe, Anne J. 2000. "Social Welfare Effects of Structural Adjustment in Trinidad and Tobago." *International Advances in Economic Research* 6 (3): 593. http://dx.doi.org/10.1007/BF02294984.

Cairoli, M. Laetitia. 2011. *Girls of the Factory: A Year with the Garment Workers of Morocco*. Gainesville: University Press of Florida. http://dx.doi.org/10.5744/florida/9780813035611.001.0001.

Caldeira, Teresa. 1996. "Fortified Enclaves: The New Urban Segregation." *Public Culture* 8 (2): 303–28. http://dx.doi.org/10.1215/08992363-8-2-303.

Caldeira, Teresa. 2000. *City of Walls: Crime, Segregation, and Citizenship in São Paulo*. Berkeley: University of California Press.

Campbell, Carl C. 1997. *Endless Education: Main Currents in the Education System of Modern Trinidad and Tobago 1939–1986*. Kingston, Jamaica: University of the West Indies Press.

Caraway, Teri L. 2007. *Assembling Women: The Feminization of Global Manufacturing*. Ithaca, NY: Cornell University Press.

Carnegie, Charles V. 2002. *Postnationalism Prefigured: Caribbean Borderlands*. New Brunswick, NJ: Rutgers University Press.

Central Statistics Office (CSO). 2003. *Labour Force Statistics*. Port of Spain: CSO.

Central Statistics Office (CSO). 2007. *Fast Facts about Trinidad and Tobago*. Port of Spain: CSO.

Chakrabarty, Dipesh. 2000. *Rethinking Working Class History: Bengal 1890–1940*. Princeton, NJ: Princeton University Press.

Chapkis, Wendy, and Cynthia Enloe, eds. 1983. *Of Common Cloth: Women in the Global Textile Industry*. Washington, DC: Transnational.

Charan, Richard, and Darryl Heeralal. 2004. "How Guns Are Smuggled into Trinidad." *Trinidad and Tobago Sunday Express*. Sunday, August 8, 6.

Chouthi, Sandra. 1988. "Local Garments Have Quality . . . But Manufacturers Continue the Search for Improvements." *Trinidad and Tobago Express*. Thursday, July 7, 28.

Clifford, James, and George Marcus. 1986. *Writing Culture: The Poetics and Politics of Ethnography*. Berkeley: University of California Press.

Stuempfle, Stephen. 1995. *The Steelband Movement: The Forging of a National Art in Trinidad and Tobago*. Philadelphia: University of Pennsylvania Press.

Susser, Ida. 1988. "Directions in Research in Health and Industry." *Medical Anthropology Quarterly* 2 (3): 195–98. http://dx.doi.org/10.1525/maq.1988.2.3.02a00010.

Sutton, Constance. 1974. "Cultural Duality in the Caribbean." *Caribbean Studies* 14 (2): 96–101.

Taylor, Erin B. 2009. "Poverty as Danger: Fear of Crime in Santo Domingo." *International Journal of Cultural Studies* 12 (2): 131–48. http://dx.doi.org/10.1177/1367877908099496.

Thomas, Deborah A. 2004. *Modern Blackness: Nationalism, Globalization, and the Politics of Culture in Jamaica*. Durham, NC: Duke University Press. http://dx.doi.org/10.1215/9780822386308.

Thompson, E. P. 1967. "Time, Work-Discipline, and Industrial Capitalism." *Past and Present* 38 (1): 56–97. http://dx.doi.org/10.1093/past/38.1.56.

Thompson, Robert Wallace. 1958. "Mushrooms, Umbrellas, and Black Magic: A West Indian Linguistic Problem." *American Speech* 33 (3): 170–75. http://dx.doi.org/10.2307/453201.

Tourism and Industrial Development Company (TIDCO). 2002. *Trinidad and Tobago Export Directory 2002*. Port of Spain: TIDCO.

Tourism and Industrial Development Company (TIDCO). 2003a. *Trinidad and Tobago Export Directory 1990–2000*. http://www.tidco.co.tt. Accessed March 23, 2005.

Tourism and Industrial Development Company (TIDCO). 2003b. *Trinidad and Tobago Export Directory 2003*. Port of Spain: TIDCO.

Trinidad and Tobago. 1979. *Report of the Commission of Enquiry into All Aspects of the Garment Industry in Trinidad and Tobago*. Port of Spain: Government Printing.

Trinidad and Tobago Express. 1987. "Gordon Sets up Two Committees: Probe into Illegal Garment Imports." *Trinidad and Tobago Express*. Thursday, March 19, 3.

Trinidad Guardian. 2004. "Editorial: Speak Up, Mr. Minister." *Trinidad Guardian*. Tuesday, November 9. http://www.guardian.co.tt/archives/2004-11-09/editorial.html. Accessed May 18, 2007.

Trinidad Guardian. 2005. "PNM neither Decent nor Competent: An Interview with Dr. Charles Carlson." *Trinidad Guardian*. Sunday, October 30. http://www.guardian.co.tt/archives/2005-10-30/news12.html. Accessed June 5, 2007.

Trinidad Guardian. 2007. "CPEP Contractor Geddes Hinds: An Agent of Change." *Trinidad Guardian*. Thursday, April 12. http://www.guardian.co.tt/archives/2007-04-12/features1.html. Accessed June 5, 2007.

Ulysse, Gina. 2002. "Conquering Duppies in Kingston: Miss Tiny and Me, Fieldwork Conflicts, and Being Loved and Rescued." *Anthropology and Humanism* 27 (1): 10–26. http://dx.doi.org/10.1525/anhu.2002.27.1.10.

Ulysse, Gina. 2007. *Downtown Ladies: Informal Commercial Importers, a Haitian Anthropologist and Self-Making in Jamaica*. Chicago: University of Chicago Press.

United Nations Office on Drugs and Crime (UNODC) and the World Bank. 2007. *Crime, Violence, and Development: Trends, Costs, and Policy Options in the Caribbean.* New York and Washington, DC: UNODC and World Bank.

United States Department of State (USDS). 2001. *Country Report on Economic Policy and Trade Practices 2000: Trinidad and Tobago.* Washington, DC: Bureau of Economic and Business Affairs.

Urciuoli, Bonnie. 2008. "Skills and Selves in the New Workplace." *American Ethnologist* 35 (2): 211–28. http://dx.doi.org/10.1111/j.1548-1425.2008.00031.x.

Venkatesh, Sudhir Alladi. 2006. *Off the Books: The Underground Economy of the Urban Poor.* Cambridge, MA: Harvard University Press.

Wacquant, Loïc. 2012. "Three Steps to a Historical Anthropology of Actually Existing Neoliberalism." *Social Anthropology* 20 (1): 66–79. http://dx.doi.org/10.1111/j.1469-8676.2011.00189.x.

Walvin, James. 2001. *Black Ivory: Slavery in the British Empire.* Oxford: Blackwell.

Werner, Marion, and Jennifer Bair. 2009. "After Sweatshops? Apparel Politics in the Circum-Caribbean." *North American Congress on Latin America Report on the Americas* 42 (4): 6–10, 38.

Westwood, Sallie. 1984. *All Day, Every Day: Factory and Family in the Making of Women's Lives.* Urbana: University of Illinois Press.

Wilk, Richard. 1994. "Consumer Goods as Dialogue about Development: Colonial Time and Television Time in Belize." In *Consumption and Identity*, ed. Jonathan Friedman, 97–118. Chur, Switzerland: Harwood Academic.

Williams, Eric. 1994 [1944]. *Capitalism and Slavery.* Chapel Hill: University of North Carolina Press.

Wilson, Peter J. 1969. "Reputation and Respectability: A Suggestion for Caribbean Ethnology." *Man* 4 (1): 70–84. http://dx.doi.org/10.2307/2799265.

Wilson, Peter J. 1973. *Crab Antics: The Social Anthropology of English-Speaking Negro Societies of the Caribbean.* New Haven, CT: Yale University Press.

Wolf, Diane Lauren. 1992. *Factory Daughters: Gender, Household Dynamics, and Rural Industrialization in Java.* Berkeley: University of California Press.

Wolf, Eric R. 1982. *Europe and the People without History.* Berkeley: University of California Press.

Wolf, Margery. 1992. *A Thrice-Told Tale: Feminism, Postmodernism, and Ethnographic Responsibility.* Stanford: Stanford University Press.

World Bank. 2009. "Caribbean: Accelerating Trade Integration, Policy Options for Sustained Growth, Job Creation, and Poverty Reduction." Report no. 30, Poverty Reduction and Economic Management Sector Unit, Latin America and Caribbean Region. Washington, DC: World Bank.

World Trade Organization (WTO). 1998. *Trade Policy Review: Trinidad and Tobago.* Geneva: WTO Secretariat.

Wright, Melissa W. 2001. "Desire and the Prosthetics of Supervision: A Case of Maquiladora Flexibility." *Cultural Anthropology* 16 (3): 354–73. http://dx.doi.org/10.1525/can.2001.16.3.354.

Yanagisako, Sylvia Junko. 2002. *Producing Culture and Capital: Family Firms in Italy*. Princeton, NJ: Princeton University Press.

Yelvington, Kevin A. 1989. "The Support Networks of Female Factory Workers in Trinidad: Some Preliminary Considerations." Unpublished ms.

Yelvington, Kevin A. 1991. "A Fourth Shift? Making a '*Connec*' and Keeping Support among Female Factory Workers in Trinidad." Paper presented at the 13th Annual Meetings of the Southern Regional Science Association, Miami, April 12.

Yelvington, Kevin A. 1993. "Introduction: Trinidad Ethnicity." In *Trinidad Ethnicity*, ed. Kevin A. Yelvington, 1–32. London: Macmillan.

Yelvington, Kevin A. 1995. *Producing Power: Ethnicity, Gender and Class in a Caribbean Workplace*. Philadelphia: Temple University Press.

Yelvington, Kevin A. 1996. "Flirting in the Factory." *Journal of the Royal Anthropological Institute* 2 (2): 313–33. http://dx.doi.org/10.2307/3034098.